The Long Road to Obama!

The Long Road to Obama!

One Heart at a Time

Thomas S. Walters

To order additional copies of this book, contact:
Xlibris Corporation
1-888-795-4274
www.Xlibris.com
Orders@Xlibris.com
114736

TABLE OF CONTENTS

Essentially this is the story of George Washington to: "Martha, please one revolution at a time!" First the white man had to win his freedom, a battle of "we the people" against the British Empire and then vs. our own greed. Only when we the people won this battle could we go onward to fighting for others over slavery in the Civil War.

After that came T R's war on corporate America, then women's suffrage and freedom to the world—FDR's and Churchill's Atlantic Charter. Only it applied to us as well as the British Empire. We yelled freedom to all, yet brutally denied it in America. Dr. Martin Luther King Jr. would of course change that. Finally our disaster in Vietnam making our political opponents traitors! And finally a welcome to the 21st Century.

FORWARD

The Impact of W.W. II on America:

IN HUMAN RELATIONS, to know where we are, you must know here we have been. Only by knowing both, can you begin to understand where we are going. Trying to understand history is like trying to comprehend the world while in a sand storm because we are so much a part of it, in our own tiny little corner.

Before there was television, people gained their view of the outside world by news-reels, which were run ahead of movies. If a picture is worth a thousand words, how much is a moving picture worth—with sound? Our tiny little corners have greatly expanded, thus the causes for our hearts to change have changed as well.

In the 1930's, the news-reels were full of images of Hitler and his goons, screaming about Jews in Europe, and Japanese screaming banzai, in war ravaged China.

They also ran clips, of the German-American Bundt, screaming hatred about Jews, Catholics and blacks—here in America.

By the early 1940's, the news-reels were full of images of Hitler, and Tojo trampling all over Europe and American colonies in the Pacific.

They also ran clips, of Ku-Klux-Klan rallies, screaming about blacks and other news clips of American citizens being jailed because of their ancestry—here in America.

By 1945, the news-reels were full of images of Hitler's death camps and our own emaciated survivors, from Japanese prison camps.

They also ran clips of dead black men, hanged for crimes unknown and American citizens being released for non crimes from camps—here in America.

Many people in America made the connections, even if they did not want to. Many for the first time looking hard in the mirror at America thru the camera lens, did not like what they saw . . .

Race relations before World War II in America:

President Theodore Roosevelt 1901-1909; invited the famous Booker T. Washington a renown botanist for finding new uses for farm products like peanuts to make mayonnaise (who helped found Tuskegee Institute of WWII fame) to the White House. The other-wise popular President would be hanged in effigy all across America for this . . . Not for inviting the black man to the White House, for that was allowed. Teddy Roosevelt was however guilty of a horrendous cultural sin . . . he had invited him in—through the front door.

Blacks were always only allowed in the back door of anyone's house—so they would always know their proper place. The sad reality was; many a whites' house was burned to the ground for violating this rule of cultural law here in America.

The following story was told to me, by my brother, Frederick. Birmingham, Alabama winter of 1945-1946: My mother's story about her own heart:

Our father to be, Billy was still serving in war devastated Europe. My mother with their daughter Pauline were living in her mother's big house when the maid, a black woman asked if she could show her husband who had just returned from Europe, where she worked. My grandmother said yes.

The next day, my mother and grand-mother, were waiting in the kitchen, by the back door, for the maid and her husband to arrive. While talking about when their young men, Billy and John (my mother's younger brother) would be coming home from this war when the front door bell rang . . . "Who could that be . . . they wondered?"

It was the maid and her husband. Dressed in his army dress uniform with all his medals and campaign ribbons, simply by standing there at a safe distance, tall and proud, he was in effect quietly demanding that if he was to come in, it would be through the front door . . .

After a long pause, my grandmother invited them in—through the front door. My mother was so stunned, she said, she almost had a heart attack.

After showing the maid and her husband through the big house, they all sat down in the living room and had little cakes and coffee. They all talked for awhile, and then the maid and her husband left.

My mother then asked: "Why, did you let them in, through the front door?!?"

My grand-mother replied: "That man, just spent three years saving me from Hitler, how could, I not!"

My mother upon reflection, decided: That the old South, that she had always known, would change in her life-time. She also vowed, that she would not allow her children to be raised as prejudiced. Clearly the Long Road to Obama was being charted out, one heart at a time.

Upon Reflection:

Since I do not believe this story is unique; America had culturally been changed by World War II and the picture camera with sound in ways both big and small, obvious to some, oblivious to most. While many would resist these changes, the changes would endure . . .

Many white people having looked in the mirror at America with the aide of the camera lens realized for the first time that the constitution's "we the people" should apply to "all" Americans and how badly it did not—in reality.

In 1947 Baseball began to integrate and President Harry Truman ordered the U.S. military to de-segregate by executive order. Senator Strom Thurman launched his Dixiecrat Rebellion in 1948 and the current Civil Rights War was officially declared open.

America had and was changing, even if few could realize how much at the time and despite those who would resist these changes. We today sixty years later, are on the back slopes of these mountains of hatred and disrespect that we are still striving to overcome.

Un-fortunately there is still another mountain yet to climb before we reach the Promised Land Martin Luther King spoke so eloquently of . . . the mountain of fear . . . that story lies in your future not my past.

I sincerely hope you will join me as we together share some bread and fine wine together as we explore how we came to where we are. Okay, you must furnish your own bread and wine, but at least let me furnish the words . . .

Considering the young of America overwhelmingly elected a black man President of the U.S. of A. in 2008, I am confident of the future. For in one lifetime we as a nation have traveled a stunning distance as a society. My own journey began in the summer of 1964 when I personally realized I was at that moment the most despised person ever—a n-lover in the Heart of Dixie—Alabama by birth. I as a child had been taught to love all God's children while never realizing what it actually meant until that afternoon at age thirteen.

If I thought a black President would never happen in my life time, imagine for a moment how many blacks felt the same way. Sixty years ago blacks here in America were literally hung for crimes unknown in many states North and South and few cared to find out why or by whom. I am truly awed by the distance we have travelled.

CHAPTER I

Introduction

B ARAK OBAMA WAS not elected president of the U.S. by accident. It was a very long hard fight by people many who died long before he was even born. We are our worst enemies. Ben Franklin was legally sold by his father. In the 1780's and 90's we outlawed that act—by restricting how many years our children could be sold for. That didn't stop us. In the 1890's a century later, we sold our children for a drink. Today when charities make micro loans to 3rd world men, the response all too often is added sales at the local bar or gambling houses. We are little different.

These battles fought against our own greed, had to be won and laws passed for ever forbidding ourselves from that right to abuse our power to do harm to our selves, before white men could ever attempt to win freedom for the slaves in the 1860's, grant women the right to vote in 1920, or blacks the right to run for president in 1965. This is their story, as well as those of the modern era *to tame our greed.*

Two Bolts of Thunder:

In the early 500's A.D. the scrolls of the Emperor of China reveal a most mysterious notation: Two large bolts of thunder were heard on a cloudless day. What this meant no one knew but it must have seemed of ominous days ahead.

It is here in these two bolts of thunder that we must look for the roots of our American Democracy. The most likely cause for these two bolts of thunder on a cloudless day was the volcano of Tambora in Indonesia. Similar to Krakatau which was a mighty volcanic explosion of the 1880's which gave the world beautiful sunsets for decades to come it too originated in Indonesia. The difference was Tambora was far larger!

A few months after the ominous bolts of thunder on a cloudless day the sun began to disappear even at noon throughout the northern hemisphere. The Dark Ages were upon us. For two years the crops would not grow and starvation was everywhere.

In Western Europe with the collapse of the Roman Empire in 476 A.D. and with it civilization as then known the Dark Age would take on the name for the period from 476 A.D. to about 800 A.D. which would see the dawn of modern Western Civilization.

So to trace our Democratic roots: We should first explore the end of the Roman Empire and the birth of our democratic roots in the middle ages yet to come:

Note: In this book I aim for the truth, sometimes the truth is not nice, so if you want nice: read some other book. If you want the brutal truth read this book.

Our democracy did not begin in the ancient Athenian Demos—Democracy or even in the Roman Republic which copied and modified it. Our American Democracy begins with those very uncouth uncivilized barbarian Germanic tribes who overran and looted what remained of the Roman Republic.

Uncivilized mankind was democratic. As long as any individual could pick up all they owned and walk out, that was power. Thus the hunter gatherers of the world simply had to have tribal councils to make decisions in unity, if possible. Once man discovered how to farm the land producing far greater crops for their swelling populations, things changed. As farm lands spread from eastern Turkey (wheat) and north eastern China (millet) over the thousands of years from about 8500 B.C.—the end of the last Ice Age, they not only discovered other crops to farm, they over lapped one another as well.

In the process they formed organized governments, civilizations to protect themselves from drought, pestilence, floods and death—or the four horses of the apocalypse. While none of these governments could simply make them go away, they could insure that the survivors had the tools (food, plows, horses and seeds etc.) needed to start over again.

Their populations however continued to grow and inevitably some families grew faster than others. Over time this produced great disparities in wealth even if they started out even. Thus those families with more people than land sold their labor to the highest bidder.

Again over the thousands of years the basis of power became the land you owned and land cannot be carried away. Thus if the tribal council voted against you in a land dispute, what could you do? Revolt against the majority, I think not. Or walk out forfeiting what remained of your land? Most likely you grumbled and kept what little you still had. This scene repeatedly occurred until:

People being people, quickly those with the power moved to keep out the weakest, those with no or little land. Thus the tribal councils came to have fewer and fewer members and over time dictatorships by many different names (Dukes, Ra's, Kings, or kings of kings: Emperors) arose in every civilization.

From Turkey and Egypt to India and China dictatorships arose everywhere. Europe remained the land of hunter gatherers—democracies because the grains of Asia failed to grow in colder European climates until about 1000 B.C. with newer seeds. Gradually farming did spread to Greece and the age long battle between the historic democracies and the new civilized dictatorships began.

Granted we have no proof of these "age long battles between the historic democracies and the new civilized dictatorships" for people had to first discover writing and that would take thousands of years. By the time primitive writing was discovered around 6000 B.C. in various places originally pictographs which gradually morphed into symbols representing either things or sounds or both.

The Sumerians (ancient Iraq) about 3400 B.C. are credited with developing the first true type of modern writing. For writing was needed for civilizations to grow. From the Sumerian civilization it quickly spread with changes to Egypt and India. This is Sanskrit writing. The Chinese would develop their own system as the Western World would eventually develop the Phoenician Alpha Beta System.

Yet based on our current knowledge of all hunter gathering groups being democratic these many contests for power simply had to have occurred before writing could record them in Asia and Egypt. For by 3400 B.C. dictatorships by many names had already arisen from Egypt to Japan. In all the rest of the world in hunter gatherer societies democracies ruled and writing had yet to win.

Therefore it is only since writing developed that these "age long battles between democracies and civilized dictatorships" by many names have been recorded. That in conclusion does not mean they did not happen, they just went unrecorded before writing.

The first known actual attempt at writing a history: "The History of Greece and Persia" by Herodotus about 450 BC got almost everything wrong. Nonetheless he is remembered kindly by historians of today for he gave it a good try. The problem was no one knew what had happened before their own time. Everything before their own time was just family legends remembered mainly for their own family gain, let alone when it actually happened. That of course does not mean history began about 500 BC, but that only our feeble attempts at writing human history began then.

In Athens under King Solon and Pericles of about 590 BC the Athenian Demos—a participatory democracy arose. You literally had to be there to participate: Great for a small city, unworkable for a great nation. When Athens expanded into Sicily and later to Italy, its Demos failed, as did Athens soon after. Nonetheless they did inspire the Romans.

The Roman Republic:

The Romans (native Italians living next door to the Greek Etruscans) who's last King loved raping his generals wives in front of them was not surprisingly overthrown. In jubilation the Romans proclaimed never again shall their ever be a King of Rome. Instead they created the Roman Republic originally about 500 B.C. reestablished about 390 B.C.—modifying Athenian democracy.

A Senate composed of the wealthy and powerful by inheritance and the House of Plebes (people) by election of the middle-class citizens of Rome. The Senate would nominate Consuls to rule and Generals to fight; the House of Plebes would then elect them or not.

This was rarely a harmonious relationship: as the Senate used large bags of money to bribe other Senators and many smaller bags to bribe the House of Plebes to cut taxes on the rich. While the House of Plebes constantly voted for new taxes upon the rich to pay for new aqueducts to Rome and to raise armies against the neighbors because the small holders of land needed more land for their many sons.

Reality was in the ancient world; war was almost inevitable. Every little city state or nation was constantly presented with an ever growing population and a finite fixed amount of land. It was either conquer or be conquered. With one big difference: When the neighboring King's Army met the Roman Army the soldier subjects fought out of fear for their King. After all they lived at his mercy—**subjects** or property of the King. If they won the battle, the King took what he wanted and parceled out the remainder to his generals. Rarely was anything left for the common rabble except all the women they could rape.

When the Roman Republic's Army won however, the House of Plebes insisted the senior citizen soldiers of Rome get their share: a plot of land of their own. Thus the enlisted soldiers of Rome fought for themselves. Not surprisingly Rome conquered all.

In a few centuries the little city state of Rome covered most of the civilized world of their knowledge. Many states hating their rulers as much as Rome despised their former kings, over thru them and petitioned Rome for annexation. By offering some of their ex-kings lands and joining the Roman Republic they knew they too could join this wonderful creation. By the second century BC the proudest boast from Egypt to Iberia (Spain) was **"I am a citizen of Rome."**

What a citizen of Rome meant was if the local general controlling the local courts stole your goods or daughters you could protest to your Plebe (representative) and sooner but probably later an investigation would be launched and the general would be no more.

That is power and the generals administering the many provinces knew it. Thus the Plebes protected the middle class citizens whose citizenship could be purchased. The poor non citizens—slaves, were at every one's mercy.

This success caused a major problem. We do not know how many Plebeians made up the House of Plebes, but as the Republic grew so apparently did the House of Plebes and we do know they did become more of a mob than a dignified house of discussion.

In 1787 we divided our states into districts of 30,000 people meaning our four million people elected less than 80 representatives allowing for "other people not including Indians not paying taxes"—i.e. slaves; counting as 3/5 of a whole person. Granted the first census would be held in 1790, thus this first assessment of the seats was by guesswork. If we used that same standard today we would have a mob of 10,000 representing our 300 million Americans of today all fighting for that microphone—the current 435 fighting for it, is bad enough. This is why representatives scream bloody insults at one another—to gain recognition.

The End of the Republic:

Apparently in Rome they had something like 10,000 fighting to be heard above the mob. The solution chosen in the end was to abolish the House of Plebes. This was disastrous; the House of Plebes meant that a

Greek merchant lived without fearing the local General could walk in; taking his wife or his goods. But with the House of Plebes abolished . . . there was no one to complain to, for the local court was run by the local General. The military ruled with only the Senate who cared only for the rich, all too often the General in question who was probably a nephew or brother of a Senator.

With the House of Plebes abolished, the Senate quickly began awarding newly conquered lands to their sons only—the officers of the army. Thus the enlisted citizens no longer wanted to join and the army became an army of mercenaries composed of the poorest only. Their loyalties were no longer to the Republic but to the generals that paid them. The proudest cry of the ancient world: *"I am a citizen of Rome"* grew fainter each year. In about a century after the abolishment of the House of Plebes, Rome was dominated by individuals commanding armies of mercenaries and in 27 BC General Octavian proclaimed himself Emperor Augustus Caesar. Rome which had vowed to never have a king again, now had one by a different name.

The Republic was dead, long live the Empire. The Senate quickly became a house of ceremonies only, effectively perishing as a real factor in governing. The emperors usually glad to keep it for the façade of legitimacy for themselves. Now the Emperor could seize the daughters and wealth of the former high and powerful and they gladly did so.

By 180 AD the Emperors were at the mercy of the Praetorian Guards whose job was to protect them. They quickly discovered they could kill the emperor and put the job up for sale. For they and the army alone had the power. Selling the title to the highest bidder the pay of the army rose and its discipline fell apart. By the 300's AD the Empire was in full retreat everywhere.

Gradually as the centuries of anarchy went by a new proudest yell emerged: Of the many religions of the Roman Empire only Christianity stood against the Roman Emperors yelling what amounted to "We would rather be lion food than a willing subject of the Empire!"

Thus Christianity grew in strength as almost every one gradually grew to hate the Empire now on borrowed time, ever declining as it hollowed out what remained of the republic.

Finally embracing Christianity trying desperately to save itself in the late 300's AD and divided by Emperor Constantine but the now Western Empire despised by the Christians finally collapsed in 476 AD when it could not pay its victorious army of German mercenaries that had just defeated the Huns—modern Hungary.

The strength of all societies is the many, many little guys. In America we had Ben Franklin the son of a candle maker (the poorest of the little merchants of the time) who would invent a stove bought for over a century, bi-focal glasses and a printing empire. Two brothers in Ohio who figured out how to make their bicycle fly—the Wright brothers and more recently a few friends working in garages to invent our personal modern computers.

It must have been the same for ancient Rome, where the little guy was free to invent a better mousetrap without worry about the powerful stealing their inventions. *Thus the Roman Republic invented concrete among many other things which the modern world could only marvel at for nearly two thousand years!* What a loss. Only the mudflats of the Adriatic survived—Venice out of reach of the marauding armies. Unfortunately the inventors of concrete and other things of value are rarely known to us for only the truly rich could afford either parchment or the laborers to carry stone books.

Medieval Europe:

When the hired mercenaries (the Germans) over ran the Western Empire they were ignorant savages only partially Christianized. Yet it is to these barbarians that we owe our democratic roots. All primitive peoples are democratic. The strength of any tribe is its numbers. If any member can pick up all they own and walk out—that is real power. Once people began to farm i.e. become civilized they lost the power to walk out for land is very hard to carry. Dictatorships by many names soon followed. So it followed for the barbarians over running the Roman Empire since they had to eat; they had to learn to farm as well.

If we lack detailed knowledge from the ancient world, who did know how to read and write but did not have newspapers or written histories and only dates like in the twelfth year of Solomon's rule—than our knowledge of the Dark Age is immense.

In about 800 AD the King of the Franks, a German tribe, Charlemagne whose vast empire stretched across France, Germany and Northern Italy had a new cause. At his capital Aix le Chapel (Aachen, Germany) he ordered universities or schools to be built all around his vast empire. ***This act is***

considered the Rebirth of Western Civilization. The early Middle Age had begun where gradually reading and writing would once again flourish outside the church.

The rise of the British Empire:

At this same time still other Germanic tribes the Angles, Saxons and Jutes had come to rule the ex Roman Britain now called England while the people became known as Saxons. In 1066 William the Conqueror of Normandy over ran England. A century and a half later, one of his ancestors King John decided to become an absolute dictator. The Norman officers, the knights of the kingdom and the Saxons—the people together rose in revolt and forced King John to sign *the Magna Carta* in1215 which led to eventually creating the English Parliament.

Despite the similarities knowledge of the Roman Republic in 1215 was as buried as can be. The House of Lords for the Dukes, Lords and Earls of England and six commoners stood representing the commoners which eventually became the House of Commons for the non rich and powerful according to the well known and powerful towns and villages of 1215.

While the House of Commons was never meant to be truly representative of the whole population by selecting towns and villages across the whole of England its design was to reflect the people's needs to representation when taken as a whole. Thus censuses of where the people actually lived were not needed—at least not in 1215.

Over the next 500 plus years however a lot can happen. The mid 1300's brought The Black Death which wiped out at least one quarter and possibly half the population including entire towns and villages throughout the known world, but populations would recover despite leaving terrible memories.

A lasting influence may have been the sudden loss of excess labor and the sudden need for labor saving devices. For as always those with good and adequate food tended to live while as usual the poor were the first to die.

In the 1500's came the sudden rise in agricultural efficiency as farmers discovered if they saved the best yields to plant new crops they tended to get whole crops of the better yields. Since this was being practiced in France as well as England suddenly both had extra crops to sell to one another.

The end result France won, with its better sunlight compared to dreary old fog bound England. French lettuce was big and green while English lettuce not so big with yellow and brown mixed with the green. In the

1600's came *Enclosure* where the wealthy of England choosing the French lettuce drove the English Dukes, Lords, Earls, and squires (small land holders) to find better crops suited to foggy cool England. These better crops proved to be cattle and sheep and only grass to feed them with.

This was disastrous for the many landless peasants of England. Growing grass needs very little labor, herding cows and sheep only a little more. The vast majority of landless peasants were now redundant or unneeded. The misery of the English peasants forced off the land by the land owners 'enclosing' their fields can not be described.

This of course was the majority of the population. The House of Commons fought against it like hell, but economics has no mercy. Neither did those who had any money as the towns and cities were continually swamped by the starving masses.

During this same time period a Priest named Martin Luther nailed a protest letter of complaints to Wittenberg Cathedral in 1517 Germany. Even more importantly a copy was reproduced by a printer on a newly invented device: the printing press using still another recent device; cheap paper. Very quickly Christian Europe was ripped upside down by many, many people agreeing with Martin Luther's objections plus their own additional ones.

Note: This truly marks the difference from the ancient and modern worlds—the basis of power. In the ancient world, power was based on who controlled the armies. In the modern world; power is based on who controls the press. In the ancient world the written word existed but was controlled by the rich who alone could afford the very expensive pedaled flowers—trimmed and sown together to make parchment or have others carry the clay tablets for them. As Europe was about to learn in the modern world—those who control the press (and cheap paper) quickly control the armies. Now we have the internet and twitter—but still in our ever changing world, control the spread of knowledge, you control the people and thus the army.

Since few people agree with their world turned upside down—Civil War quickly engulfed the whole of Western Europe until 1648. The protesters—Protestants were divided into many sects. While the Roman Catholic Church counterattacked by reforming itself and pushing the Kings, Emperors, and Dukes to crush the Protestants. Generally those closes to Rome remained Catholic and those furthest away broke away.

Henry VIII and his six wives of course chose the opportunity to seize the English Catholic Church and remake it as his own Anglican Church. Hanging Catholics as traitors to his realm and burning outspoken Protestant critics as heretics, England was not merry.

Settling a new Continent:

Thus not so merry ole England, Protestant Scotland and newly conquered mostly Catholic Ireland sent tens of thousands of starving peasants with out land to the New World, most to be sold at auction to pay for the three month voyage across the Atlantic by sail. Sold for years anywhere from four to fifteen years depending upon the supply and location of the sale; this in the hope that they the illiterate starving masses might somehow acquire the tools for surviving in the New World and a piece of land of their own. For land was the basis of power to the poor everywhere.

Make no mistake in the 1600's they perished in the New World by the tens of thousands for to the illiterate, any education is very difficult. For not only have they not learned how to read and write, but to a large degree they have also failed to learn how to learn. In the Old World where they came from, virtually nothing had changed in centuries, except for their impoverishment. In the New World, everything was different: the crops that grew and an axe to defend oneself with and if successful guns which were expensive.

Yet those who did acquire the necessary tools (quite often just the determination to pick oneself out of the dust of defeat and try, try again) to survive in a hostile world on the frontier of Native Americans wanting to kill them and wild forests and animals wanting them for lunch, soon formed the majorities of most of our colonies.

By the late 1600's the flow of desperate Englishmen, Irishmen and Scotsmen willing to sell them selves into slavery fell behind demand so a very old trade flourished: the selling of actual unwilling slaves from Africa (first sold in 1619 Virginia) began to take their places in North America. While initially black slaves were freed after a number of years the same as whites, this proved unprofitable. So people being their natural greedy selves changed the colonial laws to make it permanent for those not entitled to the birth rights of Englishmen, this of course was very profitable.

New England was the big exception to the above. Farming the cold hilly and rocky soils of New England required great efforts of work with farming techniques being very primitive by today's standards to raise barely enough food to eat and no cash crop to sell in Europe. This could and only appealed to the Puritan middle class, who were far more interested in escaping the beggars, thieves and prostitutes—the desperate, that England was then overrun with.

The great efforts of work appealed to the Puritan work ethic even for no cash return but to few others. But no return impoverished the middle class Puritans and they were forced to welcome fishermen who worked hard but in dirty and dangerous work that did produce a cash income from the cod banks off Newfoundland.

Dirty and dangerous work had no appeal to the Puritans, but shipbuilding aha, that appealed to them and with dirt cheap lumber from Maine, Boston was soon the third largest builder of ships within the British Empire by 1700.

Meanwhile most of the desperate stayed in England or Scotland and either starved or learned new industrial trades—in the colony of Ireland the desperate Catholics were not allowed to for their manufacturing would mean competition with England, so if they stayed, they simply starved. Thus cabinet making, sewing dresses, anything to earn a few pennies in England by hand or leg powered tools took off, just to survive.

It is widely believed that the population of England and Scotland fell from ten million to about eight million between 1600 and the early 1700's. This is the origin of the Industrial Revolution in Britain, out of necessity it occurred before the steam engine. As always, progress is painful to those left behind.

Of the estimated 300,000 Briton's fleeing to the New World in the 1600's about half went to the Sugar islands of the Caribbean (life expectancy about five years, but riches to the survivors) and the other half to the swampy mosquito infested tobacco lands of tidewater Virginia (life expectancy perhaps 20 years and rising plus some wealth for the survivors) while only about 17,000 went to New England—a full 70 years life expectancy: far greater than in England and bringing their wife's and even a few children, they quickly multiplied.

Thus by 1700 both New England and the Chesapeake were about equal in population with the Caribbean still islands of wealthy sugar plantations with few whites and many, many slaves.

Meanwhile South Carolina was getting started now that Englishmen and French Huguenots—protestants driven from France) under the protection of Britain had learned how to grow rice from their slaves and North Carolina as an overflow southward from Virginia.

The English neglecting the middle between Virginia and New England was now seized by the Dutch—New Amsterdam (soon to be New York) and Swedes—Delaware and New Jersey (settled with mostly colonist from Finland) which were quickly seized by the Netherlands—or Dutch containing Holland with in.

The Netherlands surged from a very unhappy Protestant colony of the super rich but oppressive Catholic Spanish in 1570 to a maritime superpower by 1670. They did so by picking on a much weaker but lucrative foe. While Spain had conquered the rich Aztec and Inca Empires of the New World, Portugal had discovered the coveted route to India around Africa and China beyond. While the French, English and the rest of Europe fought over the Spanish gold and silver fleets to Europe, the Dutch seized most of the Portuguese Empire.

Soon from Indonesia to South Africa and Sri Lanka to the coasts of Africa plus a few sugar islands in the Caribbean and New Amsterdam the Dutch flag soon proudly waved. Controlling the sea routes bringing the silk of China, the cotton and jewels of India and the slaves of Africa to both Europe and the Americas; Holland soared in wealth. Unfortunately booming Holland made for few settlers for New World colonies.

Naturally this soaring wealth soon brought jealous and more powerful enemies. While Europe tried to storm the Netherlands, Britain seized most of her empire, including the above New York, New Jersey and Delaware. New Amsterdam with 5,000 people, more than half non Dutch, mainly Germans, English and Jews facing a British fleet and rebellion by its own English quickly surrendered.

In these late 1600's Lord Baltimore founded Maryland as a refuge for English Catholics but soon being overrun by Protestant Virginia planters, partial religious freedom was granted. Finally Pennsylvania was established by William Penn for the Friends of God-called Quakers (because they quake in their boots by detractors) of England in 1682 though soon over run by German settlers, Pennsylvania rounded out the first twelve colonies of the 1600's.

Georgia established by George Oglethorpe in 1733 as an attempted solution to the indolent lazy beggars—the poor of England prohibited slavery, rum and almost everything fun. A few thousand people attracted by free transport and free land despite dying off in the usual numbers were soon fighting for all they were denied. Blaming their heavy deaths and poverty-growing rice in the hot mosquito infected swamplands of the coast was very labor intensive hence only poor returns at a high price in lives; in 1750 Parliament granted Georgia their rights. This quickly proved most beneficial to South Carolina planters moving southward. Owning a hundred slaves each producing a small return, quickly added up with dying slaves easy for them to replace.

In Britain however this transformation of the locality of the people effectively created large numbers of false seats where no one lived in the villages or towns that elected members to the House of Commons in the 1700's for the towns and villages on roads expanded and those many towns and villages without roads soon died. These seats in the House of Commons were taken over by the land owners or literally sold to the aristocracy at every "election."

Into this mix George III arrived determined to obey his mother's command: "George, be King!" In the 1760's the new king pleaded poverty gaining a pay raise to bribe still more members to grant him still another pay raise. Soon both houses were commanded by the king who was determined to crush these Americans who dared to say no to him.

The people of Britain could not stop George III despite agreeing with the Americans who initially were simply demanding their rights as Englishmen. The people of Britain also demanded the House of Commons reflect where the people actually lived in the 1700's not once upon a long time ago—in 1215. Thus many did refuse to join the army forcing the king to buy mercenaries from Germany—called Hessians to fill out his army, but that only cost money. *Many bolts of thunder would soon be thundering.*

CHAPTER II

The Life and Times of
Thomas Jefferson

T HOMAS JEFFERSON WAS born April 13, 1743 in Virginia, the son of a self made man who died 14 years later in 1757. Graduating from William and Mary he began practicing law in 1767 and was elected to the House of Burgesses in 1769. In 1772 Thomas Jefferson married Martha Wayles Skelton, together they have six children, three dying in infancy. In 1782 his beloved wife dies, never legally replaced.

For Jefferson born into success, victories would come easily, inheriting his wealth early with an easily bought college education and a brilliant mind born to think far ahead of his day, his life was quite different from many Americans of both his times and today. He like all our founding fathers should be graded by the times he lived in, not ours:

The Times of Thomas Jefferson:

Ben Franklin, running away from his near en-slavery to his elder brother in Boston, would have to climb upward in Philadelphia. George Washington born inside a tavern in Virginia, fighting the French and Indians 1754 to 1761, he too would have to earn his fame and fortune. Neither of these two would ever have a college education, just life times of experiences in the schools of hard knocks.

Anther point to be understood, if life is hard today and truth is; it is mostly only as hard as you chose to make it for yourself. In the 1700's life was truly hard, not just in the lack of our technology but far more personally. Most people in America were sold upon their arrival to pay for the three month voyage here. If you were born here quite often you were sold as a child to who ever had the money, such as Ben Franklin above. Slavery by many different names was common place in 1700 America.

If you were female life was doubly hard, not only were you likely sold but with virtually no rights, you were literally at the mercy of your owner for the duration of your contract which you rarely had much say, if any.

If you became pregnant no matter who the father was, the contract owner could and quite often did stop by the court house and get the contract extended after all as a female you had no say what so ever.

Yes, for whites it was usually for four to fifteen years with some rights, for blacks it quickly was extended to lifetimes with virtually no rights, but the point was slavery was common-life for most people was hard, very hard. In America with a chronic shortage of labor—with wages more than twice that of Europe, in 1700 perhaps three times Europe's. Those who had the money ruled as colonial legislators by buying drinks in the taverns and in their assemblies they as usual voted in their own favor. If you were a free white male and could work, you were by definition middle class, again, if you were free.

By the early 1700's life in England had improved since the early 1600's and the English no longer poured into America as England was in fact industrializing before the steam engine. To replace the hordes of desperate Britons, human importers now went further and began importing Protestants from Scotland, Ireland, France, Germany and of course Black Africa—only colonial Maryland tolerated Catholics in America. New York: Jews, if they stayed quiet.

If life was very hard for many white males, doubly hard for all too many white women, for blacks in the America's life quickly went from hard, to harsh to virtually unspeakable in the 1600's. At least whites had people who looked like them in the colonial legislatures, blacks obviously did not. If conditions gradually improved for whites especially since improving conditions were needed to recruit more whites, not so for black Africans.

When the human cargo is presented to you in chains, by free blacks in Africa, it was quickly discovered, it was best not to release them. If you keep your cargo locked up, why give them fifty square (5x10) feet of living space, when that living space could be additional cargo. Thus fifty square feet quickly dropped to two square feet. Try living in two square feet for a three month voyage, not surprisingly many did not survive the voyage. It very quickly became a financial game of absolute cold statistics: A 90% survival rate was excellent but rare, 80% was good, 70% profitable, and so on.

In the colonial legislatures of America, few objected anywhere, after all they quite often were the buyers, to them the cheaper the cost, the better. After all if the survival rate for whites on the untamed frontier gradually rose from perhaps 30% in the early 1600's to about 80% by 1700 surviving their initial contracts, for 1st generation blacks it was undoubtedly even lower for surviving the equivalent period in a strange new land totally alien to all that they had known before. Granted statistics on the above are few and far apart, but everyone agrees life for the poor male indentured servants was terrible, for females all too often horrible and slaves just short of murder:

In 1669 Virginia legalized the murder of blacks by the High Court writing into the law of Virginia* the "casual" murder of blacks by the owner or their hired help as legal. Exactly the meaning of "casual" we can only infer that no one would be prosecuted unless the owner chose to prosecute which was soon clarified:

In the 1680's the Slave Codes were approved by the High Court of Virginia which passed into law: 1: Blacks were required to have written permits to leave their plantations or trying to escape their plight. 2: Blacks were no longer permitted weapons. 3: Twenty lashes required punishment for all blacks for violating laws 1 or 2. 4: Thirty lashes for any "black lifting their hand against their owner." Twenty lashes were considered life threatening; thirty lashes were considered a death sentence.

Not satisfied with there own greed, Virginia decided to force the hand of God by ordering in 1682: . . . "it is enacted that church wardens read this and the other act, twice every year, in the time of divine service, or forfeit each of them six hundred pounds of tobacco," . . .

Many other colonies soon followed Virginia's lead and added such penalties as branding a runaway slave with an "R" on the cheek and/or cutting their ears off or even scalping them.

While this concentrates on Virginia even Massachusetts supposedly founded for religious purity passed into law in 1641; ". . . lawful captives taken in juste warres, and such strangers as willfully sell themselves or are sold to us . . . . This exempts none from servitude who shall be judged thereto by Authoritie." Apart from spelling not being standardized then; we clearly see Massachusetts was not far behind Virginia in dehumanizing colored people. No matter how we interpret "juste warres" or judged thereto by "Authoritie."

Let us remember that life everywhere was cruel by our standards. Whether we are talking about England, France, Russia, Africa, the Middle East or China life for the poor was one poor harvest from starvation, or any of the other Four Horses of the Apocalypse. Their always were more people than the technology of agricultural knowledge could support if one harvest should fail. The exception was America where by their standards new technology had reached a fertile land of the Earth just waiting for people to tame the untamed frontier: a whole new world literally awaited them. For blacks and Indian slaves however their only purpose in the New World was to benefit their owners, period.

The only difference between us and the deer in the forest and the rats beneath our homes was that we humans could now write laws governing our behavior in obeying the yet unwritten but very real "law of survivor of the fittest" or perish. For like it or not this law had existed and governed our survival for millions of years during our evolution. Only now with our rapidly rising technology and thus our ability to grow more food, the stage is being set for: Unknown to all, the times are a changing . . .

For the natives living in the New World, however the arrival of the white men, quickly spelled disaster. The Spanish arriving in 1492 decided in exchange for being taught Christianity the natives were to be the willing slaves of Spain. The natives had no say and confined to the islands of the Caribbean and confronted with the iron weapons and amour was quickly subdued. What their bows and arrows could not stop the white man's diseases quickly finished off. The estimated native population of Hispaniola Island (Dominican Republic and Haiti) fell from 300,000 in 1492 to 500 in 1548—Spanish estimates. These few survivors quickly disappeared surviving only as a few Mestizos among the many Africans and Mulattos of the Caribbean.

For the white man and his cattle, sheep, goats and pigs plus the wheat, hay, and barley brought to sustain them the first year also unwittingly brought the microbes of the Old World with them. These unseen microbes and bacteria were unknown to anyone then, but they were just as real. Influenza, the Black Death, Measles and Small Pox perhaps the biggest killer in the New World quickly felled Native Americans. New World killer microbes like Syphilis were no match. Among the little islands of the Caribbean the European boot was just too heavy and swift for the Natives to develop anti (defensive) microbes for their hosts to survive.

Old World microbe killers had developed with man over thousands of years with the human populations of Europe, Asia and Africa to some extent. This was because trade went mostly east to west and back again where people lived along the Silk Road in cities and towns—feasting grounds for these microbes. In the North, South of the New World cities and towns only existed in Mexico (the Aztecs) and Peru (the Incas) with only scattered exceptions, between them was the scarcely populated tropical Central America where few Native merchants ever ventured to cross.

When the first English colonies were settled in Virginia (1607) and Massachusetts (Plymouth Colony 1620), they too were astonished that their neighbors, Native Americans died off so quickly to epidemics that claimed only a few of the whites.

With the astonishing quick elimination of their New World slaves and no desperate population in Spain willing to sell their freedoms for the enormous cost of a three month sea voyage available, the Spanish turned to Africa for their slaves. African slaves were partly endowed to Old World diseases by ancient trade across the Sahara and generally lived long enough to pass on their newly developing immunologic to their children. Thus they proved very profitable. They also proved deadly to the Europeans who were only poorly prepared for their microbes of Malaria and Yellow Fever—but poorly prepared is far better than no defense at all.

Thus the Caribbean was quickly a land of a few Europeans and many African slaves growing sugar for the Old World. Mexico (ex-Aztec Empire) and Peru (ex-Inca Empire) having far larger Native populations scattered over far larger lands for survivors of the many epidemics sweeping their populations away, far more survived gradually developing those ever so needed anti microbes. Nonetheless the Native population of Mexico fell from about ten million in 1500 to about one million by the early 1700's only from that low figure would it grow in the future.

By 1769 the vast majority of white males of the Thirteen Colonies were middle class farmers, some with a few slaves, most with-out through-out the colonies. In New England with its lack of good farm land very few slaves, except on their slave ships and personal servants for the wealthy. In Virginia, there were many slaves, most on large coastal tobacco plantations. By 1769 many would be farmers heading north, south and westward from Virginia looking for new lands to be tamed, that its coastal plantations were selling far more slaves than buying them. This was one reason that the overseas slave trade was abolished in our constitution—coastal Virginia could see its future after 1805 as a seller of what would become a limited and valuable resource—slaves.

Otherwise little had changed since 1700, except that since 1760 George III was now king and he was determined, "to be King" in the old sense where we the people would be his true subjects with our British lives at his mercy. Having overturned in effect the Magna Carter and its creation Parliament all that was left was to crush these colonists who dared to say no to his absolute dictatorship.

By 1775 with roughly a third of both houses of Parliament bribed and still another third political allies (mostly in the House of Lords) and a compliant Prime Minister to take the heat, if things went wrong, George III was truly king in the old sense. That is dictator for life with both houses of Parliament and the Courts effectively at his command.

The Life of Thomas Jefferson:

First let us begin with why Americans wanted independence from the British Empire. Many wanted independence so they could cross the Appalachians and settle their. George III by the Proclamation of 1763 had prohibited this. Still others like Washington wanted to sell the lands they had already purchased west of the line through the Appalachians. Others wanted to build hat and clothing factories to employ the excess populations building up in land hungry New England—prohibited by Parliament. The king had feared losing control of people living far from the sea while Parliament had feared competition from America.

Simply put many people wanted independence because they could vaguely see the future, where Ireland ruled by Britain for Britain's benefit was sinking into utter poverty, and soon would be utter starvation in the great potato famines of the 1800's.

India ruled by Britain for Britain's benefit would sink into the same disastrous situation in the 1940's and 1960's when many highly educated people (The Club of Rome) argued that sending food to the hundreds of millions was simply a waste, for India was beyond saving. Fortunately many countries stepped up and sent millions of tons of food aide to the hundreds of millions anyway.

The war for Independence:
and the rise of a New Republic:

While these events had not happened yet, *many in America could recognize the strangle hold Britain was strapping America into,* for the Crown feared losing control of people living far from the Atlantic. While allowing colonist to make hats and clothes would mean competition for British factories—Parliament objected to this. Building ships was okay, because if not built in America they would be built by who else had the good ship building wood—Scandinavia.

Nonetheless many people in 1775 still hoped for reconciliation with Britain especially in the then thinly settled middle colonies. Among these was the most famous person from America, Benjamin Franklin who as the representative of Pennsylvania, Massachusetts and other colonies was called to the Cockpit Arena in London for a meeting over the Boston Tea Party—where Bostonians dressed as Indians through a cargo of British tea into the harbor rather than pay the tax on it.

Revolutions are naturally led by the young, those who have learned to question everything but not yet accustomed themselves to the way life has always been. With education they have learned that in other worlds life is different. When they ask; why not here? The seeds of revolution are planted. If there is enough educated youth wondering why not here? Revolutions are made. The elders are naturally the slowest to join . . .

There for three hours Ben Franklin, now in his 70's, was mentally torn asunder by professional speakers hired for the occasion to mentally torture him. I find ten seconds difficult enough, but three hours! As the saying goes: in walked a loyal "**subject**" of the British Empire, out walked a proud and determined "**citizen**" of a nation about to be born: For the king, had already decided to crush these beyond pity criminal commoners, who had dared to say "**no to George III!**" And now Ben Franklin was young at heart!

The no of course, was no to taxation without representation. In the colonial mind we were British subjects which meant no taxes could be passed on to us directly by Parliament because we had no representation in Britain's Parliament. We could and did pass taxes on to ourselves in our own single house assemblies but our taxes were in fact quite low, mainly because we never accumulated the £120 million (a staggering sum; roughly $600 million in 1790 dollars) in debt nor did we pay any of the king's exorbitant £600,000 personal annual salary. By comparison we paid only $15 million for the Louisiana Territory in 1803 stretching to Canada and the Rockies which France must have thought a handsome sum.

Every colonist could see that if Parliament could pass taxes upon us we would be in the same slave state as Ireland—or soon to be India. Most Briton's agreed with us and the minority in Parliament called for reform:

That representation should be based on where the British subjects actually lived, not where they supposedly lived over five centuries previously in 1215.

However the majority of even the House of Commons enjoyed only having to face a few voters at election time let alone being able to buy a seat as the highest bidder. The House of Lords was held by inheritance and of course no American of common descent was eligible. This House of Lords even today is under attack in Briton for being un-elected.

Still there were a few others who differed with the British Empire for other reasons. Exactly when Thomas Jefferson came to this I can not say, but by the 1770's as a young man, he did. Britain then as now was in theory a Constitutional Monarchy. However George III had decided to obey his mother's command to him: "George, be king." To be king, in the since of traditional kings, George III pleaded poverty, to gain a bigger allowance from Parliament. Gaining a bigger allowance he bribed still more members of Parliament into still another increase and so on until he controlled Parliament.

This was openly done as people routinely had been legally bribed as the Royal Falconer, who received a hansom salary and did nothing. Except of course, obey the king's wishes in Parliament. Even a popular leader like William Pitt the Elder the Prime Minister who led Briton to victory in the Seven Years War 1756 to 1763 in Europe known as the French and Indian War 1754 to 1761 in America, was bribed by accepting the title of Earl of Chatham and the £300 per year bribe that meant he would gladly retire from the House of Commons and move to the less powerful House of Lords.

Jefferson later living in Louis XVI's France during the Revolutionary War 1775-1783 and visiting Ireland and Britain after the war; was disgusted with its king, dukes, lords and earls and its whole class structure towering over the impoverished millions. George III's yearly allowance of £600,000* (£1 ='s One British Pound Sterling or one pound of silver) dwarfed the British working person's earnings of £5 to £20 per year—and that income was that of those who could claim steady year round jobs, depending on their level of skill.

For the desperate, all too often the many poor incomes of probably £4 to as little as £2 per year reduced them to beggars and in desperation thieves—a hanging offense. The very idea of £ or pound thinking to the poor was absurd, they thought in Farthings (960 ='s £1) and half pence (or half pennies, 480 to £1). A six pence coin to the many was a small fortune. A shilling, almost a weeks pay equal to 12 pence each or 1/20th of a £ was true riches to the impoverished.

Even the dukes, lords and earls were quite satisfied with the King's annual bribes of £300 and up, commoners (the Gentry or middle class) in the House of Commons with less. All these people looked down on the true commoners as peasants desperate on their handouts literally of a few farthings for bare survival. This £5 to £20 per year incomes was the poverty that Parliament and George III meant to drive Americans to in a good year, let there be famine and we too would join the Irish and hundreds of millions of India in starvation. In 1799 famine struck the poor of England-London was quickly torn by riots.

None of this was spelled out of course as the Irish had yet to starve in the millions, Londoners in food riots let alone the hundreds of starving millions of Indians in 1775, but the attitudes of the English upper classes were clear to any who could see them. These attitudes were common in America as well.

Our wages were higher because of our traditional shortage of labor, perhaps £30 per year for a fulltime laborer and higher still for those with skills or those who could afford to buy slaves. The rich in America like Washington or Franklin might "earn" incomes of perhaps £600 per year but their attitudes were naturally inherited from the old continent from the people they had looked up to for all their lives. This is normal and explains why Hollywood actors and actresses are routinely asked to endorse products and ideas though why one might ask should they know better than anyone else?

George Washington (born in 1732) hoping to reach royal blood status by earning that honor, by fighting in the French and Indian War (1754-1761) in America—officially fought between 1756-1763 between France and Britain and others in the "Seven Years War" in a century of warfare over which country would rule the world. At Waterloo, in 1815, Britain was crowned (for the moment) champion of that very different world!

Most unfortunately for George, though following perfectly legal orders from above in Virginia, Washington was blamed by London for violating the truce between the two powers. Thus crowned in America for returning with the given up for dead, he was badmouthed in Britain. Then came Braddock's Retreat. Where George seized command of the leaderless army and led most of them to safety. A hero he was proclaimed by all survivors, including the wounded King's officers!

Most unfortunately for George, General Braddock who had won victories in Europe had not understood fighting in the wild untamed American forests was very different. And now General Braddock is dead . . .

Who to blame? Never could the British blame a fallen hero—a blue blood, obviously so . . . The commoner Colonel Washington, an officer of a lowly colony, Virginia was blamed for the disaster!

Thus George Washington crowned not once but twice as an American hero was hanged not once but twice by the British press. George waited forlornly for the world to come to his rescue. When in 1763 George Washington learned that his one true love, Lady Fairfax, had given up on him ever attaining knighthood (an officer of the King's Army) had instead consented to marry a blue blood by birth, in England. George the revolutionary, was born by his victories in America and his insults by Britain.

Declaring war upon the only world he had ever known, marrying Martha Curtiss as a rag to bind his deep personal wound. Washington would have to await a nation willing to tear up all that it had known, to join him. It is easy to forget our war of independence, was an uproar against those who declare "you there, you shall obey me, by the right of my birth." We colonial Americans, had finally grown tired of obeying these orders given by people, who in our mind, had never "earned" that right. Thus:

Our War of Independence!

These are the reasons Civil War within the British Empire broke out in 1775. These are the reasons America declared its independence in 1776. These are the reasons that every person signing that Declaration was willing to put their heads into the noose of the King's justice. These were the reasons worth dying for, if necessary.

For eight years British and other "Hessians" foreign troops, rampaged across America, but thanks to our continued faith in George Washington we gradually outlasted the British Army. Nonetheless not all thought the same way. The future Federalists would propose an upper House of the well bred, college educated and wealthiest Americans—in short our own House of Lords for the officers of the Revolution. Thankfully this was rejected. But they still thought that way.

This, his hatred of the upper class despise-meant of the working classes was what separated Thomas Jefferson from virtually all others of our founding fathers:.

We the people vs. the rich and power full.

Washington among others hated the British despise-meant of them personally, but not that of the average workers. To Washington, Adams and Hamilton among the future Federalists those who worked with their hands were of a lower being. With the American Revolution won the future Federalists would soon, if not already despise slavery mainly because to them there was little difference between slaves and whites who worked with their hands.

This was the cause of Jefferson's Democratic-Republican Party for to them there was every difference that mattered. **The white working classes had fought for their freedoms in the Revolutionary War, the slaves had not**—quite often freed by the British to fight the whites enslaving them. But the British officers quickly proved to be as bad as the Patriots. That might not seem important to you, but to the worker who had withstood bullets and cannon fire it was damn important. See: WWII and the black man: That was damn important to them too!—Chapters 4 & 6.

The white working man had earned his freedom and saw no reason to give it up to the officers who had commanded them in war. The war was over, sacrificing one's liberty to fight the common opponent was no longer necessary.

Just as the commoners of England had joined with the Dukes, Lords and Earls against the hated King John in 1215 and demanded and won the House of Commons as an equal body to the House of Lords for their officers, our working class whites saw no reason to surrender their freedoms either. Just as the aristocrats of Europe looked down on the starving peasants around them, so too did our aristocrats. This was natural; it simply was the way the world had worked for thousands of years with only the occasional exceptions like in ancient Athens and Rome and in 1215 Britain.

Now, perhaps we can see the absolute bitterness between the Federalists and *the abomination in their mists: Thomas Jefferson*. This champion of the French Revolution (1789): killing thousands who described it simply as "a few deaths to the liberty tree, as its natural manure of both patriots and tyrants." *To Jefferson the Federalists were the tyrants in our mist.*

This should not take anything from the Federalists, after all they were patriots, and with-out Washington's leadership victory would never have crowned our efforts.

Jefferson was far from perfect. Thomas Jefferson was a thinker not a man of action like Washington. Jefferson could never have crossed the Delaware. Colonel Ben Franklin of Pennsylvania upon meeting the much younger Colonel Washington of Virginia in the French and Indian War (1754-1761) wrote in his diary about Washington: "Now there is a man I would gladly follow into battle." Only Washington could stare total defeat in the face, raise an attack force, cross the Delaware River and charge to victory. For with-out that victory at Princeton Christmas Day 1776, our revolution most likely would have died by spring as the British thought it was about to.

Jefferson convinced that women existed only to give pleasure to men. Native Americans tied to ancient hunting and gathering, were simply destined for oblivion or extinction. On slavery he fully realized its evilness, only he knew not what to do. Dependent on the wealth it generated for him personally, he lied to himself, but at least he knew it was a lie:

Criticizing slavery in many letters but not publicly he wrote among many such letters: "I tremble for my country when I consider that God is just; that his justice cannot sleep forever."—"a revolution in the wheel of fortune" might lead to "an exchange of situations between slave and master." Jefferson knew slavery was evil, but he knew not what to do.

He lived in Virginia which at the time could be described as overrun with slaves. A practical politician, he knew he could never free them in Virginia and if he did he feared their retribution as God's wrath. Further he personally was dependent on the wealth the slaves produced for him. In the end he knew he lived a life drenched in sin. But again, he could not see the future but he knew his fellow Southerners dependent on their slaves for that wealth, would never free them with-out a terrible war.

You could say he foresaw the Civil War and Reconstruction to come, perhaps even the resulting reaction in the Jim Crow South but being human he could not see Dr. Martin Luther King, Jr. and his message of "love your opponent." For Gandhi and King were not born yet and no one had lived *since Jesus Christ had ever preached "forgive them, for they know not, what they do."* What they did of course was crucify Jesus. Jefferson clearly did not want to be crucified by his fellow Virginians.

Yes, Thomas Jefferson deserves to be criticized for this stance especially since he knew he was drenched in the evilness of slavery, however if we admit that we too are human, perhaps we can forgive him for this sin, as horrible as it was.

I recall hearing many times: "I have nothing against blacks; I think everyone should own one." To this I was expected to laugh! That is the reality that Tom Jefferson should be judged against. For it was his reality as mine too growing up in white racist America. As evil as this thought was and still is, it still sadly exists, even in San Francisco of today, and few of us are as brave as Dr. Martin Luther King, Jr.

On the rights of women he simply believed what most men thought in his era. We should remember that if Morristown in New Jersey granted single women property holders the right to vote in 1801, that the grand State of New Jersey rose to the occasion and prohibited it in 1807, least others continue with such a dangerous idea!

It would be 1890 before Wyoming entered the Union as the first state granting women the vote. Only by 1920 would we as a people help lead the 20th Century in recognizing women as people deserving rights.

The Cherokees and colonial Native America:

On Indian rights the Cherokees in the Southern Appalachians stood as an exception to the Native American rule of fight until you die as a people, but they still refused to give up their extensive traditional hunting grounds wherever possible. Having watched their traditional bully the Tuscarawas exterminated in front of them, the Cherokee's in the mid 1700's had begun to seek the secrets of the white man's super power:

A Cherokee chief went into a white man's town and asked the blacksmith if he could make him a tool he had seen a white farmer use. The blacksmith pulled a log off the shelf and turned its many leaves, looking at its many scratches and drawings before asking him if the drawing in the log was the tool he wanted? Replying yes, he asked about this log and its many leaves. The blacksmith replied this was a book written by all the greatest blacksmiths of all time. A how to do it book of the 1700's.

By Jefferson's era they had begun to learn to read and write their own language and the white man's too. In doing so they also learned that after the French and Indian War, to the white man, the only good Indian was a dead Indian. Refusing to fight the white man except in their courts of law, even when usually losing, they knew to fight otherwise would only mean their own extinction.

In the end of course having won their rights to their lands in the U.S. Supreme Court, President Jackson to applause North and South in 1836 ordered all Indians remaining east of the Mississippi to move to Oklahoma or die—"Let the Supreme Court defend them, if they dare." This Jefferson understood would happen, no matter what Jefferson felt. The Trail of Tears or extinction would happen sooner or later.

Jefferson's other contributions include something we usually take for granted, freedom of religion, it should not be. In colonial America only Maryland founded by Lord Baltimore as a refuge for English Catholics, had partial religious freedom. All twelve other colonies had an official religion, usually Congregationalist north of Maryland and Episcopalian, south of Maryland. Uniting to fight Britain, religious restrictions obviously fell by the wayside, except to the established clergy in each of the now states. Jefferson disallowed the state church in his 1786 Virginia's Constitution. Gradually the other twelve states would follow. Note our constitution only forbids the national government from promoting any religious sect—though this would later be re-interpreted to apply to the states as well.

We the People,(Tom Jefferson) as President:

Finally one last contribution by Jefferson: his hatred of war. As all the above clearly illustrates the world of 1800 was far, far from perfect. The French Revolution had drastically changed the world for the good. Alas, the French poor and middle classes un-used to self government quickly devoured their own revolution but its dream of "The Rights of Man*" would live on in the 1800's to revolutionize Europe.

Our Federalists euphoria at the news from France quickly fell into despair. The French trying to make their world perfect at once, violently turned it upside down, and many everywhere objected. In France, the guillotine went into over drive; royalist Europe declared war and in America our Federalists half expected Jefferson to do the same—rip their heads off, to them. In 1799 Federalist America declared an "un-declared" war against revolutionary France. In 1800 when we the people elected Jefferson, it seemed too many Federalists, the end of our revolution and there own lives to follow shortly.

In short America had changed between 1775 and 1800. **In 1775 we were British Colonists, looking upward in awe; in 1800 we were mostly Americans looking at each other as equals.**

As Americans, our know it all elites, were no longer held high in esteem for President Adams (1797-1801) was not President Washington (1789-1797) and we the people knew it. For clearly Adams would never have crossed the Delaware either. When he was criticized, Adams allowed the press to be silenced and one critic, a congressman who dared call Adams a tyrant, thrown into jail, for doing so and his wife and child thrown into the street. Washington would as he did, just accept the criticism, no matter how much it hurt—and it did.

When in Jefferson's inaugural speech of 1801 his "we are all (Democratic-) Republicans, we are all Federalists" signaled his acceptance of **the loyal opposition.** Jefferson understood the meaning, though it would take a few decades to sum it up that "we were all patriotic Americans, even those who disagree" in a short phase.

In 1801 Britain and France made peace as we did. America prospered and Jefferson was able to buy Louisiana in the interlude. All was good. In 1805 they went back to war. Both countries began seizing our ships, Britain if our ships traded with Europe without inspection for an ever growing list of contraband. France seized our ships if we had them inspected by Britain. It was the 1790's all over again. All was bad. The Federalists had chosen the French Revolution to fight. Naturally the Democratic-Republicans, the lovers of the French Revolution, quickly demanded war with Britain.

In December 1807 Jefferson prevailed upon congress to suspend all trade with both. This was a gamble that both Britain and France would back down. Instead they both tightened the screws still tighter. Now, all was worst. Our exported raw materials prices hit the floor, while our manufactured imports soared in prices. Jefferson refused to back down. He knew peace hurt, but war against the British Empire would hurt far more and endanger our unity, for still mostly Federalist New England favored trade with Britain only, under almost any conditions.

In March 1809 a new President: James Madison lifted the embargo. The march toward war quickly resumed. In 1812 it began, and once again our coast was ravaged highlighted by the burning of Washington D.C.

The world is far from perfect today, in 1801-1809 it was if anything, far worse. Especially for a little country squeezed between the super powers of the day.

After Jefferson's retirement in 1809 he gradually struck up a letter exchange with his fellow ambassador to Louis XVI's court, John Adams—with Ben Franklin in the 1770's who died in 1791. The stubborn John Adams would of course live to see our fiftieth anniversary on July 4th 1826 that Adams had pushed so hard for back in 1776. These two men who with John's wife Abigail had been the best of friends, before falling apart in bitter political warfare in the 1790's while never abandoning their positions, gave us a great insight into their politics.

John Adam's last words: "Jefferson still lives!"—The afternoon of July 4th 1826. Two patriots to the bitter end, only Tom Jefferson had in fact died a few hours earlier on this our fiftieth birthday. Two patriots with a capital P to the bitter end.

T J in hindsight:

We now know that Thomas Jefferson was in fact guilty of the heinous crime he was accused of; keeping an African Venus at Monticello. DNA tests prove that the one known male child of Sally Henning was fathered by someone in Jefferson's male family and Thomas Jefferson, by his own notes was the only Jefferson at Monticello at the time of his inception. Further Jefferson listed the fathers of all his black children except those of Sally Henning and he requested that Sally Henning and her children be freed upon his death. Deeply in debt, this was granted; Jefferson did not request this for any other slaves.

Jefferson married Martha Wales Skelton in 1772; together they produced six children by 1782, when as often happened in his time she died along with three of their children in infancy. He never officially remarried. He quite apparently loved Martha deeply, and never could replace her. So what did he do, he was human.

Sally Henning was there and we have to think that to some degree she was willing,* had he legally married her, his political career would have been totally destroyed, and the marriage quickly annulled by Virginia, if ever allowed. If they married in the eyes of God, he simply joined thousands of other married couples on the frontier where preachers were few and far between. After all, he truly believed that women existed for the pleasure of men. He may have been totally wrong on this, but who is ever totally right on everything?

Finally in conclusion, you might have noticed millions of people voting in our primaries all across America in 2008 and in 2012. That was Jeffersonian Democracy at work, **we the people**, deciding who our next President would be by our votes in the primaries. Still to this day, no other country allows its "we the people" (no matter how right or how wrong we may be) to make that decision. Their political aristocrats only, elect who their "we the people" finally get to chose from.

This difference might be said what de Tocqueville described as America's "associational vitality." Or we the people of America expect more of ourselves than what government requires us to do—for example: volunteering for the public good. The thousands perhaps more than a million volunteers taking the time to campaign for our politicians of all creeds are truly the inheritors of Jefferson's fondest hope about our future. Thank you to all of them regardless of the candidates you supported and the same must be said of those who volunteer for thousands of other worthy causes, I know Jefferson would applaud you as well. For you are the spirit of "we the people."

This chapter began with an oblique attack on Jefferson for being born into a rich privileged life. He was. Credit to him I say, for over coming that natural bias towards his own class. Jeffersonian Democracy might have happened with out him. America was inherently heading that way as British Colonialists, looking up in awe, became Americans, looking at one another as equals, just as we were heading for religious freedom as well. No one person can change the world, but someone has to push on that door blocking change for it to fall away. How the world would be with-out them, we can not know, so let us praise them for pushing.

In 1776 besides our Declaration of Independence, Edward Gibbon published the first of six volumes of *The History of the Decline and Fall of the Roman Empire.* Our founding fathers may have learned the following about that most successful republic founded more than two thousand years earlier by 1787:

This the most celebrated work in the English language—*Oxford Encyclopedia of World history*. These volumes of that ancient republic was studied by our founding fathers, which might have learned the following:

The Roman Republic:

What they did right:

1. A two chambered congress with ultimate power in the lower chamber.
2. The smaller Senate somewhat removed from the people, so that wisdom might prevail over the spur of the moment.
3. The larger House of Plebs (people) closely connected to the people to force the Senate to act upon the needs of the ordinary citizens.
4. A citizen army whose loyalty was to the Republic.
5. Taxes paid by the rich, which created a long term feedback of wealth to the working classes.

and, What they did wrong:

1. A divided executive, which meant whenever they disagreed nothing was done, necessitating the appointment of dictators who only once voluntarily surrendered their powers once granted—Cincinnatus.
2. No separate judicial system.
3. No limiting mechanism to keep the House of Plebs, or representatives from becoming a disorderly mob.

and in the end:

4. A professional army whose loyalty ultimately passed from the Republic to individual generals. Who in the end destroyed the Republic.

While our constitution was written by James Madison (our 4th president) he was a student of Jefferson then serving as ambassador to France once again in 1787. Madison using Jefferson's Virginia constitution of 1786 as his guide must share with Thomas Jefferson the honor.

In crafting our constitution it was felt that a professional army was required to police our vast areas. Therefore as a guard against individual loyalties building toward generals it was decided that our soldiers and officers must transfer regularly from post to post.

Let us end this chapter by praising a few Democrats for making America better: Pres. Jackson for restoring Jeffersonian Democracy and F.D. Roosevelt for giving us hope in the Great Depression. Now let us give praise to a few Republicans for making America better: Pres. Lincoln for freeing the slaves and Teddy Roosevelt for breaking up the giant corporations and trusts strangling America. Finally there is one other person: Dr. Martin Luther King, Jr. who would push very hard on that door to change America for the better.

In memory of Thomas Jefferson: A lifetime well spent making this world better:

1776—Writes draft of Declaration of Independence.
1777—Proposes Virginia Statute of Religious freedom.
1778—Helps persuade France to join our war against Britain.
1786—Religious freedom established in Virginia.
1801-1809—Revolutionizes America with Jeffersonian Democracy.
1803—Purchases Louisiana Territory—doubling U.S. land area.
1807—When push comes to shove, chooses peace over war.
1825—One of his dreams is fulfilled—the University of Virginia opens to even the poorest citizens. Though by this time several states had opened state supported institutions, thereby beating Virginia to this honor.

AUTHOR NOTES

*Note 1: These money amounts used can be very loosely translated into the dollars ($) of today by simply adding 00 on to them. Thus Franklin and Washington in our actual buying power earned several 100's of pounds (£) or 10,000's of dollars ($) per year. Probably about $60,000 per year each; that hardly sounds rich to us but our technology has allowed our average incomes to buy about 16 times what their incomes could buy. So in that sense £600 in their money ='s $60,000 in our money adjusting for our technology almost a million dollars per year ($960,000) in our actual incomes. Thus a £30 annual income for a full time laborer is $3,000 in our money and $48,000 annual income allowing for our technology. A £5 annual income is $500 in our money, $8,000 in our technology. Near starvation wages anywhere.

In our world living on £30—their money or $3,000—our money per year is very difficult yet they survived in the 1700's by living with-out our technology in homes without electricity, in door plumbing or glass windows—usually glazed thin paper so even the poorest home could have light in the day. Even by their standards they were the working poor. On the £5 or $500 per year in our money that the poor of Europe lived on, you might understand why thievery and prostitution were rampant.

How much would Tom Jefferson have paid for a computer? Far more than the £20 equivalent in 1790 money for a computer, monitor, printer and software etc. that we pay today (by the above math £20 in 1790 = $2,000 today); is a very safe bet. Multiply the $2,000 by 16 (our technology vs. theirs) and you get $32,000; a small fortune in 1790. Yet Jefferson probably would have gladly borrowed $32,000 from Franklin to buy one or a second one for Franklin, I have no doubt. We gladly paid millions for individual computers for doing far less a few decades ago.

*Note 2: Reference to slave conditions in America is largely drawn from "IN THE MATTER OF COLOR" by A. Leon Higginbotham, Jr. a study in: Race & The American Legal Process; The Colonial Period.

*Note 3: Sally Henning, at the age of 13, in the late 1780's visited both London and Paris while escorting the youngest of Jefferson's daughters to see both the Adams in London and Jefferson in Paris. In both cities after more than a year in Europe she simply had to know she was free legally, for slavery was not allowed in either country.

Why would she choose to remain a slave? We cannot say for certain: However, if she looked around at the desperation of the uneducated poor around her in both countries; her relatively high status as a trusted house servant and with her family in Virginia, were most likely the reasons.

*Note 4: "The Rights of Man" the guiding principle of the French Revolution—1789. Tom Jefferson as the ambassador to France was consulted on this: "Men are born and remain free and equal in rights." The French Revolution would be subverted from the top by Napoleon; despite this his triumphant armies would spread its principle across the face of Europe. Defeated in the end (1814-15), the spirit would rise again and again until Europe freed itself from its ancient class structures in the 19th Century and in Russia beginning in 1905. Though in Russia's case they too would find their freedoms usurped by Lenin and Communism.

Also the Latin American revolts of the 1820's were against this spirit: "The Rights of Man" by Spain (overrun by Napoleon, but now freed) trying to reform itself and thus the towering elites of Latin America over the impoverished millions below their feet. Those towering elites objecting quickly rebelled and won their independence; the elites, freedom from Spain so they could continue to tower over the millions below their feet. The little "we the people" of Latin America since then are still trying to scale these heights with varying success.

*Note 5: Much of this work comes from JOYCE APPLEBY's book: THOMAS JEFFERSON—a great work of art and throughout this book the Oxford Encyclopedia (desk version) of World History to check all facts.

CHAPTER III

From Andrew Jackson to the times of Abe Lincoln and the birth of Modern America

URING OUR REVOLUTION the British having failed at crushing the rebellion in New England in 1775 met a frustrating no win but non losing scenario in mid America than in 1780 invaded the South looking for that victory so tantalizing just around the corner, or so they thought. Capturing Charleston on a second try the invaders moved inward where among others was the Swamp Fox (Francis Marion) and a teenaged Andrew Jackson awaited them en route to their final crushing surrender at Yorktown in 1781.

After Jackson and a friend failed to kill British troops they were captured and Jackson then aged thirteen was brought before the British Colonel and commanded to polish his boots. For daring to say no to British Tyranny the Colonel raised his sword to halve this arrogant teenager's skull. Young Andrew raised his hand and deflected the sword into disfiguring both his hand and skull but survived to change his corner of the world.

Over the next thirty years young Jackson shooting game for a nearby tavern in east Tennessee earned a law degree by many years of trial and practice on the frontier with his law book in one hand and a rifle in the other.

With the outbreak of war in 1812 the Tennessee Volunteers and by now General Jackson were called to action. Fighting the Creek Indian Confederacy all across Alabama finally slaughtering their mostly women and children at Horseshoe Bend—Indians had slaughtered mostly white women and children at Fort Mimms, north of Mobile a few years earlier, as our mutual slaughters continued, as we moved across America.

At the end of 1814 flush with victory over Napoleon in Europe a British Army laid siege to New Orleans which controlled the Mississippi River's outlet to the sea and thus the vast interior of North America in this world before the rail roads. General Jackson was ordered to save the city. In

January 1815 Jackson delivered a Waterloo type disaster to the British—see the movie "The Buccaneers" for a great portrayal of this battle.

In 1824 General Jackson won the election for President but by "we the people" standards was cheated out of it. Thus the Democratic-Republican Party of Jefferson blew itself up. In 1828 Jackson to popular acclaim North and South won the election on the new Democratic Party's ticket. We the people—free at last, free at last (yes the white males only) free at last was a new development; what shall they do?

This is a strange concept but the white male was truly free for the first time in some two thousand years. A king or emperor shall not rule nor a tiny arrogant few (like the Lords of England or our own Federalists) shall not rule either, the many little we the people (as in Commoners of olde England) themselves of America shall rule. Only once this concept was a given understanding, as we truly became Americans could other's freedom become a concern to the white males. Their own freedom naturally came first, so now, what shall they do?

First we shall destroy the banks. We the people hate them, so why keep them around at all? Because industry of all kinds, grind to a halt with-out banks. With no banks you can not borrow money, so very little gets built.

So President Jackson warred upon the banks but did not destroy them. He in effect forced them to lend money cheaply. Interest rates like the 23% today's banks charge you if you make a mistake disappeared. Laws were passed making lending rates of more than 10% criminal. Usury Laws we called them.

His detractors, the rich, said America will now collapse into financial ruin. Yet, we did not! Nonetheless, despite their claims of ruin, many of these laws would last for over a century. In the 1970's facing double digit inflation our congress wiped them out. Our rich (Wall Street) have jumped for joy ever since. It took them a hundred and forty years, but Jacksonian America was dead at last. The rich now rule. That is, since the 1970's. Don't tell me you haven't noticed the rich getting richer and the middle class sinking into oblivion! Now at least you know why, **a Teddy Roosevelt* we are in deep need of!**

Otherwise in the 1830's, we the people wanted land, cheap land. The Native Americans have it and too much of it, so we the people say let us take it! So President Jackson tells the U.S. Supreme Court to take a hike or literally "defend them (native Americans), if they dare." The Army, the

President and we the people vs. the Court and Native Americans—the Court agreed to a short hike and the Cherokees (and many others) to The Trail of Tears—abandoning their traditional homes of their many, many great grand parents in the East for Oklahoma. For their only alternative was extinction, what else can one do?

Most of this land would soon be lost as well. This might have been wrong, but it simply was reality; go to Oklahoma or die as a people. We the people (white males only) are free, free at last, free at last, now what will we do?

Old World Reality at lasts sets in upon us:

Unfortunately now that we are free (the white males only) the world conspires against us. Our population is literally soaring upwards, from zero in 1600 to about 300,000 in 1700 to over 5,000,000 in 1800 as our prosperity and power as the first truly free people on Earth soars upward and so does our en-evitable doom.

Until now our number one problem was labor, or the lack of it. People were always needed, everywhere in the old world people were not needed, hence people were as cheap as they, the people could tolerate. Not true in the USA people had the exact opposite view, people were as expensive as people could demand. Granted this is difficult to understand but true, America in 1776 was a great place for a white male!

Not able to recruit people fast enough, we started en-slaving them and forcing them here to meet our insatiable demand. Even so our founders cared about those less fortunate than us whites therefore even as we en-slaved people, others fought on there behaves. Greed naturally being stronger, people laughed at them and their silly ideas, but their dreams would not go away.

Some states having far fewer slaves than others, were far more willing to tackle the issue than others so: In 1790 to keep the peace between the now states we agreed to automatically send all ideas regarding slavery to the trash can of "for further study."

But doing so did not make our greed go away. For people everywhere are greedy, and we are no exception, as our population continued to soar upward to 7 million in 1810, to ten million in 1820, to over thirteen million in 1830 and onward and upward it continued without relent.

So too did our greed, as long as demand for labor grew as fast it was no problem. Reality however soon set in for a different reason. Even as we were still very short of labor as a new nation-technology soon brought changes. How to haul cargoes of potatoes, apples and wheat eastward from the lands now open to us on the route to the Pacific eastward was soon a major problem, needing a major solution.

The Erie Canal and our Modern World begins:

In these still olden days there were but two ways to haul cargo, over land by human or beast or by water. Since by water is vastly easier than hauling cotton over a mud soaked hill just to try controlling one's descent on the other side lest we get dirty cotton and us as well, so water was definitely the best route.

To make a long story short the Erie Canal soon launched New York City to greatness. For this canal cut right thru the Appalachian Mountains. Opened in the 1820's using canals, dykes and pumps it was powered by horses and mules pulling barges from Buffalo to Albany and then down the Hudson river to NYC.

This route previously discovered by mother nature to drain Lake Ontario when the St. Lawrence River was choked with ice in Canada during the last Ice age. Now that the river was free of ice and therefore the vastly greater lake shrunk to today's size, this route was now powered by many workers guiding the many barges up the canals in both directions with the help of many dams. Only our modern world soon came up with a newer and better idea:

The steam powered railroad. An Englishman (Thomas Newcomen) among others discovered the coal fired steam (water) engine to pump unwanted water from Cornish tin mines in the early 1700's. Needless to say other people (most notably James Watt) quickly wanted to find new uses for it. About 1800 a Frenchman built the first steam powered locomotive, which soon tipped over and crushed him. Great idea . . .

In 1805 Robert Fulton of the U S built the first steam boat. Gradually, Englishmen discovered if you put the locomotive on rails first of wood but soon of iron the railroad with steam powered locomotives soon followed in the early 1830's. Thus even as the Erie Canal caused a severe labor shortage to spur Irish to flee to America our first railroad was built to replace all the suddenly un-needed labor.

Thus the Irish arrived in New York City only to discover they were not welcomed in the 1830's. This was new in America. Previously we had always welcomed everyone even Native Americans if willing to live by our rules—but rarely happening.

While we still had a shortage of labor across America, in New York where the Irish were pouring in on empty cargo ships returning to the US—ships carrying huge cargoes of wheat etc. to Europe but smaller cargoes of manufactures to the US took humans to fill their otherwise empty holds. The impoverished of Europe gladly took whatever space available.

In Ireland the great potato famines in effect told all Irish stay and starve or go anywhere you can. So unwanted or not they the majority of Ireland, poured into America. Unwanted except by those willing to employ those willing to work for less; and in America as everywhere there are always the privileged who gladly look down on all others.

Thus in America the old world of the privileged and the down trodden began to appear even among whites. This was new to America but old as humans in the old world. For the first time there is an abundance of labor so the I'll do it for less driving wages lower and lower made its debut in America.

Thus, The birth of modern America begins:

For modern America began to grow as the unwanted of Europe the Irish, and soon followed by still more unwanted peoples of Europe and soon Asia continued to pour in despite being called daego's, white niggers, pollacks and every other insult imaginable by the native American laboring class. For competition willing to do my work for less is never ever welcome.

Reality is: if at home you are in effect are told stay and starve or go and be insulted, again what choice does one have? Just as my eldest ancestor in America sold himself for eight years hard labor, if the choice is between dying or being insulted, insults here we come and the Poles, Greeks, Italians, Chinese and Japanese poured into America especially as the roads are paved in gold stories filtered back home and the cost of transport fell with steam powered ships.

Granted our roads have never been paved in gold, but if you think a dollar a day is good money, great even, how does several dollars a day sound? For even in New York City the teeming masses of the old world are welcomed by manufacturers as the world's impoverished will always work for far less than native whites. So gradually, modern America begins to grow even as General Jackson sets the white man truly free.

The Life and Times of Abe Lincoln:

About the same time General Jackson was fighting the Indians in Alabama—General Harrison defeated still more Native Americans in Indiana at Tippecanoe (and Tyler too) thus our near west of Alabama and Indiana were opened to settlement. Soon followed by now President Jackson ordering all surviving Indians east of the Mississippi to the strange foreign land called Oklahoma still more lands were opened to settlement and white America jumped with joy.

For we were determined to take those Indian lands and if the Indian chose to fight and die for them, so be it—for we the white males were free and all we needed was more land. Soon with Manifest Destiny the Pacific Ocean was quickly our goal and nothing, not Mexico or British Canada could stop us.

And so an unsuccessful farmer in Kentucky could give farming another try in Indiana, whose son was borrowing books to self educate himself. His name of course is Abraham Lincoln. By his adult times he was practicing law in Illinois and America has finally started moving forward as well as westward.

According to the Commerce Department from 1820 onward U.S. per person real income has begun to grow at 1.4% annually remarkably continuing thru today. That doesn't sound like a lot, but over 200 years of compounding it has meant: Factoring out inflation, a doubling roughly every fifty years, thus:

In 1820: $ 400 was our average income or $ 4,000 in our dollars of today.
By 1870: $ 800 was our average income or $ 8,000 in our dollars of today.
By 1920: $1,600 was our average income or $16,000 in our dollars of today.
By 1970: $3,200 was our average income or about $32,000 in our dollars,
      and in 2020: about $ 64,000 should be our average income in dollars of today.

Thus in real 1820 terms our incomes are up by a factor of 16. Inflation adds about x10 to the 1790-1960 figures. These are real triumphs of technology applied to the needs of all of us, in very real concrete terms. The old world average was probably in the two hundred dollar range. By that standard $400 let alone $800 a year our streets were seemingly paved in gold! Especially because our incomes were reasonably balanced.

By the 1850's our already high incomes were getting noticeably higher breeding confidence in all of us. It's difficult to explain the world of the 1850's but the government is selling western lands at dirt cheap prices, raising all the income it needs with-out income taxes, times are good. Then that same government decides you can't interfere with others property—as in slaves, who will take your job for half your pay; because a slave does what they are told. Or at least that is what is said. People get mad:

Suddenly a new party is born with Abe Lincoln the standard bearer for the Republicans who will soon claim to be the Grand Ole Party—GOP; as a joke that holds. In the 1790's Washington a believer in American manufacturing had declared we had none to protect. He was correct for the British Parliament had prohibited them.

Gradually we had built a base of manufactures and by the 1850's these factory owners wanted laws to aide them thus new pro manufacturing laws along with anti slave laws formed the basis of the Republican Party.

Thus the Whig Party which had elected several presidents on the basis that slavery was taboo from mentioning quickly disappeared while the Democratic Party with its slave half and non slave half quickly became bitterly divided. To us today the issue of slavery seems as if it would have dominated politics from 1776 to 1860. But that was a different world:

In 1776 as we declared our independence the only issue on hand was the British Empire trying to ram its tyranny down our throats. Our differences, no matter how serious paled into insignificance compared to that.

From 1783 to 1812 Washington, Adams and Jefferson while having many disagreements all in effect agreed on Washington's declaration that we needed thirty years of peace to solidify as a nation. From 1812 to 1815 as we again thwarted the original evil Empire's attempts at re-instating its tyranny again, our differences seemed minor.

For those who survived enemy armies trampling across our nation doing as they pleased, they certainly believed we must stand united or surely we shall hang separately. This was not an idle statement, it was the firm belief of a new nation trying to survive in a world of kill or be killed.

The world of our founders, no matter how entrenched, did die, as it must for it was not our destiny to remain but a footnote to Europe. Thus Abraham Lincoln born in 1807 Kentucky just west of the Alleghenies raised on a steady diet of hard fought battles, and of course great victories and the knowledge that we had won while witnessing first hand our spreading across a continent developed their own truths. This truth was very different from their elders.

Their elders growing up fighting desperately against Britain from Boston in 1775 to New Orleans in 1815 and from Charleston to Detroit in between was we must stand together or surely we will hang separately.

Slavery was an inconvenient trap spelling our doom if spoken of nationally. For the majorities North and South agreed we could never agree on slavery, thus we did what to most people is inconceivable today: We simply agreed to disagree on that and will talk about other things civilly.

Thus people simply agreed to disagree on slavery as we had on religion. One should remember that in the 1500's and 1600's both Protestants and Catholics had butchered one another throughout Europe. In fact one German village of Protestants united and burned out and murdered their Catholic neighbors on the same night that their Catholic neighbors burned out and murdered their village. This mutual savagery in the name of God only ended in 1648.

Thus the discussion of slavery nationally was taboo, except when our frontier entered new lands where the issue had yet to be decided. Thus with the exception of the Missouri Compromises of 1820 and 1850, slavery and Civil War were both taboo because to both the North and South the one equaled the other and the British Empire stood watching us closely.

New times call for a change, in politics:
The Republican Party is born.

Then came the 1850's: and a new generation was arising, we had built an industrial base and factory owners wanted new tariff laws to protect them. Others growing up on stories of our victories; while watching our country pour across the interior plains and heading for Oregon and the gold fields of California, simply never feared the British Empire.

Thus the Republican Party was born in 1853. While the existing parties refused to discuss slavery while supporting agricultural interests, thus the GOP grew in the North among younger voters who simply never feared the British Empire as their elders had. In 1856 with the Northern vote split between the Whigs (who never spoke of slavery) and Northern Democrats (who only spoke of slavery when the South was elsewhere) and the tiny Republican Party, The Southern Democrats (who never spoke of slavery with Northerners) won; even though President Buchanan was from Pennsylvania with decidedly pro slavery views—for he supported the Supreme Court's decision:

In 1857 the Supreme Court made its **Dred Scott Decision**. By this court decision a slave owner was legally protected in his property—slave rights in all parts of the country. Including in the North, where previously slavery had been declared illegal.

Suddenly slavery and Civil War was in heavy discussion everywhere. This decision also lifted Federal Law over states rights as in freedom of religion referred to earlier.

In 1858 the Democratic Senator Douglas of Illinois running for re-election was challenged by an upstart politician named Abe Lincoln. Since Douglas was favored to win the Democratic Party ticket for president in 1860, Abe Lincoln's incessant demand that Douglass answer yes or no to supporting the Dred Scott Decision attracted America's attention. A yes answer would destroy his Northern support while a no answer would destroy his Southern support.

Douglas eventually said no, opposing the Dred Scott Decision thus winning his senate seat and the Northern Democratic Party's presidential nomination. The Southern Democrats quickly broke away; the Whig Party broke up as the nation was about too. In the presidential election of 1860 Lincoln narrowly swept the North into the White House with just under 40% of the national vote, all in the North, while in the South, Lincoln was not even allowed on the ballots. Thus 40%, all in the North was the majority in the Electoral College and victory for Lincoln.

For the South, it was clearly now or never for the slave owners. What would the four out of five non slave owning whites choose to do? In seven states they were given no choice. The governor and state legislators being of the wealthier fraction also owned slaves. So like most people they voted on their own behalves. They voted for slavery and succession.

In four Southern states however the people demanded that the people be given the choice. The majorities of these four states: Virginia, North Carolina, Tennessee and Arkansas voted for continuing the union candidates. But South Carolina started the shooting at Ft. Sumter guarding Charleston Harbor.

Unfortunately many of these four choosing state legislators were also slave holders now forced to choose between the people who elected them and their own wealth—their slaves. Shockingly they voted for themselves and succession. After all they knew it was now or never for slaveholders.

We the people, were simply tossed overboard.

In two states Kentucky and Missouri the Governors disagreeing with their legislatures fought mini Civil Wars within their states while Delaware awaited what would Maryland do. President Lincoln dispatched the Federal Army to save them both for the union.

The Birth of Modern America:

The Supreme Court's Dred Scott decision of 1857 literally put the torch to our unity by prohibiting the majority in congress from preventing the further spread of slavery into the territories or even their transit through Free States. Extremists on both sides quickly took the lead, highlighted by first "Bleeding Kansas" and in 1859 John Brown's raid to free the slaves by storm by seizing the Federal Arsenal at Harper's Ferry, Maryland at the junction of Virginia's (and West Virginia's—today) border.

Many people ask was this bloody war to follow necessary? I say it was inevitable. If the Dred Scott decision had never happened some other event would have sparked the towering powder keg that had built up since 1775. Fundamentally this was because the America of 1850 and beyond held a very different inner truth then those Americans who had so desperately fought the British Empire between 1775 and 1815.

The generations that had fought the British Empire lived by the truth that we must stand united, or surely we will be hanged separately. Our republic had in fact barely survived both wars highlighted by the British burning Washington D.C. in 1814 and many leaders plotting the succession of New England in 1815. Since people everywhere have a great deal of pride and we are certainly no exception, we chose to remember our glorious victories and to forget our humiliations. Thus:

To the generations that followed, naturally not feeling the pain and fears of the previous generations, felt young, strong and vigorous. For they witnessed firsthand, America spreading across the continent, feeling our ever growing might and choosing to remember our victories and forgetting our many defeats to the British Empire—after all we had won hadn't we?

Therefore with each passing decade after 1815, the old sacred truth of the previous generations: We must stand united or surely we will hang separately; was gradually replaced in the North with that other sacred truth that had also been around since 1776: That slavery in the land of the free must be abolished, no matter what the price.

By 1850 the generations that had fought the British Empire were passing away and the younger generations that thought so differently were taking up the places of leadership both North and South. Thus the powder keg rapidly grew between North and South. Between those determined to abolish slavery and those who's power stemmed directly from it.

Any possible compromise possibly acceptable to the South ending slavery would have required compensation to the owners and all freed slaves to leave the South. Most Southern states not wanting free blacks had passed laws requiring newly freed slaves to vacate the state; if not they would be seized and resold. This was because free ex-slaves were a direct economic threat to working class whites. These terms would never have been acceptable to either Northern tax payers or Northern workers. We are all too self-centered for that to have occurred. For in the North resentment toward the Irish willing to work for what was now all too often being called nigger wages was building.

If the South would have been left to itself to abolish slavery it would have been a very, very long time before the South would have done so. The proof of this is that even when the North abolished slavery by force of arms, the South re-imposed its near equivalent: The Jim Crow South as soon as they could. Even when the Jim Crow South was abolished by Northern congressional action in 1964-1965, the middle class white South seriously considered going to war even then to preserve its privileges. I know, for I am one, though only a teenager then:

The main reason this second Civil War did not happen was the simple fact that the outcome of the first Civil War had so deeply been burned into the South's consciousness.

In 1965 I remember Jesse Helms as a commentator on the Raleigh, N.C. local TV news saying: "A hundred years ago we lost that war, and surely we will lose this one." Not long after he would be elected to the U.S. Senate as an arch conservative.

The reason the South would have taken a very, very long time to abolish slavery on its own was simply because there were so many slaves. The South's elites owned them and working class whites did not want to have to compete economically against them.

Yes if the slaves had been sent to fight the alleged supermen of Nazi Germany and the Samurai soldiers of Japan they would have returned determined to stand on their two feet and their children would have fought a bloody war of liberation in the 1960's and 1970's but that is my guess how long it would have taken for the South to free the slaves on its own. The North determined to abolish slavery in the land of the free could never have waited so long.

The American Civil War:

Due to the rising industrial power of the North and the rise of the anti-slave Republicans, in 1861 the Southern slave holding elites feeling that it was now or never for them, led their states out of the Union. They did this by using the firebrand anti-slave radical rhetoric and actions like John Brown's raid as attacks on the Southern way of life. The question that has been argued ever since is whether the Civil War was fought over Slavery or States Rights? The answer is in fact a three part answer . . .

> The majority of Southern people fought for States Rights.
> The majority of Northern people fought to preserve the Union.
> All fought over the state's right to have slavery and to succeed from the Union if necessary, to preserve it.

The primary reason for this debate is that people are far more self-centered than we sometimes prefer to think. The political leaders on both warring sides fought primarily over slavery while the rest of us fought primarily over states rights to succession. The Northern Republican leaders led by Abe Lincoln could never have sold a bloody war to the majority in the North only to make others free.

As proof of this the Emancipation Proclamation did not pass until 1863 even with-out the South's votes to bloc it for two years. The North could unite and would fight a bloody war however to preserve the Union. The war to free the slaves could only be a part of the war to preserve the union.

The Southern Democratic leaders could never have sold a bloody war to their majorities of non-slave owning whites only to preserve slavery . . . Several Southern states popularly elected representatives that rejected succession—but once the fighting started . . . The South could unite and would fight a bloody war to preserve its way of life.

In 1865 after four bloody years 350,000 Yankee soldiers lay in their graves, the exhausted North was victorious. The Union armies had every reason to be proud and to celebrate their triumph . . . Yet at Appomattox the proud and bloodied Army of the Republic first saluted and then fed the surrendering Rebel Southern Army that had been starved into finally surrendering. There can be little doubt that these simple gestures, at so painful a time for the war shattered South did much to undo the hatreds of war . . .

Reconstruction:

The North's attempt to mold the South into perfection after the Civil War: Let me start by saying: I do not have any sympathy for the former slave owning elites, including some of my own ancestors. When they chose to lead their states out of the Union, contrary to the wishes of the majority white let alone black populations of their states for their own sinister selfish reasons, they forfeited any right to anybody's sympathy.

Then after losing the war instead of accepting their loss of power they chose to use hate to regain it. They were evil people even if only by their chosen ignorance of the consequences of their actions. In this book I am simply trying to tell the truths as I see them.

With (the South's Elites) choices of war and hatred 620,000 Americans lay dead in the Civil War and a wasteland filled with racial hatred after the war. With these hatreds we are still paying for today, they deserve no one's sympathy, indeed not!

Immediately after the Civil War came Reconstruction. Would the South march boldly into the future or retreat back into the past . . . The victorious North was determined to force march the South forward. The old Southern ex-slave owning elites fighting for their survival inevitably became their mortal enemies but which way would the majority of white Southerners march?

First very briefly the Northern version: After the Civil War the North's effort to politically reconstruct the South was a noble* experiment that primarily due to the endemic corruption in both the North and South failed but did little lasting harm.

I could not disagree more. Corruption there was plenty of, but that was almost an incidental fly on the wall compared to the real problems: Every society has its elites and regardless of what you may think of them, they are a powerful force that when dealt with severely, will comeback if they can—with a vengeance . . . *so, do not let them!*

Since there was no "Marshall Plan" for rebuilding the South economically, the would be middle-class whites had no interest's in supporting the "march forward to an enlightened future" imposed governments. To make matters worse the North had taken the opportunity of the South's succession to erect high protective tariffs on foreign trade to protect its manufacturers, other countries responded against Southern cotton and tobacco exports.

This would keep the Southern economy depressed for many decades to come. With so few good jobs available, out of their many economic frustrations the white South quickly and deeply resented the promotion of "black rights" as being at their expense . . .

In Germany after World War One, their elites were hammered with heavy reparations with the "German war guilt clause" adding insult to injury. Rather than allowing themselves to be wiped out, they elected (like elites do) to make the German middle-class pay instead of them. This resulted in; the four trillion marks to the dollar middle class wipe-out and a nation filled with hate which in turn eventually brought Hitler and his Nazi thugs to power.

In the American South before the Civil War the plantation slave holders were most of the elites. Freeing the slaves' without even a token of compensation wiped many of them out, the largely unavoidable corruption that resulted from a world being violently turned upside down wiped still more and middle-class whites out as well . . . Then to add insult to injury many if not most of the old Southern elites were barred from voting, holding office and many occupations such as running newspapers. You can not under estimate the hatred that built up as a result among these displaced elites.

Under Reconstruction, political not economic, their places were taken by Scalawags*"—Southern opportunist traitors as far as the old elites were concerned and "Carpet Baggers"—Yankee exploiters (with their rug type satchels) of the South using the freed blacks as their tools while the old elites became outlaws, the original leaders of the Ku Klux Klan—though they usually called themselves other names like The White Camellias or The White Citizens Council.

The snobbery and fear toward blacks of the pre-Civil War (Antebellum) Southern elites now was outright hatred. Prior to Reconstruction the elites had acted "in a sense" on behalf of slaves because they were their property. Unless they tried to runaway, let alone rebellion, then death usually followed preferably slow agonizing deaths, before other blacks. For blacks existence in America had been for their benefit only, the very thought of any black ordering the former elites about let alone actually doing so caused unfathomable hatred immediately.

Otherwise quite often they had their slaves trained as black-smiths, foremen and carpenters—middle-class occupations then, at bottom class incomes. This was naturally resented by Southern middle-class whites who could not economically compete and in fact were being driven out of the Antebellum South as a result of such competition.

Reconstruction brought the old plantation owning elites and the would be middle-class whites together in the Ku Klux Klan as outlaws trying to overturn the imposed carpet bag governments. Thus a temporary alliance of the "old" elites and the white-working class united by their hatreds; the old elites for their loss of power and the middle-class for their loss of jobs when they were so few in the war shattered post-war Southern economy was formed.

Here lies the key to why Reconstruction went so wrong: Because Reconstruction was only political the South remained a land of economic ruin through-out this twelve year period. All people want jobs, good jobs, and when they can't get them they become frustrated and look for someone to blame. Thus the Great Depression in Germany led directly to Hitler and his slaughter of the Jews.

In the Old South the ex-slave owning elites though justly hammered and driven from power were now able to seize upon this middle-class frustration and use it to eventually drive the reconstructed governments out by illegal means, thereby marching the South back into re-instating the past, as much as possible by the leaders of the original Ku Klux Klan.

This was disastrous for race relations in America . . . Because this alliance was to use illegal means in order to drive the imposed carpet bag governments out it had to become socially mandatory for all whites to vocally insult blacks repeatedly to continually prove their loyalty to the "Old South." Otherwise they were denounced as scalawags—traitors to the "Old" South and make no mistake the Ku Klux Klan hanged many whites as traitors to the "lost cause." For the K.K.K. was determined that the "Old South" would rise again . . .

Twelve years and many tears later the frustrated North abandoned its perhaps noble attempt to mold Southern society into its image of perfection—as their "lost cause." When the federal troops were withdrawn most Yankee civilians wisely left with them and the Southern Scalawags did their best to blend in or headed north or west.

Thus all this built up hatred was focused on those that were left behind to blame: The southern blacks—this was the unmitigated disaster for race relations in America caused by the failure of Reconstruction.

The leaders of the original Ku Klux Klan now took power legally and they acted to insure that the Southern blacks would henceforth always "know their place" at the bottom of the social, economic and political pyramids. When the old Southern elites returned to power the original outlaw Ku Klux Klan organizations were disbanded. In their place the "Jim Crow South" was legislated in legally. To the extent possible the Old South out of hatred was reborn . . .

Blacks were now prohibited legally from voting and their civil rights in the courts against whites were forbidden as well. Soon however the old elites/working-class alliance broke down as managers of businesses sought out the best workers at the lowest wages which all too often turned out to be blacks—as far as the white Southern "would be" middle-class were concerned. This then led to the re-birth of the Ku Klux Klan's as they are remembered today:

The failure of Reconstruction:

Technically reborn in Indiana of the 1870's, for the hatred quickly spread northward where the already hatred of Irish quickly spread to all new foreigners entering the country for millions of new laboring class workers were pushing our wages downward nationally.

For now with Negroes moving north, and East Europeans moving to New York—the white niggers, were everywhere and in San Francisco the

Asiatic hordes—the Mongols of Genghis Khan were soon pouring in. The uneducated masses everywhere looking for good jobs at ever decreasing wages, it was war upon the would-be native white middle class!

Hatred, economic hatred now ruled supreme!

The new Ku Klux Klan's purpose, now run by the Northern and Southern non-elites, was to enforce the "know your place in the back" mentality on blacks that the Southern upper class gradually no longer cared to enforce legally. The same can now be said of the Northern K. K. K. also arising in the post Civil War, as people moving northward looking for good jobs became a threat to those who had just liberated them.

Because this hatred stemmed from economic competition and blacks were moving northward along with Southern whites looking for jobs, good jobs this "disease" or "virus" of hate spread with them and infected many Northern working and middle-class whites as well. This Southern hatred or virus now became a national disgrace, which most un-fortunately is still with us today . . . Only with the gradual acceptance of "political correctness" are the very deep psychological wounds of this disease beginning to heal.

The lasting damage of Reconstruction was that by making the old elites into criminals it became acceptable for middle and working-class whites to murder blacks which previously only the elites could legally do but very rarely in fact did and indirectly by making it socially mandatory for all whites to repeatedly vocally insult blacks to prove their loyalty. The temporary alliance against the "carpetbag" governments resulted in the "Jim Crow" legislation being passed when the old Southern ex-slave owners regained their power.

These three things:

The old elites becoming criminals to regain their lost power . . .
The non-elites "right" to murder blacks and "disloyal" whites . . .
The social obligation of all whites to repeatedly insult all blacks to prove one's loyalty to the Old South, now reborn out of its economic frustrations . . .

would never have happened at least not in their severity
with-out Reconstruction as it actually happened. An economic
reconstruction might have avoided this tragedy.

The hatred as symbolized by "Damn Yankees" did not come from the Civil War. The Germans do not hate us for beating them in two world wars nor do the Japanese hate us for fire bombing their wood cities with both napalm and atomic bombs. This is because people everywhere recognize that war is hell on earth. Very few Southern Rebels could hate Northern soldiers after their salute of respect at Appomattox . . .

The hatred came from being kicked and trampled upon after the war. Yelling Damn Yankees became another way of proclaiming ones' loyalty to the Old South and opposition to the imposed carpetbag governments. The children of the Civil War Confederate veterans mis-learned the origins of this message of their parents.

To a child understanding the politics of Reconstruction was difficult. Understanding how one might hate from being crippled or "burned out" was easy. Therefore, they decided early on that Damn Yankees was hatred from the Civil War when in fact it was hatred from being kicked and trampled upon after the war. Once they and future generations made this "verdict" as children they had little reason to question it later.

America triumphant after W.W.II remembering the hatreds caused by "kicking and trampling over" the fallen, extended helping hands to re-build both Germany and Japan. Little wonder that both nations post war societies had a deep love for America, which could not otherwise be explained. Just one example: General McArthur in September, 1945 ordering every supply ship in the U.S. Navy heading for home, to reverse course to feed a starving Japan.

Having condemned Reconstruction as I have, I should say one lasting benefit of reconstruction was the spread of public education though-out the South for both blacks and whites alike. Nonetheless in my opinion it would take the generation after World War II with the advent of television and a full century after the Civil War to only begin to undo the harm of Reconstruction which so effectively criminalized Southern society.

Thus only in 1965 with the murder of four little black Sunday School girls—disgusting even many racist whites in 1963, passage of the Civil

Rights Bill of 1964 and the Voter Rights Act of 1965 did we begin to return to 1865 in terms of race relations in the South and to a lesser extent in America as a whole . . .

Reconstruction was perhaps a noble attempt at reconstructing Southern society into what the North thought was perfect or at least far better than the previous legal by law but morally criminal slave society of the antebellum or pre Civil War South. Reality however is one person's view of perfection is not another's. That is why we so disagree on so many things today.

One might say that Reconstruction was the attempt to "speed dial" the then present reality of the South in 1865 perhaps a hundred years into the future overnight. Unfortunately people and their societies can not be speed dialed forward by anyone but themselves . . . Attempting to do so can be disastrous . . .

Or to put it another way: **Horse Trough:**

There is an old saying: You can take a horse to the water but you cannot make her drink. Any attempt to try to make her do so will invariably result in a violent reaction. We are still paying for that violent reaction today.

The Aftermath of Failure:
The Bad Guys Rule, the Gilded Age:

Hatred only caused more hatred on both sides of the black/white divide, a self-perpetuating cycle of hate that spread all across America like a virus that still plagues us today. Only now with political correctness is this sickness beginning to heal.

While it is easy to say; "stop the hate" and it cannot be said too often, the reality of human nature is once a person does hate, stopping is very hard . . . Saying "stop the hate" and "to love all God's children" however, does help us gradually to end our hate-filled past in the future because anything repeated often enough does with time become at least a part of reality . . . That reality is Martin Luther King's Promised Land that he saw from the mountain-top, that I too will probably not live to enjoy, but I sincerely hope to . . . for I was taught to love all God's children, no matter what others may call them, period!

When the Old South re-born out of hatred would die only time and future events could tell . . . World War II, the news reels depicting the evils of the world both abroad and here at home plus our black service men fighting the Nazi devils of the so called "Aryan super race" would prove to be the events . . .

A New America is Born:

When in 1946 that black soldier appeared in his dress army uniform before my grand-mother's front door in Birmingham, quietly demanding to be let in thru the front door—and was, the New South and a New America was symbolically born (see Forward), formally announced by Baseball and President Truman desegregating the military in 1947.

The Civil Rights Bill of 1964 and the Voter Rights Act of 1965 marked America's recognition of a "New America" reaching adulthood. When Senator Lott of Mississippi was forced to resign his post as majority leader in December, 2002 for applauding the late Senator Strom Thurman of South Carolina's stand in defense of the Old South in 1948.

This clearly symbolized the New America and perhaps a New South as well were reaching toward maturity. Most unfortunately he was re-elected in Mississippi, so clearly the Deep South is still far from marching boldly into the future.

This New America is not yet dominant even in the rest of America as our still segregated society bears witness to. But at least our openly racist history is all but buried in the past. The mountain of segregation has been climbed; the green valley Martin Luther King dreamed of was reached with the election of a black man president of the U.S. in my life time, I am truly awed . . . again.

Most unfortunately, **America the land of hatred** now ruled as old world reality set in, as the forces of kill or be killed took control in the ashes of war with Abe Lincoln's death. For the price of victory was high and 350,000 Yankee lives must be paid for:

Like WWI the price is high and America will pay dearly as Germany spread its pain to Europe, America too would pay dearly for vengeance by definition brings out only the worst in us all . . .

Unfortunately Lincoln and John Wilkes Booth became among the last to die for lost causes—John Wilkes Booth for slavery and Abe Lincoln for "we the people," or the good guys. Yes, we can argue for ever who are the good guys and who are the bad guys, but we can also let history decide.

In the decades after Lincoln's death, racial hatred of all kinds spread across the nation. Industry spreading across the Union as always needed little hands to do little jobs, so we—yes we, sold our children to the factories for peanuts. Factories quickly became Wall Street and gobbled up most of America.

So unless you believe racist hatred, selling our children or Wall St. owning the locks, the stocks in and the barrels outside our stores are the good guys, the bad guys ruled. However, while the Republicans ruled this era (1865-1901) the lone Democrat to be president in this era, Grover Cleveland elected twice, was probably the worst of them all. The only president to use the Sherman Anti-Trust Act, during this period, he used it to crush . . . the labor unions who dared to try saying no to domineering industry.

We the people need new schools, better hospitals and help facing new times as industrialism sweeps America. Our elected leaders say: farmers take to the factories, townsmen obey the big city railroads and rich people tell us what it is that you want, because we the politicians want your money!

The rich people demand: crush the labor unions who dare to say no to our right to lower wages and lengthen the work week. The Republicans, raising the flag of the Republic; yell: "Vote for the rich in the name of the U.S.A." The Democrats having shed slavery say now: "Elect us and we shall out do the Republicans"—and they meant it! This was soon called the Gilded Age, because it was the day and age to get rich! All ready rich, now is the time to get super rich. The Vanderbilt—railroads, Carnegie—steel, Rockefeller—oil and J.P. Morgan—banks are quickly upon us, sucking we the people dry.

In 1860 we were a nation of overwhelmingly middle class people both North and South with much in common with 1776. By 1900 we were dominated by the rich beyond rich owners of corporations squeezing Middle America out of existence with far more in common with today. So what were our politicians doing besides getting rich themselves?

In these rapidly changing times, ignoring us and our needs, telling us it is inevitable the rich will get richer as the laws of survival dictate the rich will get richer and there is nothing that can stop time itself. In short this was today's world of modern industrial America arriving. But in the late 1800's it is new—in America.

Europe dominated by the Dukes, Lords and Earls from antiquity and the rising rich from the middle class industrializing Europe, this was old hat. The rich have always been few, the middle classes a few more and the numerous masses impoverished. Think for a moment how desperate would you have to be to literally sell your freedom for up to fifteen years of slavery. Yet tens of thousands of English did just that to escape the starving in Europe in the 1600's. With the union of England and Scotland under the Scottish King James IV—the First of the United Kingdom, the Scots soon joined the English in America.

To poor to pay for the three month voyage to America, it was either surrender your freedom or die in Europe. The same realities in the Third World of today explain why people stuff themselves into crates and pray someone will open the crates thousands of miles away in the First World of today.

In the 1800's the steam engine powering ships forward even when the wind blew ships backward, the time required quickly dropped from several months to eventually a week or so and the price for crossing the ocean fell drastically. Soon the masses of impoverished Europe were pouring into America.

Welcome to modern America.

Politicians getting rich are as old as Roman Plebs taking little bags of money and naturally bigger bags if they can. Some things do not change. In George Washington's time politicians bought drinks at the local taverns along with a good speech as local entertainment to win votes. They paid for those drinks so they could make far more money in office. As criminal as it may be, some things do not change. So what makes this modern America?

How one earns a living. In 1860 we were a nation of overwhelmingly agriculture. Even New York Sate was mostly rural in population. It literally took 3.9 million residents of New York plus most of New Jersey—the Garden State plus Connecticut to support the nearly one million residents of greater New York City.

Without mechanization there were severe limitations on how much farmers could grow and get to market. Even with horses and wagons you still had to carry your apples, potatoes and wheat the fifty miles to the nearest railway station at about two or maybe three miles per hour—and if uphill? If it rained! . . . Each farmer requiring many loads before it was done.

This was the Achilles Heel of our economy. Think about pushing or pulling a cart of potatoes mile after mile to a market for a few seconds, yes having a horse to actually do the work helps a lot, but how many of us would look forward to spending day after day doing it and don't even think of uphill or mud in the unpaved world of 1900.

Obviously by 1860 this was changing. Every tiny little town was demanding its own railway. As a result railroad mileage shot upward from zero in 1820 to 30,000 miles in 1860 and to 200,000 miles by 1900. Yes, there was a severe demand for a trucking industry and in the 1900's it would start to grow in a hurry. But by 1900 with the above distance cut to say twenty miles, each farmer with horse pulled machines could get a crop to market and return in a day or two. As farm to market efficiency rose; the relative number of farming related workers fell drastically.

In 1860 about 30% of all workers in America were farmers; the majority of the rest were somehow getting that produce to market. By 1900 the percentage of farmers had been cut in half along with the number getting the produce to market as well. Thus the percentage of all workers in manufacturing shot upward from 8% in 1860 to about 20% by 1900. By 1940 it would almost reach 40%. Today were going back toward the 8%, but that is mostly automation.

From 1860 to 1900 our economy changed radically. From 1607 to 1860 our economy had only changed minimally. What changes that had occurred were by growing in volume not method. But of course with the steam engine that was changing. Changing gradually before 1860; in a hurry after 1860 again i.e.—modern America.

Every one recognized these stunning changes, many people welcomed the changes. Certainly our average incomes rose and that made many people happy. But while our average incomes doubled from 1850 about $600/year to 1900 about $1200/year the top one percent soared while the bottom fifty percent didn't grow at all, many in fact shrinking. Needless to say those shrinking incomes were not happy. Our politicians yelled and screamed about it but what could they do, stop time itself?

Radical changes were required. But when you have a constitution that served our fathers and grand fathers well, you don't simply propose radical changes, if you want to get elected. People naturally resist changing, especially radical changes. As time went by and the need for changes grew ever higher and higher the demand for radical changes by growing numbers of people being left behind in these ever changing times gradually overcame the resistance.

By the 1890's the call for real change in our government reached critical levels. After all at Homestead in Pennsylvania, labor fighting bitterly against the Carnegie Steel Mill, seven guards and eleven workers and supporters were killed. Labor was organizing and industry were arming guards as the gulf between the haves and the have-nots was ever widening into a seemingly unbridgeable gulf.

Thus the Progressive Party was founded to fight for we the people along with the even more radical Socialist Party not to mention the Communist Party while both existing Republican and Democratic parties claimed nothing could be done to stop progress or time itself.

The Republicans dedicated themselves to manufacturers and the Democrats claimed vote for us and we will out do the Republicans—and meant every word of it. At the same time calls for two other radical changes reached the critical level as well: Women's Suffrage and Prohibition. These three movements; were in fact:

revolutionary . . .

A storm was brewing beneath the Gay 1890's:

1—We the people ruling ourselves once again—always revolutionary.
2—Women's Suffrage, yes the right to vote, with-out which no other right matters therefore: revolutionary by default to many—who preferred to laugh. and
3—Prohibition: Outlawing the right to be happy—as many would describe it and therefore worth fighting both for and against.

A new revolution was brewing deep inside which would shake the world like no other previous revolution, yet it would be so big, that it would not acquire a direct name; for it was won in so many small revolutions that no one thought to put them together:

In America we would call it our Civil Rights Revolution.
In Europe they would call it their 1960's Age of Revolt.
In Africa they would call it Independence day—many times.

Elsewhere it would take longer to arrive but it would soon shake the status quo to pieces as it had in the above countries.

In Eastern Europe the mighty Soviet Empire would collapse before it. In the Middle East the revolution would be called the Arab Spring—still occurring today!

The proper name for it was:

The United Nations
as designed by Eleanor Roosevelt.

But, that's a secret, so do not tell, dreamed by the dreamers of 1919, who yelled in joy at a proposal by a 'slave' Democrat Woodrow Wilson to the world:

A world without empires,
a world governed by
we the people,
of the people,
by the people,

(While many started to add;)
of *all nations*.

Once again that's a secret, for who could dream the impossible dream; of a world with-out empires in the 1890's? Few in deed. But by 1919 they would number millions in the Western World and a few dreamers like Gandhi elsewhere.

AUTHOR NOTES

*As a Southerner I might take great pride in the North suffering 350,000 deaths compared to the South's 270,000 dead. Truth is they were all Americans and no American should take any pride in their deaths.

Furthermore, the main reason in the difference was not the individuals that fought the battles—they were all from the country, even the North. The real difference was the South's generals listened to what their doctors said: Get your drinking water from the left and use your natural toilets to the right. after a few days the Southern troops were noticeably healthier than the Northern troops despite having greater access to medicines.

*Teddy (or Theodore) Roosevelt. That is someone who will truly represent the middle class (and working poor) by declaring war upon the rich. It can happen for Teddy Roosevelt did in fact happen and was president

1901-1909. Tom Jefferson is the only other president in my opinion in the same class. Though he hardly qualifies as modern. Andrew Jackson would qualify but his shall we say, un minority views disqualify him.

*Scalawags: Olde Scottish for a horse cheater. Taking a favored to win horse and changing his colors, thereby cheating the un suspecting.

CHAPTER IV

The Roosevelt's Teddy, Franklin and Eleanor plus a Truman

PEOPLE ARE PEOPLE. We are our own worst enemies. Given a chance we would sell our children for a pittance. Yes, we are that mean, and most unfortunately I have proof:

From 1775 to 1800 we talked a lot about freedom and "we the people" and it's many connections so we abolished slavery for our white children by abolishing our own right to sell our own children to whoever had the money. We as a nation said we would no longer sell our little Ben Franklin's for a little money today for our own selfishness. Guess what? Time passed, and we fought a war over slavery 1861-65 for others not so lucky, and "we the people" lost. Yes, we lost, big time. Yes we won the war but lost the real issue with Lincoln's death.

For while there are good people in Washington in both political parties, unfortunately both also have bad people who put most people at the end of the line. While it is difficult to distinguish the good from the bad, because they all claim to put you first, regardless how big the lie. And in politics the bigger the lie the better, so how does one tell? I wish I had a magically easy system, but I don't. So we just have to watch the results:

Manufacturers said we need small hands, so we the people said hey, my kids have small hands; how much will you pay me for them? Yes, we the people took the money, and the factories quickly took our children and their little hands. Welcome to the world of the 1890's. We once again are our own worst enemies . . . in 1900 America produced 62,000 High School graduates in a nation of 76 million to tackle the 20th Century. Where were the missing million plus others?—At work.

Welcome to the world of **Theodore Roosevelt (T R)**. Born in 1858, from his home in New York City he watched the body of the beloved Abe Lincoln being carried back to Springfield, Illinois for burial. Theodore was about to join him in the grave. At age ten after years of asthmas, Theodore's wealthy father sat down on Theodore's death bed and said: "The doctors have done all they can, they can do nothing more. You will have to find the strength to climb out of this bed or you shall die in it."

The next day, T R found the strength to climb out of that bed and adopt a physical strengthening program eventually including boxing, to fight for his own life. It was with this determination that T R came to the New York City Police Commission in the 1890's as a Republican of the rich. When asked to vote on banning cigar making in people's homes, T R actually went into their homes—virtually unheard of and was shocked at the poverty in America.

For this was a world of newspaper reports by journalist including many liberals but edited by people dependent upon companies buying advertising—the life blood of every paper. Thus while the writer might want to write of utter poverty in America—the editors want to paint paradise in America to keep their advertisers happy.

For while our incomes as a whole have doubled those at the top have not only doubled but tripled or even quadrupled while those at the bottom (now mainly emigrants and blacks) have actually fallen. Perhaps black incomes in New York have fallen, otherwise little more than the slave wages of the past.

This is why the English, French, Scandinavians and Germans (certainly no Dutch or Swiss) now only rarely come to America. Only the poorest of Europe find the poverty in America attractive. For we have now reached the £5-$500 per year wages George III had tried to, in effect, impose upon us.

T R found to his shock typically two sometimes three families sharing what had been built for one poor family apartment, with tobacco scattered with food and children rapping both into cigars and eating both at the same time. T R born among the rich, privately tutored until Harvard; rejected their indifference, and declared war upon those who would buy and sell these children. For the evil ones were not just the factory owners, they were also the little guy saying to the rich, give me the money, because I want a drink, take my children, do as you wish with them. Of course they never used such words, but that is what they meant.

Even today would be money lenders in the third world trying to lift the poor out of there poverty experience their lending result in rising local bar sales and little else. Make no mistake we still are our own worst enemies. Women do far better at this—if they are allowed to have some business power in their own home. They seem to actually want their children to have a better future. We men unfortunately just want a drink and if our children can be sold to buy one, so be it. Naturally we lie about our intentions—some things do not change.

After all how many times did husbands tell their wives I'll vote yes for women's suffrage at night and again in the morning, then in the afternoon vote no?

Therefore this 1890-1920 reform period is perhaps the most important era in American history. For this era was when the world truly changed. The world had seen democracies before in ancient Greece and the Roman Republic plus in hunter gatherer societies the world over. Now for the first time, planet Earth would see three movements reach ascendancy.

The first was woman's suffrage, the second was prohibition and the third was once again we the people ruling ourselves, but not for long! In British South Africa, Gandhi would soon launch the rudiments of his eventual "Quit India Campaign." While some might argue over whether any of these movements were truly firsts—our history is both very long, complex, and spread out over many lands. Certainly it can be said that never had a powerful nation welding influence worldwide ever tried to grant women true citizenship as political equals as well as prohibiting the sale of liquor throughout the nation.

These were revolutionary goals even if we were smart enough not to declare them so. No point in alarming the Loyalists, err opposition, if not granting women the vote and taking their drinks away somehow didn't already alarm them. This was truly revolutionary: and more yet to come: for people were already starting to dream impossible dreams like:

We the people of all nations ruling themselves for the good of all the people.

No, it would not happen overnight, these were dreams which in the world of 1900 were covered in Empires, even America now had an empire! But, before something can happen, people must first dream of it. By 1900 people were dreaming the un believable, like a world with-out empires. How many in 1900 could imagine the world of 2000, where all empires would be ancient history?

Granted there are a few unhappy colonies such as Tibet and Sinkiang within the Chinese Empire of old. Russia, I prefer not to think about . . .

Yes, even now the world is far from perfect. But compared to the world of 1900, a world covered in empires, how many in 1900 could believe in our world of almost no empires of just a century later? Yes, a worldwide revolution was looming just over the horizon. Turn on the news and watch it happen, even now!

Our world of today, increasingly governed by we the people, of the people and for the people, now of more and more nations. Even in the Middle-East, the monarchies are rightly worried. The world is a changing for both dictatorships and monarchies alike. But before that revolution can happen, we must get back to the mundane of this actual world:

Many may argue that women's suffrage is good and prohibition was just plain stupid. The Moslem world has prohibited alcohol for over a thousand years. So do not think it cannot be done, whether it is worth the price is entirely another question. My point is they are linked.

They are linked because in the 1800's we the people wanting a better America chose to link them. From 1775 to 1860 we talked a lot about freedom and what it would mean. We the people chose to abolish selling our children to long periods of servitude—slavery by a different name and in the Northern states slavery itself. But soon others took up other causes exemplified by Martha Washington's objection to our constitution saying nothing about women's rights.

While I agree with George's reply: "Martha please, one revolution at a time." For George knew firsthand how his many bills to grant both women and slaves some legal rights had been ridiculed in Virginia's House of Burgesses (and Ben Franklin's requests for women's rights in Pennsylvania) likewise had been "passed for further study"—a polite method of saying to your ideas: "to get lost."

Anti-Slavery, Prohibition and Women's Suffrage movements would all slowly get started in the 1800's. None of the above would be taken seriously by us men in our drinking establishments also called legislatures. Yes. we as a people drank about six times what we drink today per person. It was simply normal for every man to get drunk virtually every night—women drank but probably far less than six times today, so men, probably more than six times!

In the 1850's slavery exploded (see chapter III) resulting in the Civil War and its legal destruction. While Prohibition and Women's Suffrage were pushed aside as both political parties Republican and Democratic chose to act toward them as previous parties had ignored slavery.

But now with the rising tide of reform movements in the 1880's and 90's, the world beneath the politicians are a changing . . . whether they like it or not. Most of them do not like it, for they represent the rich and powerful who genuinely believe they are powerful because God wants them to be.

People always love it when people tell them what they want to hear, and now science tells them God wants them to prosper as in the survival of the species as God's plan. Newspapers depending on their purchase of advertising promote those writers who please the rich and powerful. Thus the middle class, the purchasers of the vast majority of newspapers are painted a beautiful painting of the wonderful life in America—thus putting so many to sleep.

Yet the tide of those calling for reform continues to grow as virtual Civil War breaks out in Colorado over falling wages; the same in Chicago over layoffs and less pay in the Pullman Strike. Eugene Debs leads the workers and threatens a national railway strike. Democratic President Grover Cleveland sides with the company and throws Debs into prison and crushes the strike.

In 1890 Wyoming entered the union with women having the vote, legal citizens, with the power to pass laws protecting themselves as equal human beings. One should never underestimate the importance of this right: Martha Curtiss, forced to remarry in a hurry or lose her wealth—being at the mercy of any man in court was lucky to find a good man in George Washington. Throughout the world women were legally protected by their fathers and husbands and no one else. Many men are good but many men are bad and some are simply evil. How would you like to have an evil monster as your legal protector? Or, if your husband dies no protection at all—Martha Curtiss case.

Wyoming's constitution declaring women as equal citizens in 1890, declared a new reform era now at war by a nation that effectively did so by accepting the new state's equality statute: with those who promise one thing at night and vote the opposite during the day. How many times this must have happened one can only imagine, but many, many times must be accurate.

While many of these battles would be fought at the local state levels such as Women's Suffrage and Prohibition to get the individual states to pass the constitutional amendments to make them national laws. They were nonetheless a critical part of what became a national movement to elect people who would actually represent "we the people."

Teddy Roosevelt at the helm:

By 1901 T R had been a western cowboy, an N Y State Senator and Assistant Navy Secretary besides N Y C Police Commissioner and of course Colonel of the Rough Riders against Spain in Cuba. Shortly after as the V P, he became the youngest President at age 43, of the U S after an anarchist*1 killed McKinley. (J F Kennedy would be the youngest elected president.)

Many liberals today do not like Teddy, but his world was not ours. In 1901 there were both liberals (like Lincoln and Teddy or T R) among the Republicans and conservatives like Grover Cleveland among the Democrats. So Republicans T R, and Taft plus the Democrat Wilson formed a string of three "we the people" presidents in a row.

With the fire of a cowboy Colonel and the determination of a boxing Police Commissioner the Republican T R came to the White House (1901-09) and quickly declared all out war on Wall Street. Declaring his enemies are the surest revolutionaries ever born by their selfish greed. **By rejecting my reforms "they aid and abet those who call to over throw our whole system of government."**

His enemies were numerous and very powerful: J P Morgan (banks) who at times lent gold to the treasury as a patriotic act, John D Rockefeller (Standard Oil), Andrew Carnegie (U.S. Steel) and the Vanderbilt railroads—all these literally had more money than Washington! The war was all out using tools that had been sitting idle for decades—The Sherman Antitrust Act used only once previously by the lone Democrat Pres. Cleveland against . . . big labor! Now T R used it to batter the truly big guys. Many of the wealthiest Americans would never forgive Theodore. After all he was determined to take their guaranteed money tickets away from the rich.

Being rich himself, he was no socialist; he just wanted the rich to actually earn their wealth!—An old American concept, forgotten over the previous four decades. T R literally chose to do what many had said was impossible; turn time backwards, now for the rich! Simply by ending their right to crush the little guy—in this case, the middle class.

By now Darwin's Origin of the Species was widely accepted as the defining reality and now used as the inevitability of the rise of concentrated wealth. It was now routinely said you can't stop progress and therefore pay homage to the rich as the natural selection of the species.

Declaring that America was the home of the middle class, Teddy warred upon the rich. Never intending to abolish wealth, he just wanted to tax it according to its rewards. This too would be passed on to the states to win constitutional passage in 1913.

For T R realized there was a need for bigger government to pay for enforcing the law, national infrastructures like the Panama Canal, to create a National Park Service and a bigger Navy. A bigger government needed more revenues and T R thought the rich should pay a bigger share as in the income tax. Now perhaps you can see why T R is absolutely hated by the Tea Party Republicans. Liberal Republicans like me, absolutely love him.

When asked what would his foreign policy would be? Teddy replied in his most favorite quotation: "Speak softly, but carry a big stick." This he exemplified by signing a Panama Canal Treaty with Columbia, but when the Columbian legislature rejected the treaty, rather than renegotiate a new treaty . . . A convenient rebellion by Panamanians was soon enforced by a heavily armed U.S. cruiser, blocking the only road to Panama. Very quickly the treaty rejected by Columbia was accepted by Panama and we recognized the new country. Construction soon started and in 1914 the canal opened.

Thus Republican Teddy Roosevelt turned America upside down, with the help of Sinclair Lewis writing "The Jungle" about criminal labor and unsanitary practices in the meat packing industry. With passage of the Meat Inspection Act, The Pure Food and Drug Act and creating our National Park Service;*2 this was a gentle turnover that "we the people" deeply loved as existing laws were brought against the giant Trusts strangling Middle America.

Still new laws were pursued and amendments introduced to define unfair practices by business that the rich and powerful hated. **These were literally Revolutionary Times with-out the violence of actual war.** Bravo to T R for pulling off the near impossible: While not actually making time work backward, he did reverse the rich getting richer by default for twenty years and indirectly until the 1970's. Teddy should never be forgotten for he truly earned his berth atop Mt. Rushmore!

During these wonder years of we the people gradually breaking up the "Trusts" dominating corporate America; T R presided over the White House wedding reception of his younger brother's daughter, Eleanor and his namesake 4TH cousin Franklin Delano Roosevelt joking "so you decided to keep Eleanor's last name, with-in the family."

In 1909 T R turned over the keys to his political friend and V P William Howard Taft. The always affable Taft besides being the only president to get stuck in the bath tub, affably tried to maintain T R's war on Wall St. while welcoming them and their big money to many White House dinners. T R could face the Morgan's and Rockefeller's down—with a smile, while fighting for all of us at breakfast, lunch and dinner.

The jolly good fellow Taft could not. Gradually Taft's War on Wall St. inevitably fell, a victim to the hired hands—slick special interest people who care nothing for the people, but most definitely care about the bill at hand that could cost their company millions. Thus Taft's affability was turned to the standard war on Main St. against "we the people." Even as the war in the courts against the monopolies continued.

In 1912 T R running for the Republican nomination won all of the states conducting polls by "we the people." That was five states; the other 43 listened to the big money and re-nominated Taft. The Democrats, having elected all of one president (Cleveland) in the past 52 years 1860-1912 nominated Woodrow Wilson a reformist Governor of New Jersey. T R stormed out of the GOP creating his own Bull Moose Party and in Nov. 1912 won more votes than Taft, but Wilson won the election with the Republicans divided. Thus both parties had powerful progressive groups with-in them.

The Re-Birth of Jeffersonian—Democracy:

The election of 1912 marked the rebirth of Jeffersonian Democracy in its modern form: the primary system. When the Republicans finished third, a shock to both political parties, the drive to re-start the primary—we the people selecting our candidate system for president was re-born. For finishing third as the Taft Republicans had, should never be their intent again. Once again, bravo to Theodore.

Democrat Wilson restarted T R's war on Wall St. but was quickly asked by events if he was a Slave Democrat of old. The New Jersey democrat replied to the bartender killed in Texas by a Buffalo (black) Soldier, that no one would step forward and say kill me for I killed him. Everyone knew that was the required price, no defense by a Buffalo Soldier could ever be tolerated. Since no one could be blamed legally, President Wilson proved he was indeed a Slave Democrat of old by firing every black in the U S Army from easternmost Maine to the westernmost Philippine Island. Thus at the time of Pearl Harbor the only blacks in the military were Naval servants for officers and coal and ammo stevedores.

Otherwise Wilson restarted T R's war on Wall St. but was soon engulfed by WWI breaking out in 1914. The rich and powerful buy their way into White House dinners, and power lunches and yes even quiet breakfasts. They do this regardless of who owns the keys to the White House for the current four years. They gladly pay for those times with the president so they can push their ideas and concerns to the president. Guess why?

Presidents are human. If they ever cared about "we the people" their caring all too often gets lost outside the fence of the lawn surrounding the White House. Because we the people rarely get invited inside for a power lunch; we the people are for show, and little else; much like the Roman Senate to the Emperors. This is reality, some things do not change. Only a very strong president can stand or actually sit against the rich and powerful at dinner and fight for "we the people," against their continuous concerns for the few.

Thus the Republican Taft's War on Wall Street was converted to War on Main Street, and now Wilson's Democratic War on Wall Street was converted to war period. In Nov. 1916 Wilson ran for a second term screaming "he kept us out of war" to victory. Five months later he led America to war. Vietnam crept up on us. WWI exploded on us like an atom bomb.

By 1917 everyone knew Europe was committing suicide in an all out war to prove which side was tougher than the other and precious little else. Democratic France, fighting to avenge its defeat in 1870-71, plus the kings of Britain and Italy and the Czar of Russia vs. the Kaiser of Germany and the Emperor's of Austria-Hungary and Turkey—one group as bad as the other.

Neither group cared at all for their "we the people" no indeed not. Europe's mighty admit that "we the powerful" made a mistake in 1914 when we gladly declared war. Never, should we ever bring an end to this senseless slaughter. For it is only those who count for nothing getting killed. No, never, continue the slaughter! For we the powerful are perfect! So the mutual slaughters continued year after bloody year.

Do not think the leaders of Europe were alone in this arrogant thinking. It is common wherever people have real power, a few other examples: The Army of Japan thru assassination decided what the Emperor decided, having decided China should supply the answer to Japan's Great Depression woes only China refused to cooperate, therefore the Army decided the Imperial Navy should supply soft easy America to fill the bill—thus Pearl Harbor.

Richard Nixon Republican, firing in effect J Edgar Hoover (yeah!!!); decided the FBI and the CIA were literally at his control; fortunately a security guard at the Watergate was not (yeah!!!). Bill Clinton, Democrat decided America was welcome to tear itself apart defining the word "is" challenging us to impeach him, if we dare risk our constitution, rather than the arrogant Bill Clinton simply saying "will not happen again." That alone would have silenced the uproar, but also that Bill Clinton was a mere mortal, never! Hillary's claim to fame was "she had stood by this arrogant man!"

Thus in April 1917 war, war the headlines suddenly screamed in America! While we the people asked: On whom and why? Our ships have been sunk at sea in a war zone . . . Our crews were well warned and paid, what did you expect?

It is time for those many power lunches again. The rich attend them, you and I do not. Even more importantly the rich send their hired help to lunch, dinner and breakfast with the president. Every waking moment the rich and powerful want to drench the president with their concerns, not yours or mine.

By 1917 the rich and powerful have loaned Britain billions of their precious dollars, and now they are worried. The unexpected, the before now unbelievable might happen; the British Empire might lose. If Britain loses, they might not be able to repay our loans, oh dear. Wilson, the Democrat and the Republican opposition are both engulfed with their worries, thus at the first excuse—after the election; war is declared.

We the people rose in revolt. With both the Democrats and Republicans voting for war, we the people started voting for any one opposed to both like the Socialist and even the tiny Communist Party. Wilson responded by launching the Palmer Raids named after his Attorney General. With the Bolshevik or Communist victory in Russia in Nov. 1917 the Palmer Raids declare war on communism in America and quickly extend this to any antiwar act, thus Eugene Debs of the Socialist Party as their real enemy—serves six years imprisonment this time, (yes, again) for standing with "we the people" against the war.

One thing Democrats and Republicans can agree on; they are the only two parties in America, period. Thus the first Red Scare was launched continuing into the 1920's.

Meanwhile the Republicans voting to reject the Versailles Peace Treaty won the 1920 election, and quickly now that our rich could count on repayment of their British loans, both parties agreed we would never vote to join a world war! No, not us; The Socialists and Communists are in jail, so there is no objection. Welcome to the 1920's. Both parties controlled by the rich declare war on war itself.

Fortunately we the people had voted to pass both Prohibition in 1919 and Women's Suffrage in 1920—Martha finally got her wish. Yes Martha Washington and all the adult women in America won the right to vote. Yes, women of America, welcome to the human race. How great a step forward for mankind was this? In every home in America this debate had been going on for at least 144 years since 1776. How many times did men, our not so ancient ancestors, promise their wives yes, and then vote no?

It was no accident that this occurred during this reform era. There are good Republicans, there are good Democrats and yes, there are bad Republicans and yes bad Democrats. We can argue forever who are the good guys and who are the bad guys. The truth is they are both in both parties. Neither has a monopoly on either.

Democrats, Lincoln and Theodore Roosevelt were Republicans and they were good guys unless you support in-slavers or manufacturers buying our little children, or giant Wall Street Trusts and Corporations owning America lock, stock and barrel. Republicans, Woodrow Wilson was a good guy, unless you think the above were the good guys.

In Paris for the peace treaty Wilson gave a speech telegraphed around the world that would forever link him to the future: He proposed that the people of Europe should be allowed to determine what country they should belong to! This was revolutionary, the people be given the right to self governance! This was unheard of in Europe or anywhere else! Prior to this moment the rulers of the earth had dictated you belong there and you there you now belong to me. This was the dream of 1919 that would shake the world:

Self determination.

Democracy for all the little people—
that is us as in you and me!

The dictators of the Earth would reject his principle in the Versailles Treaty while adopting the mere words of self determination but only as mere words except for a few districts in resurrected Poland and Yugoslavia that the victors did not care or disagreed about.

Nonetheless, the idea of self-determination would gain strength throughout Europe and more and more Europeans would realize that only

Louis XIV and Napoleon wanted to rule all Germans (and all others as well).

Only the Kaiser and Hitler wanted to rule all Frenchmen (and all others as well). Not only that, but only Mussolini wanted to rule all. The average European was soon thinking the impossible, let's do away with borders, all of them. The idea of the European Union was soon born. "If any are to be freed, all must be free!" The spirit of the French Revolution still lives . . .

Thus for nineteen years (1901-1920) the good guys ruled mostly. Once again it was no accident that 32 states of 48 eventually joined Wyoming granting women the vote in this era. That is how rare the good guys rule. Yes they also approved Prohibition at the same time but one cause was a part of the other. Well in Nov. 1920 the good guys got voted out. Both parties swore no never again shall we vote for war. It's a promise.

Back to the power lunches at the White House and of course congress as well. Both parties are always invited by the rich, while you and I cannot afford them. Politics are expensive the rich can afford them, you and I cannot. So not surprising with WWI and the Palmer Raids against all those people wondering; why did we go to war at all; the bad guys retook power—in both parties.

Granted trying to prove who are the good guys (supporting we the people policies), the politicians, and who are the bad guys (supporting the few rich and powerful) is difficult since most politicians are some of all three. Most politicians of both parties want to be good. Reality dictates they should be politicians first and they are all too often buried in temptations to favor the bad guys.

Err, that is the rich. Do not get me wrong, the rich are not evil, the people they hire are. For a moment let us pretend you and I are rich. Two people offer to manage our money. They're both guaranteed, no Madoff's*8 allowed. One says he'll earn 5%, the other says I'll earn 20% for you. I can't speak for you but I'd be tempted to take the 20%. Maybe he only delivers 15%, but hey maybe 25% if it's a good year, how does he do it? By screwing the hell out of the little guy, like charging them 39% on their credit card. Forty years ago anything over 10% was called Usury—a felony. Now it's legal.

Even Obama's Banking Reform Bill failed to put a cap on interest rates—makes me wonder. Today the loan shark is your perfectly legal distant or even local banker.

In the nineteen twenties the rich soared in wealth while the poor farmers went out of business. Economics has no mercy, the congress yelled bloody hell. To be left out in the cold of an ever changing world is very painful; some things again, do not change. Yes congress screamed, but did little else; to me that equals bad guys in charge.

In 1929 the "roaring twenties" ran off the cliff of prosperity for the rich and plummeted into the depths of poor farmers who quickly became the depression for all. After three years of growing bread and soup lines at ever lengthening President Hoover-viles—shack homes, "we the people" were more than ready for a president with a good guy last name. After all, every candidate promises most solemnly that they are the best good guy for "we the people" ever. However they may word it.

Franklin Delano Roosevelt:

In Nov. 1932 Franklin Delano Roosevelt (FDR) was swept into office in March 1933 two months after Adolph Hitler in Germany as they too hoped for someone to lift Germany out of this world wide depression. FDR would play around trying a little of this and some of that and would be criticized heavily for everything.

Hitler built the beautiful autobahn highway system in a country virtually without cars for the military and the rich who naturally had Mercedes and BMW's. The Volkswagens (people's car) would come later . . . much later, as in 1949. Any and all critics were quickly arrested in Germany or worse.

FDR quite frankly is not one of my favorite good guy presidents. In my opinion he honestly tried to be a good guy president but that politician kept getting in his way. That is his own political instincts prevented himself from being what I call a good guy president. In short, he listened to his critics. That is why year after year he tried a little of this and some of that then a few years later cancelled most of the above.

The exception being Social Security, this explains why the economy picked up when he did some of this and some of that then sank back into depression levels when he, listening to critics, cancelled the above spending.

Do not blame the critics; the loyal opposition's job is to criticize. The real bad guys are the people of the same party who vote against the good guy president—when we do have one.

In a very imperfect world—like this one, some of the worst people do some things right, and most unfortunately some of the seemingly best people do many things wrong. Adolph Hitler spent money Germany did not have and then he spent more.

Building up a military for war as well as a magnificent autobahn system, he literally challenged the world as he built for war and Germany prospered and Hitler was soon very popular in Germany and feared by everyone else paying attention.

Joseph Stalin of the U.S.S.R. was another person to be feared, taking three quarters of his farmer's crops in taxes to buy factories made in the rest of Europe and forced people to work at slave wages to build them or in them when built. Just thinking about anything else would get you a one way trip to Siberia, or a bullet in the head quickly. Yes Stalin spent money, every last penny any one had at his mercy. Stalin would never be known for his mercy either. His mother screamed at him when he tried to visit. His daughter committed suicide when she learned the truth about him.

Children do not always learn from their parents. What is basic undeniable fact to one generation can be so much malarkey to the next. One example: Our founding fathers belief in "we must stand together, or surly we shall hang separately"—soon followed by "slavery in the land of the free must be abolished, no matter what the price."

Or our First World War generation were "fooled" into WWI, thus they simply refused to believe the lies told by war mongering Britain about the Nazis. Thus it took Japan's attack on us at Pearl Harbor and Hitler's declaration of war against us, to get us into WWII.

Yes, we believed as a people in 1939-1941 that Britain was the war mongering empire. The British Empire had been the evil empire since 1776 to 'we the people' of America. Our rich had made peace with the Royalists no, no the Federalists since the 1780's after all our rich like looking down on we the people as much as the aristocrats of Europe. They had in fact lied about German atrocities in WWI to "trick" us into WWI. But who listens to foreigners in America?

With both Republican and Democrats telling us repeatedly it was the British lies, not our own rich people's lies—fearing the loss of their personal loans to Britain we were convinced that we had been fooled by Britain's lies in 1914-1917 and therefore refused to believe the obvious truths of 1939-1941. That is why, we America the hope of the free world, slept so well in 1941.

Earlier in '41 Hitler's Germany invaded Stalin's Soviet Union, as one Ukrainian farmer said to the SS German invader: "Please take a quarter of my crops, half if you insist for Stalin took three quarters. The SS replied to his soldiers: "Take everything, leave nothing, burn what is left."

If you think our world is hell, try being caught between Hitler and Stalin. Gradually as Americans were shocked to learn of France's collapse and Britain was repeatedly bombed into an island of ruins, our opinions began to change. However no one loaned the British Empire any money—its days were numbered and our rich new it. Eventually our government stepped forward and cautiously began loaning our money as Lend-Lease.

But neither political party was willing to step forward as a "war party" for they both remembered WWI and its Palmer—Red Scare aftermath.

Nonetheless the exclusionary forces of the Ku Klux Klan of the 1920's and the equally exclusionary German-American Bundt of the 1930's generated its own backlash here in America. An American lawyer and singer John La Touché in 1937 composed an answer to the question are you an American? Paul Robinson (1898-1976) a negro sang in 1937 the reply in the:

Ballad for Americans:

Am I an American? "I'm just an Irish, Negro, Jewish, Italian, French and English, Spanish, Russian, Chinese, Polish, Scotch, Hungarian, Litvak, Swedish, Finnish, Canadian, Greek, and Turk, and Czech and double Czech American. And that ain't all. I was baptized Baptist, Methodist, Congregationalist, Lutheran, Atheist, Roman Catholic, Orthodox Jewish, Presbyterian, Seventh Day Adventist, Mormon, Quaker, Christian Scientist and lots more."

In November 1939 CBS (one of two major radio broadcasters) carried the song nationally. A runaway hit song it would go on to serve as the Republican theme for their convention in 1940. Like it or not, the world was a changin! Americans of all stripes suddenly began to realize what an American really was: United we (the world) stand, for surely divided we hang. But stand for war, no, united we sleep for America . . .

World War II:

So on Dec. 7th 1941 our military were caught sleeping at Pearl Harbor, and Hitler committed suicide with Japan, the empire of by declaring war on the U.S. Did you say suicide?

Japan, the Empire of, committed suicide willingly, why? Good Question. The Emperor cannot do wrong. Those who decide what the Emperor cannot do wrong—by 1941, the Army, have decided to conquer China to solve Japan's Great Depression problems. China however is a lot to eat.

China with U.S. weapons is formidable; therefore since the Emperor cannot be wrong and the Army cannot conquer China therefore the Navy must conquer the U.S. The Imperial Navy cries "were doomed!" The Japanese Army controls the Emperor so the Imperial Navy obeys and commits suicide taking Japan with it. We thought they were bluffing—do they really want to commit suicide? Never think you know. You may know, but you also may not.

Hitler, commit suicide? By Dec 8th 1941 Hitler was already up to his eyeballs in trouble in Russia. Declaring war on the U.S. was declaring "I'm going to lose this war, let's see how quickly I can!" Many would argue not fast enough. Some four years later after the Atomic bombs liquidating Hiroshima and Nagasaki, Japan it was over.

No Franklin Roosevelt is not my favorite President, but interesting . . . yes. Also the forced imprisonment of all Japanese Americans must be held against him as well, while many might argue that after Pearl Harbor, what could you expect? Our standards are either high or they mean nothing. And do note in Hawaii they were left alone, for they were "too important to the economy."

For the same reason Andrew Jackson fails while he was a true white people's president, just ask Native Americans or his slaves; or Woodrow Wilson who gave the world the dream of self rule to all but fired thousands of blacks because legally he could not hang one. Or in FDR's case Japanese Americans. Their skin might not be white, but they too are Americans and us white people should never forget it.

The choices they made was by their choice alone and we should remember Teddy invited a black man: Booker T. Washington through the front door of the White House when America was full of hate, and Harry Truman would defy a revolt in his own party. These were their choices and they should always be applauded for them.

Speaking of applause, Konrad Adenauer Mayor of Cologne, Germany was arrested by Hitler for publicly saying NO! to Hitler on Kristal naught. We should applaud him, for if we would have stood with him how many lives would we have saved?

Spending WWII in Nazi prison, when the western powers resurrected West Germany Adenauer was elected Chancellor from 1949 to 1963 during which he speed dialed Germany into the future. As a German he could do this while any outsider would have been fought tooth and nail. When a horse chooses to drink it will drink, but not a moment sooner. The same applies to people. Adenauer gave them the way by saying yes, we did these horrible things and now we vow, that we shall do better.

Yes, We can!

Meanwhile back in the good ole USA, after Pearl Harbor, big labor stepped forward and asked; what can we do to win this war? Prices are going to go thru the roof, will the labor unions accept cost of living wage increases at the end of the year and will you support our efforts to sell war bonds? *Yes, we can, was the reply!*

Management stepped forward and asked what can we do to win this war? Demand is going to sky rocket as we produce war goods and no consumer goods, will you accept a 90% marginal excess profits tax? *Yes, we can, was the reply*.

The rich owners then stepped forward and asked what can we do to win this war? Your profits will soar with this war will you accept a 70% marginal Federal tax rate plus state and local taxes raising the marginal rates to over 80%? *Yes we can*, they all sang in reply. With that kind of effort by everyone; **WWII was won!**

Are the massacres of at least 200,000 people at Hiroshima and Nagasaki—war crimes or not? Most of these victims were women and children and most of the men were non military. These events considered out of context were without question among the greatest individual crimes ever. WWII is however quite a context.

No one truly knows how many people died in WWII, a good conservative guess is sixty million which divided by two thousand days equals about 30,000 deaths every blood soaked day of WWII. Quite a context, I say just ask the millions of U.S. troops en-route from Europe heading to finish WWII in Japan by ground assault. Their answer is: "My God, I'm going to live, were going home!" Try convincing these millions that they should die.

What about Eleanor Roosevelt?

We never had a female president, so Eleanor wins my vote. Why: Franklin was a good guy because Eleanor compelled him to be. She pushed him to hire blacks in the Great Depression years; she was the driving force behind his decision to accept black men in our WWII military. The Navy selected blacks to serve their officers—they were the only blacks allowed to serve in the military at that time; servants only at Pearl Harbor.

In 1942 Franklin responded to the many demands and bedroom agreements with Eleanor to recreate black combat units.

She was born seemingly an unwanted child growing up—the daughter of Theodore's younger alcoholic brother—who left her a millionaires, alone on a New York sidewalk for hours at age eight while he was inside getting drunk at a bar and then left without her by a different door—who was mentally unstable and eventually committed suicide. People did not understand mental disorders and were afraid that this ugly child—her mother told her that brutal truth—inherited her father's ailments as well.

Yet Franklin fell in love with her, bless his heart—I suspect it might have been partially her uncle in the White House was a part of it and Franklin most definitely wanted to be President some day. He was tall, dark, athletic and handsome, and rich too! Bless him and how many future presidents get to have a marriage reception in the White House? A few years later ready to enter politics, the Democrats desperate for a Roosevelt—a beloved name of "we the people." Offered him a deal he could not refuse. On the fast track to the presidency suddenly polio struck him down after an afternoon swim.

Did I mention a last name that people adored even decades after T R? Everybody running for office claims to be a good person, how many are not only named Roosevelt but are married to a Roosevelt too! In 1932 we were ready to vote for a Roosevelt, cripple or not and Eleanor was there to push him to live up to her uncle's good name. Make no mistake, Franklin was and still is the only physically challenged president to ever win the presidency.

Yes, he tried his best to hide his inability to walk, but everybody around him in the press new it. I think they kept quiet mostly out of respect for that still very beloved name he wore . . . .

Why, was Eleanor so caring toward blacks, Jews and Catholics? Perhaps it was because growing up she had been shuttled from family to family, the unwanted daughter of insanity and ugly duckling of the rich. She did not wait until she became First Lady to care. When Franklin met her she was already volunteering in the homes of the poor in New York City.

Speaking of names, after F D R died in April 1945, Eleanor went to work for the United Nations trying to make this a better world, by fighting for her Atlantic Charter to be enshrined as a founding document, that done, she then fought for a Human Rights Council for international justice for all.

Later in 1956 in one of her last public acts she was trying to hammer out a Civil Rights Plank (or plan) for the Democratic Party with Judge George Wallace of Alabama among others. Yes, the future Governor who's most famous words was to be: "Segregation today, segregation tomorrow, segregation forever!" Out of her many, many frustrations she invited a little known man from Montgomery, Alabama: Dr. Martin Luther King Jr. to give a morning prayer for the committee; yes eventually she even managed once again to somehow bridge that gulf, bless her heart as well.

Yes Eleanor Roosevelt, niece of Theodore, wife of Franklin and friend of Dr. Martin Luther King, Jr. Here, Here; you win my vote as America's "honorary" best female president. Your time well spent. For you even managed to make Franklin look good!

Harry Truman and Post World War II:

Polio, the Great Depression and WWII probably combined to kill Franklin a few days after the start of his fourth term bringing Harry Truman into the presidency. President Harry Truman, who had never been out of the country except as an artillery captain in 1918-19 suddenly discovered the whole shattered world dumped into his lap, rose to the occasion.

Approving dropping the atom bombs on Japan with one hand then with the other he then approved General McArthur's emergency food program for a starving Japan. Fighting for economic recovery programs—the

Marshall Plan for Europe; citing our own mistakes trying to politically repair the American South after the Civil War with-out an economic recovery resulting in decades of hatred.

Then recognizing that only America could stop Stalin's Soviet Union he pushed hard for the North Atlantic Treaty Organization (NATO) in absolute defiance of George Washington's last words to America: "to stay away from foreign entanglements." Arguing that the world and America's role had changed more than a little since 1797.

In 1947 responding to Baseball inviting Jackie Robinson a black man to play ball with the whites Truman as Commander in Chief of the military ordered its integration by executive order—thus not needing legislative approval. In 1948 Truman defied the Dixiecrat rebellion led by Strom Thurmond of South Carolina winning re-election and the integrated military would continue.

Then to prove even a good president can be stupid or at least in this case, his new Secretary of State:

In 1950 Truman's new Secretary of State said "Americans will never fight in Asia in Asiatic Wars"—a month later Soviet built North Korea invaded American built South Korea both former colonies of Japan. Harry Truman told our troops to fight. The Korean War had begun, officially it still continues.

World War II, in Remembrance:

I was born the son of a WWII vet. I grew up in the world he wished he could have had, that is of Mickey Mouse, Roy Rodgers and the Chipmunks. I never had to walk his miles through the Great Depression where even hope all but died. In 1939 he married and in 1941 he and America were plunged into all out war. I never fought his battles years and continents far away wondering if peace and prosperity could ever be restored unto this shattered world? I hated war, so did he; but in very different ways. I did not understand.

We totally disagreed over the war in Vietnam, pollution and Civil Rights. Their simply was no way to bridge the gaps between us until the day he died. I'll never forget thinking to myself "I guess I'm suppose to cry for him now." Suddenly I broke into uncontrollable tears as I realized he had always loved me, no matter what I said or had done. He never understood me either, but he always loved me.

So let us try to remember our WWII vets by loving those who disagree with us for neither you or I have walked their miles in their boots.

The Second Red Scare; McCarthyism:

In the 1930's capitalism stopped working. In Britain their Labour government said cut spending to balance the budget, spending cut, revenues fell even further, the Conservatives take power and further cut spending, revenues continued to fall. In France the Rightist slashed spending so when revenues fell the Left Front took power but there spending was too little, too late and on the wrong things.

For Hitler's Nazi's had already spent Germany's money correctly and was on the march. Stalin too had spent Russia's Communist money as well, and his Red Army was getting ready to roll.

Meanwhile in America the greatest capitalist country, F D R spent money, the rich cried, so he slashed spending. The economy faltered, so once again he spent money, the critics cried, so once again F D R cut spending; the revenues fell even faster as the Great Depression continued to prove capitalism a failure.

In Germany the critics were arrested, in Russia now called the Soviet Union, any would be critics were given long trips to Siberia whether wanted or not. Thus Nazism and Communism were on the roll advancing across Europe.

After the fall of France (their spending: too little, too late and wrong) in 1940, at last F D R ordered American spending to soar and got it right. Thus in 1944-45 America roared across Western Europe to meet the Soviet Red Army in central Germany. So capitalism had triumphed after all.

But in America where people are usually allowed to think out loud, many people's thoughts had strayed from the center i.e. capitalism. The American version of the Nazi's was the German-American Bundt of the 1930's (or KKK of the 1920's). In 1941 Hitler declared war on America; the German-American Bundt disappeared overnight after Pearl Harbor. Their thinking did not—reverting to the KKK of old—but that is old American, so it's okay—too many!

Now, about those communists; by definition they are the sworn enemy of the rich and normally powerful. After all whose money do they want to spread around? Communism had rolled across Eastern Europe. They too claimed victory. The Cold War was about to begin.

In 1947 Senator McCarthy (Republican of Wisconsin) yelled communism in America must be crushed! For the next seven years McCarthyism ruled America: the land of the free and the home of the brave. As he shook a piece of paper claiming he had a list of over 100 communists in our State Department, he also gave Americans something to watch on that new device called TV.

At the 1939 New York World's Fair all kinds of futuristic devices like flying cars were on display. Unfortunately the world chose war as the future. A black and white TV was on display at the Empire State Building, and most definitely not on display anywhere was the Atom Bomb, yet these two devices would in fact dominate the future. In 1947 almost no one anywhere had TV; by 1960 virtually every one under 60 in America had at least one.

Why, one must ask. Why was McCarthyism allowed to dominate America for seven years; from 1947 to 1954 why did America allow this hatemongering to rule the land of the free and the home of the brave? Why? Why?

Perhaps it's because from 1933 to 1947 the normally rich and powerful had been relegated to the back seat. If your use to the front seat; the back seat gets old in a hurry. Fourteen years was more than long enough. The Reds are arising, it is time to take the driver's seat back and crush them while we still can.

America came out of W.W.II having beaten Germany with one arm and Japan with the other thinking we could bend and twist the whole world into whatever shape we wished it to be. Yes we were overconfident—and very arrogant.

Yes we are still prone to being the "Omnipotent Americans." The ones who think they can bend and twist the whole world into whatever shape we wish it to be. For better; most of the world is in great need of reform, and for worse; while we may have the might, 5% dictating to 95% can never be right.

We all too often forget that our victories won over both Germany and Japan were won in large part because of the support both big and small from virtually the entire world. The Soviet Union, Britain, China, India, Canada, Australia, New Zealand, Brazil, and yes even the Ethiopia's*5 of the world contributed to "our" victories.

This is not to even mention the sacrifices made by those countries overrun by Germany and Japan. This would include still another long list of countries from the Korea's to the Philippines to Burma and from Greece to Norway.

In short we can be omnipotent, but only if the world supports us . . . So, why did we endure seven years of McCarthyism and then get into the quagmire of Vietnam?

A good place to start is with a question asked long ago: A young man was working in Paris at a fancy restaurant while attending the Sorbonne University when the Allied leaders were debating the Versailles Treaty ending the First World War. The young man was curious about what President Wilson was trying to get into the peace treaty, so when the President sat down in his restaurant, the waiter asked: If he meant the people's right to self determination applied to the colonial world also? Quickly shooed away he never received his answer.

I feel confident President Wilson did not want to answer that young man's question since the other Allied leaders already objected to this popular idea. That young man—born Nguyen That Thanh later renamed Ho Chi Minh. Whether this story is true or not I do not know, we only do know that Ho Chi Minh would repeat it several times. In any case true or not it certainly deserves an answer.

If we truly believe we are "a nation dedicated to the proposition of liberty and justice for all"—Abe Lincoln. Then while many of us may feel that we are intellectually superior, I think we all would agree that every people should be entitled to self-determination to the extent possible. Therefore the answer must be: Yes.

This of course should mean that if a people freely chose a government not to our liking, that decision is their business, not ours. This does not mean that we should not try to influence them to do what we think is right, but the choice must always be theirs.

Remember George Washington was a slave owner, few people in today's America would be proud of that. Even Thomas Jefferson his leading critic of that very different world owned slaves!

With these principles in mind let us now re-trace our steps into our:

Vietnam Nightmare . . .

In W.W.II President Roosevelt ignored both Free and Vichy French opposition and supplied the Viet-Minh with arms and ammunition. I believe he did this because he had no interest in restoring French colonial rule after the war and in the meantime the Viet-Minh were fighting the Japanese and every Japanese killed by the Viet-Minh was one less that we ourselves might have to kill.

After W.W.II, President Truman made the decision to "switch sides" in Indo-China (Vietnam, Cambodia and Laos). You and I, may think this was a wrong decision, but his reason for doing so—to help prevent the communists from winning the 1947 French elections certainly too some extent justified his actions.

Most un-fortunately after the French elections, he elected to continue American support for French colonial rule, on the grounds that the Viet-Minh were communists. This was only partly true, but they were largely communist led. They were also all "freedom fighters."

To support French colonial rule, no not that! To fight the freedom fighters, yearning to breathe free, no not them either! To fight the "communists" in Indo-China, yes, finally: President Truman dispatched a few hundred U.S. Army technical and support troops to Vietnam. In reality this is when our "nightmare" began, in 1947. Meanwhile, we were watching on our new TV's:

The McCarthy hearings pouring his hatred's directly into our living rooms destroying many good Americans in both government and the private sector for daring to think out of main-stream America or sometimes just knowing someone who allegedly did. For year after year his hate and the fear his accusations instilled in others of communists among us poured into our hearts. The impact of his hate mongering and that of many others of both political parties trying to yell their accusations even louder, so as to capture the camera lime light cannot be understated. In this **feeding frenzy of political ambitions,** America the home of the brave became the home of the afraid.

Though the hearings the Anti-American Activities Investigations never produced a shred of evidence against most of the accused their careers were still ruined. People literally fled the country rather be led before the cameras and be so publicly repeatedly accused of thinking "un-American" thoughts.

How could you defend yourself against the accusation that: You were a friend of the previously accused were you not? Any yes answer was effectively saying yes I was a cohort of that communist sympathizer. If you answered no, evidence of your repeated contacts with the previously convicted by accusations only would "prove" your guilt of sharing their alleged beliefs before the public's eyes.

Soon our elites of both the press and politics were afraid that if they dissented in any way, they too would be accused and ruined in the court of public opinion. Because now with television pouring all this hate and fear into the public's heart—we the people were so afraid of communists everywhere amongst us, the accusations would be believed by many just as Herr Goebbels said about any lie repeated often enough.

When the investigations proceeded to the Army-McCarthy hearings my brother tells me our mother said: "Now that man is going to try to destroy the Army." If she did say that, it was extremely prophetic. While McCarthy failed to destroy the Army in the 1950's he did set the climate for its destruction twenty years later . . .

When General Marshall, commander of the entire army during WW II rose to the defense of the Army in 1954, at last the witch hunt was ended. One should ask; why was this witch hunt allowed to last for so long, doing so much harm.

The conservatives in both political parties benefited initially, so why not . . . The Press was un-aware in the beginning of the true power of televised accusations . . . The Liberals were its many intended victims . . . many in reaction out of fear, joined in! We the people were in fact its many victims, both conservatives and liberals alike, because we were now all, so, so afraid . . .

Levittown*7 and it's off to Suburbia!

At least however our economy had sputtered as expected in 1946 and 47 as the war economy of WWII came to an abrupt end. But regearing for peace the economy took off at almost light speed if it weren't for all them laborites demanding a doubling in wages to match war time inflation.

Given a little time prices started falling, but with demand now soaring as workers borrowed on their WWII earnings to buy new houses in Levittown—suburbia now exploding at the limits of new growth, prices stopped falling and everybody rejoiced as the economy soared into 1948 onward and upward, with the sky the only limit.

Unfortunately with congress controlled mainly by Slave Democrats err, Southern Democrats the booming economy was not entirely shared. Blacks were not allowed to participate. Just one example of the Jim Crow South now ruling all of America: Of Levittown's initial population of 82,000 on Long Island how many do you think were black? Ten thousand you might say based on black percentage of the overall population . . . Not a chance, try again?

Five thousand. Ha, where are you from? Two thousand? This is America run by the Jim Crow South, in case you haven't figured that out? But this is New York! Care to make a new guess?

You're kidding me, not zero? Finally you reasoned it out, in what country you are in! Yes zero is correct, for the American Jacksonist Slavocracy*6 rules supreme. In Pennsylvania a few determined blacks integrated, violence quickly ended their dream. We will hear more of this later . . .

In this climate of the post McCarthy years, our American idealism became subverted by our anti-communism (and anti minority-ism). Now every president, congressman and senator had to prove "they were tough on communism (and minorities too)."

We now supported anyone who opposed communism whether they might be French colonialists or brutal dictators like the Shah of Iran. Even when the Republicans retook power in the 1950's they now promised America vote for us and we shall out do the Democrats, and they too under Eisenhower, meant every word of it (including the anti minorities). For the Ballad of America was forgotten like Lincoln, himself.

Thus when the French colonialists decided to pull out, President Eisenhower decided to stay and back the government of South Vietnam installed by the departing French—and minorities would you just disappear for we Republicans are trying to outdo the Slave Democrats!

Our decision to fully support South Vietnam's decision to cancel the 1956 elections that we had in effect guaranteed only two years earlier, fell victim to McCarthy's "tough on communism." And none it seemed paid any attention to blacks, screaming . . . "what about us!" Let alone other minorities screaming what about their dreams of living in the promised land of liberty to all. Clearly Eisenhower, the congress and the press were all very wrong in not denouncing these decisions by their utter indifference. But in this climate of hysteria, very few felt brave enough to scream foul . . . for the truth, was painful and very few whites wanted to hear it.

This is the world Dr. Martin Luther King, Jr. would have to open the door of change into; to force a reluctant America to reform itself.

AUTHOR NOTES

*1: Anarchists: The modern world's first terrorists. Their motto might read: the world of 1900 was rotten; the only way to save it is to destroy everything so we can start all over. Anarchists among many other crimes assaulted J.P. Morgan's New York Bank, murdered err, assassinated President McKinley just after the start of his second term and participated in the assassination of the Crown Prince of Austria which set off World War One (WWI).

*2: Nat'l Park Service: Theodore Roosevelt had climbed the Matter horn in Switzerland, noticing not a single wild animal anywhere. Thus a big game hunter; was determined to prevent this in America. Therefore in creating the National Park Service he put more than 200,000 square miles—more land than Switzerland, Austria and Britain put together, aside to protect not just the land, but the animals he hoped would forever be allowed to roam them.

Now perhaps you understand why he is one of only four Presidents atop Mt. Rushmore, his gentle turning 1900 America upside down was truly appreciated by "we the people" as a non violent revolution. The other three, Washington, Jefferson and Lincoln definitely deserve to be beside him as well. T R unable to save the Grand Canyon in Congress; declared it a national monument, to save it from the miners already tearing it apart who had blocked T R in Congress. In the courts T R would continue the fight against local Arizona interests, fighting for we (America's) interest. Thanks, Teddy, your time well spent.

*3: Madoff: A notorious thief who promised high returns and lied and lied a lot more until finally caught and sent to prison. Yes, his name was Madoff as in Made Off—that much was true about him.

*4: In the 1600's England fought the English Civil War beheading King Charles I, inaugurated Lord Cromwell's dictatorship as Lord Protector. But after five years of enforced Puritanism upon his death, forced his son to resign and welcomed King Charles II in the Grand Restoration. Thus in the end, Parliament did nothing—the hard way!

*5: Ethiopia: An independent kingdom dating back at least to the three wise men visiting at Jesus' birth. It became Christianized when St. Thomas brought the teachings of Jesus on his way to India. A member of the League of Nations when Italy invaded with airplanes, tanks, machineguns and poison gas in 1935. When Italy declared war on Britain in 1940 Christian Ethiopia rallied to Britain's defense. In 1941 Ethiopia was liberated and would continue to fight against both Nazi Germany and Mussolini's Italy until final victory was won—for all.

*6: American Jacksonist Slavocracy: My own term for America as a whole from 1829 to 1963 with Lincoln's term a major exception. Jackson's terms in office 1829-1837 largely defines "white American" by definition. Gradually his slave—supporting anti minority views would spread nationwide after the Civil War encouraged by the Northern working classes not liking minorities taking their high paying unskilled jobs away. You see I too can attack Jackson two centuries later. But I defend him for being a white male "we the people's" president still, for even they are rare.

*7 Levittown: Three towns in New York, New Jersey and Pennsylvania built by Andrew Levitt having gained experience in mass construction during WWII.

Primary source material for most of chapter IV comes from JAMES MACGREGOR BURNS and SUSAN DUNN'S "*THE THREE ROOSEVELTS*"—definitely great reading.

A great secondary source material was "***The History of White People***" by Nell Irvin Painter. She paints a very different but nonetheless enlightening picture of America today.

CHAPTER V

Gandhi and the World of Today

First a little history—
Why did Europe explore the World?

LET US BEGIN this story in the past, those days of old. In most lands in the America's, Africa, Asia and Europe the King, Raj or Emperor ruled. The law was simple, in the lands called civilized where most people lived by farming, what the king wants, the king gets; that is the law. Except in Europe, after the collapse of the Roman Empire:

The barely civilized and Christianized German barbarian rulers of the now ex-Roman Empire had kept their ancestral rights as hunter gatherers . . . The law can most easily be explained by a little French story. This story is from the time when all Europe could marvel at the wonders made by Rome, and wonder . . . how could they have made such wonders? Forgive me I forget the names, so I have to make them up, but the story is true.

Once upon a time about a thousand years ago, the King was seizing a palace and he decided to award Sir Bartholomew with any piece of gold or art as his reward for his services. Thanking the King he chooses a beautiful vase with a fancy name. So the King goes home with his trunks of gold, silver and art being carefully carried behind him.

His daughter greets him and his treasure with cries of glee. You brought the vase home to me, she screams with delight. The king does not understand; what are you talking about? She tells him, you promised, you promised don't you remember when you were leaving I ran after you and you said don't worry, I'll bring it to you.

The King now remembers, he was thinking of many other things and to dismiss her, he had simply said "do not worry, I'll bring it (whatever it was; in his mind) home with me" to be done with her.

So the King says do not worry, I'll get it, that wonderful vase for you. So the King summons Sir Bartholomew and his vase to him. The King says to him, I must have the vase, I offer you any three pieces in exchange. I am sorry your highness but you said it was mine.

The king then says take any six pieces if you must but I must have the vase. I am sorry your highness, you said it is mine and so it is mine.

The King is angry but the law is the law. A year later the King assembles his army to storm another castle. The King walks up and down his ranks of knights, frowning at Bartholomew but walks onward. Walking down the next rank he stops behind Sir Bartholomew and smashes his head wide open.

The King then shouts: "The vase may be yours, but you are mine."

This distinction in law and absolutely no law is why Europe forged far ahead of the America's, Africa, and Asia. Since most people were wise enough to not say directly to the King "Sorry your Highness" and thus live. The Kings of Western Europe could not simply take as they pleased. For the Germans and their many descendants which over ran the Western Roman Empire had kept their Germanic hunter gatherer rights regardless of which tribe they belonged to; even those who had adopted the Latin languages.

While to most people this distinction in limited rights and none at all might seem minor. This distinction in law is what propelled Europe to conquer the world because individuals were protected in their property.

Many people wonder why Mexico is so poor despite oil to sell to that rich country to the North—the USA. Well its property law. This can be explained by answering who is the richest person in the world? A Mexican is, not Bill Gates any more. If you want to buy something wholesale in Mexico, you best know who to buy from; otherwise you may have a nasty accident, bullets included and I haven't even mentioned the drug cartels.

That is why Mexico and so many third world countries are so poor. China without democracy and India with democracy learned this lesson beginning about 1980. Our world is a changing . . .

Thus if we view Western Europe in say 1500, we see a world with many rich merchants flaunting their wealth. While elsewhere we see merchants hiding their wealth from all others. They are all more or less equally poor societies by our standards but Europe is growing richer—at least for a few, while the America's, Africa and Asia remain frozen in the past.

This in effect meant the freedom to make a buck. That might not sound like much too any king but when the bucks started mounting up it meant riches galore. So in short order:

Conquistadores free to make a buck soon conquered the Aztec and Inca Empires—for no king would ever travel so far from home* and Africa and Asia would of course soon follow. Granted Africa took longer because of diseases, but Europe would soon be upon their shores as well.

The times of Gandhi:

Thus while the British Empire was losing its old empire in America, Britain conquered still a new empire in India. For the power to make a buck sends us everywhere opportunity beacons even today, so it did then as well. Thus in the 1800's India is ruled by British law which the merchants of India find fascinating with the freedom to make a buck, but they find the British law confusing for having mastered the English language they are at a total lost when Habeas Corpus and other Latin terms are used.

So in 1888 a wealthy brother sends his younger brother to Victorian England to become a British trained lawyer. Graduating from the University of London, he stays long enough to practice law pro bono—free of charge, before the Court of London. That way he cannot be denied elsewhere.

The lawyer of course is Mohandas Gandhi (born 1869), who proves to be a bust in 1892 India, upon his return. Almost fainting in his first trial in India he reluctantly accepts an offer from South Africa. There he discovers the inner strength that he so lacked in India. Winning the case at his victory going away party he learns that the Indian merchants he had represented had no idea what was in the newspaper. Naturally it was written in English using the Phoenician Alphabet and while able to converse in English they could only read in Sanskrit.

What was written in English was a proposed law before the Natal (a province of South Africa) legislature to strip Asiatics of their voting rights. Mohandas Gandhi quickly realized in South Africa it was him only, who could fight for Indian rights. Thus for a £300 annual minimum retainer fee from the merchants, he agreed to stay and fight.

For the next twenty plus years Gandhi batters the iron barrier of utter indifference of South Africa's courts. Winning what amounts to a half way station in South Africa. The whites are above the clouds, the blacks are below every one else's feet with Indians in between.

Meanwhile traveling back and forth to India his efforts attracts great attention throughout educated India, thus:

How Mohandas became Mahatma (Great Soul) Gandhi:

It is hard to imagine that a man who dressed himself as the poorest of the poor changed the world—but Gandhi did just that. An Indian national trained as a British lawyer, he chose to transform himself into the poorest of the poor of India—arguably the poorest country on Earth by the 1940's. By adopting their lifestyle soon the poorest of the Indian laborers of South Africa saw he was one of them, fighting for their rights as well as those of the middle class Indians. When he returned to British India this lessoned learned was repeated and soon he became the Great Soul of British India and in the newsreels of the times—to the young at heart the Great Soul of all human kind.

Meanwhile he learned:

From his father: As a boy he stole a piece of gold; his father forgave him when he quickly owned up to the truth. Thus, to forgive those who are not perfect even to him personally; or to say it another way, not to hold any grudges and eventually to feel genuine sorrow for his abusers and thus change or win their hearts, by non violent protest—also from his wife below.

From his mother: How she so cared for sick strangers until healthy again and a deep love for religion though which he would later study ancient Hinduism, Buddhism, Christianity—the New Testament, and Mohammed's early life. Seeing how all these founders struggled through many miles of suffering before discovering what Mahatma Gandhi would later call Satyaorahy: the power of truth by non-violence or the more general term ashami: group living in (all) religious non violence. From Buddha he learned: Hatred cannot be cured by more hatred, but by love.

From his wife: To which he was married with his two brothers in a joint three weddings in Hindu India at the age of thirteen. He learned the power of non-violent disapproval for his all too often childish behavior.

From South Africa: He learned Satyaorahy first hand by experiencing the sufferings of the poorest Indians and their great strength at suffering the pains inflicted by their many abusers.

By believing one should practice what one preaches Mohandas Gandhi realized immediately that the 250 Indian voters—the merchant class had zero power in Natal out of the approximate 10,000 legal voters by Imperial law. To gain any real power they must gain the power of the Indian poor laboring classes who numbered perhaps half the total population of non-blacks in Natal.

Thus Gandhi quickly learned how to cut his living expenses to perhaps £5 per year plus traveling money; by using the spinning wheel to make his "untouchable" clothing, and giving up on all other non-necessities like a fine house. Founding a village to teach what he gradually developed as satyaorahy asham to both learn by experimenting and to gain the trust of all the laboring class.

To make a long story short Gandhi lost the battle of voting rights but did win a sort of middle ground of rights for Asiatics—Indians over twenty plus years of fighting non-violently in South Africa.

In 1913 Mohandas now almost universally proclaimed Mahatma Gandhi returns to India to in effect take charge of the Indian National Congress Party. This is a party of the elite, worshipping in effect at the alter of: To make bucks by British Law—but the times are a changing.

Gandhi's first act is proclaiming he will do nothing for a year, for he has been mostly out of India for more than twenty years, so he must reclaim his heritage by re-experiencing Indian life. Needless to say, many are befuddled by this.

In 1914 Gandhi launches his first non-violent protest but WWI breaks out and Gandhi still hopes to awaken British eyes to the truth about India. So Gandhi recruits for the military only to discover that in one village where he had personally recruited a small army for non violent protest, he is not even allowed in by the elders and waits for two days just outside with a lone assistant with not one visitor.

Fortunately or not, Britain and Gandhi would have more success elsewhere and over a million Indians are recruited as volunteers for the western front vs. Germany as well as the Middle-East vs. the Ottoman (Turkish) Empire in response to Britain's offer of "near-like" Dominion status or self government like British Canada and Australia after the war.

Then the Massacre of Amritsar occurs:

There are many versions of this story but this is mine: In 1914 Europe declared war and the armies tore into one another and no one won. In 1915 they all tried again and everybody lost. In 1916 they tried even harder and they died by the millions and still no one won. By 1917 they are all exhausted but make peace? Hell no. Continue the slaughter! This war is called WWI, "the war to end all wars"—a very sad lie of the time.

Britain is desperate so to make a short story shorter Britain made many promises about after the war to get help in the war to many peoples in many places. To India they promise near autonomous status—almost independence. India is thrilled and more than a million troops volunteer to be sent to Europe so they can be slaughtered like everyone else.

America enters the war and victory is won in 1918. Time to deliver: Unfortunately the whole purpose of empire is to rule others for your benefit and no others . . .

In 1919 Britain decides what is "near like" Dominion status is: The same old Imperial rule with many minor—though some actually substantial for Britain to give up concessions. In summation: A lot for Britain to surrender but peanuts to Indian nationalists, depending strictly upon your point of view.

In 1919 also new commanders arrive in Punjab Province—divided between India and Pakistan today. A new law is passed and people riot in the streets of Amritsar the capital. The commanding Brigadier's wife somehow gets mud splattered upon her dress. She gives her husband bloody hell for the insults she has heard. Going to the Governor he declares a prohibition of any gatherings of people for twenty days.

A few days later the farmers of the countryside walk into town for their annual farmer's market festival. The Brigadier is alerted and sends his Army to execute them "for not recognizing that Britain rules" with their bullets tearing into the startled farmers, their wife's and children's flesh. How many were killed? Undoubtedly, in the many hundreds but there are many counts up to well over a thousand.

So this is India's reward of semi-independence in reality. Britain would soon grant many reforms but they never amounted to semi or near independence, for that would mean the end of British rule for Britain's benefit.

The people of India are in an uproar, but they know not what to do, for the British have the guns and many in India love this whole idea of being free to make a buck. For years many people of India had been begging Gandhi to return to India to take charge of their efforts to force real reform in India.

The official Inquiry into the massacre exposed its hand when it announced no changes in command for the Punjab at the beginning so the finding of correct behavior for its conduct is of little surprise. For most Indians this was more than enough, but for Gandhi he still held out hope for the defeated Moslem, Ottoman Empire.

When the Treaty of Sèvres (1920) a sub page to Versailles; revealed this ancient empire (successor to the Christian, Byzantine Empire) would be destroyed and divided amongst the Christian victors, this was the last straw for Gandhi and Moslem India. When the Ottoman's signed this treaty; Mustafa Kemal (soon to be Atatürk or "Father of the Turks") would lead a rebellion to expand modern Turkey and modernize the country to its present boundaries and democratic laws helping prove just how hollow "the war to end all wars" was, but that is another story, not this one.

At last everyone in British India have reached the same page of history that we recall them as being. From 1920 to 1936 the Gandhi led non violent rebellion against continued British rule both from with in jail and from with out results in thousands of dead Indians. Many of these deaths however do not die in vain for many register in Britain as they watch their own government ruthlessly beat British rule into the heads of Indians on the newsreels of the times.

Winston Churchill having served in British India in the 1880's as a young officer of the crown remembered the India of the 1880's which of course after Amritsar and the Treaty of Sèvres is now dead as can be. Thus Churchill and the Conservative Party in Britain truly believe India ruled by Britain is "the white man's burden" that must be borne for the sake of Indians and all other non whites.

Even the aristocrats of India had changed; during the 1880's they were as stuffed shirts as the worst of the Kings, Dukes, Lords and Earls of Europe. Churchill naturally saw their backwardness and therefore he thought just how better "enlightened British rule" was, than their backward rule. But fifty years of continued British rule had changed even their stuffed shirts. For now many were willing to give up their inherited titles and privileges if doing so would drive the British out.

Now this was a sea change in thought; comparable to "our founders" no longer willing to discuss slavery in public (1790) to our welcoming the Civil War—Abe Lincoln to abolish it (1861-1865); that unfortunately Churchill failed to comprehend like our elder statesmen failed as well to comprehend. Again the world was a changing . . .

As a part of the 1919 India Constitution Act in 1927 a review of it was launched; which finally produced a revised Indian Constitution of 1937. This revised constitution granted some real powers to the people of India:

With about a third of the national budget granted to the partially elective assembly and perhaps half of the budget granted to the elective Parliaments of the directly ruled by Britain states. Those states still ruled by the remaining Indian Princes would remain un-changed and they would appoint their representatives to the national parliament—about a third of the total. The budgets and revenues needed for the military, police and courts would remain the privilege of the crown and its appointees with veto power.

Debating the pros and cons of this constitution in 1936 the Congress Party devoted to both socialism and independence decided to run for office with-in the capitalist Imperial Realm of British India to give it a try. In the elections of March 1937; Congress wins about half the seats nation wide.

Forming governments in six of the larger states they proceed to try revolutionizing elementary education—to make it of practical value to the poor i.e. to teach how to make handicrafts and other useful items to their impoverished families. Not surprisingly many British officials find "it is hard to serve where you have ruled"—Phillip Mason.

Naturally the socialist independence advocating National Congress Party has its opponents besides the British. Most importantly the Moslem League led by M. A. Jinnah which fails miserably in this 1937 election, for Gandhi has captured the hearts of poor Moslems and Hindu's alike. While Jinnah is well dressed trying to represent middle class Moslems; soon charging "the fact is the Congress wants domination of India under shelter of British bayonets" and "to subjugate and vassalize the Muslims under a Hindu Raj and annihilate the Muslims." Gradually Jinnah's support grows and by 1939 is a force to be reckoned with for his rhetoric captures the fears of Muslims . . .

World War II:

On September 3rd 1939 the world suddenly changes with the proclamation by "I, Victor Alexander John, Marquess of Linlithgow, Governor-General of India so hereby proclaim that war has broken out between His Majesty and Germany."

This declaration of war was done so with-out any discussion of any kind with any Indian. India is in shock. For while many and probably most had supported Britain's stand against the hatred of Hitler; the almost universally felt contempt for continued British rule is profound. For if one's opinion of war or peace does not matter, than any participation in so called "ruling" is of no value either.

Quickly the Congress Party led by the equally well dressed Nehru demands complete independence for India and we will join Britain in the war as equals. Soon rejected as an offer of blackmail; the Congress Party quits the government in November 1939 and demands Britain must:

"Quit India."

Lord Linlithgow calls for a meeting with Gandhi still living among the poorest, who holds no title or office to quit; for the now universally proclaimed Mahatma needs no title or office let alone fancy clothes to lead the hearts of India. Gandhi cries at the thought of London where he had lived (1888-91) and visited several times since, being bombed but no, Britain must grant independence or he could not support the war effort. He will promise to do as little as possible to embarrass the government during the war however.

In March, 1940 the Moslem League proclaims the "Two Nation Policy" for India. Gandhi's initial reaction: "Vivisect me before vivisect (split) India." But on April 6th 1940 declares: "The Muslims must have the same rights of self-determination that the rest of India has."

In May and June 1940 Western Europe collapses before the Nazi blitzkrieg; Sir Winston Churchill (a direct descendent of the Earl of Marlborough) becomes Prime Minister and soon makes his famous speech; "... **until the new world comes to the rescue of the old, we will never, surrender!"**

Quickly Britain begins arresting the leaders of the Congress Party and any non-violent acts or alleged acts about to be committed including Gandhi and Nehru. But India remains tense as everyone knows all Gandhi must do is raise a finger and India will explode even as the Axis Powers, Germany and Italy lurk in the Middle-East while the British Empire makes its brave final stand alone.

As Gandhi is quoted as saying in 1941; "There is neither warrant nor atmosphere for mass action. That would be naked embarrassment and a betrayal of non-violence;" at this so critical time.

Three days before the Japanese secret attack on Pearl Harbor and with other known battle/invasion fleets approaching British Malaya one could argue out of desperation the British announce by official communiqué:

The government of India announces "confident in the determination of all responsible opinion in India to support the war effort until victory is secured" announced that all arrested for civil disobedience, by now over 25,000 people would be released.

With the American battle fleet crippled at Pearl Harbor and the smaller British and Dutch fleets destroyed; British Singapore surrendered on February 15th 1942. With British Hong Kong and Malaya lost along with the American Philippines and Dutch East Indies—modern Indonesia, British Burma would quickly follow. Suddenly the Empire of Japan was knocking on India's door while the Bay of Bengal was totally exposed.

In 1944 a Japanese Army of 200,000 troops with perhaps 60,000 Indians of Tamil extraction recruited from ex British Malaya and former Indian POW's invaded India under the political leadership of Subhas Chandra Bose—an Indian opportunist. When India refused to rise in revolt against British rule, the invasion collapsed due to lack of supplies—when the supplies they physically carried ran out, that was effectively the end of the invasion.

On a smaller scale this was a repetition of Napoleon's invasion of Russia, with the mountains and jungles of Burma (modern Myanmar) replacing the Russian winter with the same effect. With the former Indian POW's disappearing like the Prussian's and Austrian's quickly returning homeward leaving the French to their peril. Only a few thousand Japanese would make it back to Burma just like only a few thousand French would make it back to Poland in 1813.

In April 1942 the Cripps Commission arrives offering nothing now but promises for independence after the war is concluded with every sub-division offered to opt out with several opportunities for doing so. Since to India this plan offered nothing now but promises about the future it was widely rejected for their simply was no trust remaining for British rule in India.

On July 14th 1942 the Working Committee of the Congress Party formally rejected the Cripps commission offer, declaring "British rule must end immediately." On August 7th this declaration was backed by the All India Congress at Bombay. Two days later British India arrested Gandhi, Nehru and many others.

Mobs reacted violently throughout India with the government firing on the mobs and at least in one case machine gunning them with aircraft. After a rapid exchange of letters between Lord Linlithgow and Gandhi in prison; Gandhi out of frustration declares a personal fast to stop the violence. The rioting soon stops.

On February 22, 1944 Kasturba, Gandhi's wife of sixty-two years dies. Gandhi soon after catches malaria and much to his embarrassment is released from prison on May 6th 1944. Soon after suffering from malaria, hook worm and amoebic infections he is in critical condition at the age of seventy-five. Insisting on only native herbs being used on him, he nonetheless eventually recovers. With the conclusion of WWII all other political prisoners would be released.

Before they all die let us all say thank you to the soldiers of all nations from Africa, the Americas, Asia, Europe and Oceania who suffered along the long roads to both Berlin and Tokyo. Our freedoms today is owed by us to them for their sacrifices, thank you.

On May 8th 1945 the war in Europe concludes and Britain schedules elections in July at which Churchill and his Conservative Party are thrown out of power by a huge margin.

Just what this means even the victorious Labour Party seems to be initially at a loss in regards to British India and its colonial empire. But gradually the elder statesmen of the Labour Party realize that to the British electorate: *The world had changed and Churchill had not.*

The world had changed—America the New World had come to the rescue of the old, as Churchill had called upon them to do, in Britain's darkest hour and this time the Americans decided to stay to win the peace won in war.

Churchill and F.D. Roosevelt had strongly disagreed over colonial rights to be free; for even as F.D.R. had promised the Philippines their independence in ten years in 1935, granted in 1946. Churchill had never conceded anything even with his own signature on the Atlantic Charter jointly adopted on August 14th 1941 which promised all peoples everywhere their rights to self government—enshrined as a founding statement in the U.N. Charter in San Francisco—1945. Yes, indeed:

The world had changed and Churchill had not.

Gradually and no doubt reluctantly the elder statesmen of the Labour Party promised British India in 1946 complete independence would be granted in 1947. For Jinnah and The Moslem League it was now or never. Greeting Britain's statement promising independence to India with; "we have forged a pistol and are in a position to use it."

Lord Wavel the new Viceroy asks Nehru to form an interim government—Jinnah and The Moslem League refuse to join it. Charging Nehru with "the caste and Hindu Fascist Congress and their henchmen to dominate and rule the Mussalmans and other minority communities of India with the aid of British bayonets."

On August 16th 1946 The Moslem League proclaims Direct Action Day and Calcutta immediately explodes in religious murder as first Muslims kill Hindu's who quickly respond by murdering Muslims. Soon the whole of Bengal joins in the mutual slaughter. After four days of joint suicide over 5,000 are killed and Gandhi arrives and prays for peace, the mutual slaughter ends in Calcutta and Gandhi moves on to quiet the killing fields of Bengal, soon after the state of Bihar then explodes.

By the time the rampage is quelled there the Punjab—the other directly ruled by Britain state to be divided along with Bengal, erupts in flames. On his way by train to the Punjab, Delhi explodes in violence as Hindu's, Sikh's and Muslims go for each others throats. Here Hindu's and Sikh's have been expelled from the Punjab in reaction literally go to civil war to force Muslims to abandon their homes and businesses in Delhi so they can have them.

Now Lord Mountbatten has arrived for Lord Wavel had proved unable to stop the communal violence between the Hindu's and Moslems of India. Even Gandhi could only dampen it down, but as long as Jinnah and The Moslem League felt the threat of violence served their interest what could any mortal do.

On January 13th 1948 Gandhi begins to fast to voice his disapproval of violence. On January 18th in Gandhi's presence many communal leaders of all religions sign a pledge to promise peace in Delhi, the level of violence notably drops off. On January 30th with his forearms resting on the shoulders of his grand nieces Ava and Manu—his walking sticks; Mahatma walks to his evening prayers a short two minute walk lifting his hands in greeting when three shots strike him. His final words: "He Rama"—Oh God and dies—killed by an angry Hindu in protest to his non-violence.

In retrospect:

While judging Mahatma Gandhi from the near future of 2010, he was not perfect even in his ideology of wishing as he told Lord Linlithgow in 1939 that it was his greatest wish that the whole world would resist the hatred of the world non-violently.

Perhaps it is my own selfish greed speaking in reaction to this but I have no desire to be fed to the lions of ancient Rome as the Christians were. It is my belief that doing so was the only method of fighting the power of Rome available to them in their far, far from perfect world.

On this I must agree with Nehru that this is still a far from perfect world, some people like Britain and later America, can be persuaded non-violently, other peoples must unfortunately must be persuaded by the force of arms for to quote Chairman Mao and his Little Red Book: "Political power comes from the barrel of the gun" as M.A. Jinnah of The Moslem League demonstrated so clearly in Gandhi's own time and place so violently displayed for almost all to see.

Perhaps with time the goal of resisting all non-violently may be reached, but until we conquer our own greed we will not get there. For the cold reality of the world as we know it now, dictates that at least some will always say that what you have is mine because "we have forged a pistol and are in a position to use it"—Jinnah; to take it from you.

On both Gandhi and Nehru I still must disagree on their socialism. While teaching useful knowledge to the poor might be good, it is no panacea to future wealth. It is only a ticket from the utter impoverishment of 1937 India to the poor of 1700 Britain. If £5 or $500 per person annual income is your ultimate goal that and little else can be reached. Fortunately reaching from about $300 in 1950 to about $500 in today's income India abandoned many of its socialist policies about 1980. Since then India has reached about $2,500 in today's money by acknowledging the cold reality that capitalism still works in our far from perfect world.

Even Gandhi found £300 or $30,000 in today's money acceptable in 1893 South Africa. Granted I too am far from perfect, but not even the Great Soul was either.

Having said these criticisms, I must praise, no first from my knees and bow and then praise the Mahatma for almost single handily revolutionizing our modern world. In 1914 when Gandhi launched his first non-violent protest in India, the world was covered in colonies and dictatorships.

The colonies are now long gone excepting a few by their own choice like Puerto Rico—the U.S.A. or the Falklands—U.K. Many of these ex colonies owe their freedoms indirectly to Gandhi; yes he is entitled forever as the world's Great Soul.

The dictatorships by many different names we must still deal with. Dr. Martin Luther King, Jr. and Nelson Mandela of South Africa would use their versions of Gandhi's non-violent protest to free their peoples in our ever changing world.

Our rapidly changing World, part I:

Talking about a generation gap, here is one for you: In the 1970's India wanting to educate its massive numbers of people; but lacking the resources to build wired communications to all the cities, towns and villages plus to each home, built rockets to launch satellites above the skies instead. Providing electronic education during the day and entertainment in the evening, very quickly all wanted a village TV.

With a village or neighborhood TV and a bicycle to generate the power at the locale, this was soon accomplished. If you think that soon produced a generation gap, think of neighboring Nepal.

Here was a kingdom still frozen in time. When the Emperor of Nepal journeyed from time to time thru the kingdom the peasants were alerted ahead of the Emperor. Not worthy of seeing the Emperor with their own eyes the people would turn away and bowed in prayers for the Emperor to be kind and leave them in peace.

Then Indian television arrived; almost as quickly as in India everyone in Nepal had to have a village TV and a bicycle to power them. By this time India is a democracy with its Prime Minister being heckled by the opposition and the President asking the people for their support. The elders of Nepal know that is somewhere else, for they are already accustomed to Nepal as it has always been.

Not so the children, born they know nothing but I am hungry, all else they must learn from their experiences. Their parents of course try to teach them their way, but TV tells them other ways are possible. By the late 1990's Nepal is ready to explode, not surprisingly it soon did. In 2009 Nepal abolished its royalty.

Our Rapidly Changing World, part II:

In case you haven't noticed the Middle East is a bit behind the rest of the world in a changing world. In 2010 we see protesters protesting in Iran where we the many little people actually think the "powers that be" should actually listen to we the many little people who dare to say "no" you did not win the election of 2009.

Or in Dubai where Sheik Issa bin Zayed al-Nahayan was brought to trial under intense international pressure. Charged with beating a business man with a whip, a cattle prod and a wooden plank with a protruding nail, not satisfied with that punishment he then fired bullets at the victim and finally driving over his legs with a sports utility vehicle all while being videoed—and released to the press.

The international community was satisfied when Dubai finally arrested Sheik Issa and charged him with the above crimes. However his brother is the President of the United Arab Emirates and Emir of oil rich Abu Dhabi these facts of course had no impact in the courts ruling: The three men videoed helping the Sheik inflict the above punishments were found guilty and sentenced to prison. The two photographers were both sentenced to five years imprisonment for illegally photoing the Sheik with-out his permission while the Sheik was ruled not guilty by diminished capacity having taken prescribed medicines before shoving sand into the merchant's face and the above crimes.

Or again in Dubai a British woman making the mistake of reporting she was raped by a Syrian waiter while celebrating her marriage. The Dubai police quickly ruled there was insufficient evidence against the waiter while by her own admission she was guilty of the crime of pre-marital sex and awaits her sentence w/o her passport. While we should all object to these crimes of criminal justice we should do so noting that it was just two centuries ago that a British court ruled that a "noble man" was correct in raping a commoner on her wedding night as his "ancestral right."

It was only with our Revolution of 1776 and the far greater French Revolution of 1789 that our changing world began to actually change. In Britain in reaction to the loss of America, the French Revolution, the above nobleman's ancestral rights the times are a' changing at last even in

Britain resulting in the Great Reform Act of 1832 starting Britain on her own gradual revolution.

Our Rapidly Changing World, part III:

Today I just heard that 4 billion Earthlings (over half our 6.9 billion people) can functionally speak and write English—that is how high the demand is for the internet, and people wonder if we have crossed over into a new level of existence. While I must question the four billion number, the demand for the internet is extreme and everyone today wants to be each other's neighbor. I can only say, welcome to the world! Howdy neighbor.

AUTHOR NOTES

*Note: On rare occasions Kings would flee: In 1808 Napoleon forced his brother onto the vacant Spanish throne and Portugal was soon to follow for conquering French armies. The King of Portugal fleeing to Brazil fell in love with Rio de Janeiro. When General Wellington of Britain drove the French out in 1813, the Portuguese King declined to return. In the end facing de=crowning in Portugal, King John VI returned to Portugal in 1821 leaving his son Pedro as regent in Brazil. In 1822 Pedro declared himself Emperor of Brazil in a virtually bloodless coup. The Brazilian Monarchy would last until 1889. The Portuguese Monarchy would hold out until 1910.

CHAPTER VI

The Life and Times of:
Dr. Martin Luther King, Jr.:

M ARTIN LUTHER KING Jr. was born into the soft easy life of middle class America. His father was the highly respected Reverend of Atlanta's Ebenezer Church, the largest Church in black Atlanta with a salary appropriate with that position. Sent to the best schools in the South, Pennsylvania and Boston his father had prepared him to someday take his place. But everywhere he went Martin Luther King Jr. met racism throughout America.

The Times of Dr. Martin Luther King, Jr.:

By 1900 America had changed drastically from 1700, even 1800. In 1700 America were twelve colonies of the British Empire along the Atlantic-Georgia would be created in 1733 as a land of second chance for debtors and other minor criminals as a protective buffer for the French Protestants (Huguenots) of South Carolina against the Spanish of Florida. By 1900 America had won its independence from Britain, spread its wings and spread across the continent to the Pacific.

In spreading its wings and flying like a bird across the continent it had multiplied its wealth by a factor of about four over its considerable individual wealth of 1700 per person. Having already a more than adequate supply of food the added wealth was spent on improved housing, newer clothes and of course all the new inventions like railroads and electrical lights and telephones.

We had changed drastically in other ways as well. The terrible war that Jefferson had foreseen had taken place far sooner then he could have imagined in 1826. In the 1820's America had been united by the thought "America must stand united against the British Empire or surly we shall hang separately." By the 1850's the generations that had actually fought the British (1775-1815) were quickly passing and being replaced by newer generations that had grown to adulthood on stories of our great victories while witnessing first hand our sweeping across a vast continent.

By 1860 the North which had abolished slavery in the land of the free had also given birth to a new political party dedicated to abolishing this abomination from throughout the land of the free.

The Republican Party swept the North and the still Democratic South succeeded. Four bloody years and 620,000 dead Americans later slavery was abolished throughout America.

The militarily crushed South's white's reaction soon set in as Jefferson had predicted. If slavery could no longer be fought militarily it could and would be fought socially. The Yankees were now damned as long as they militarily occupied the South. For blacks they were now the hunted by vigilante groups under the banner of the Ku Klux Klan's determination to resurrect the old South from the ashes of defeat.

At the same time the war ravaged South with no economic reconstruction only political sent several million people northward all infected with this virus of hatred looking for jobs, good jobs. This hatred of blacks and whites for each other quickly spread into a national disease. By 1877 after twelve years of tears the North abandoned the freed slaves to the restored old South now called the Jim Crow South. The slaves have been freed only to be enslaved again by a different name.

By the time the Republican Teddy Roosevelt was president 1901-1909 the North had changed as well. This very popular president would be burned in effigy both North and South when he invited Booker T. Washington (the founder of Tuskegee Institute of WWII fame) through the front door of the White House. For by now it was accepted that many a white man's house would be burnt to the ground for doing so. Blacks had been freed by the Civil War and declared citizens, but by 1900 they were very much 2nd class citizens now even in the North where they were now denied what gains they had made previously within the economy. For Booker T. Washington was now a rarity, a black man given credit for his inventions. He would be the last, for decades yet to come.

The black doctor which most unfortunately I can't find anywhere, who invented how to preserve blood so it could be transported thousands of miles comes to my mind. Blood donated in the U.S. sent to the battlefields of both Europe and the Pacific, thereby saving countless thousands of American lives in WWII was allowed to die after a post war car wreck. Yes, this doctor was allowed to bleed to death as a North Carolina hospital refused to treat him. After all, I 'm ashamed to say; he was black.

ONE HEART AT A TIME

During WWII when blacks were welcomed into the northern work forces, to fill the ranks of those whites feeling the obligation to win the war. Now after the war they were denied any rights at keeping those same jobs over newly hired whites.

Kaiser Manufacturing among many others simply fired blacks en mass. The unions that blacks had paid their dues to, simply ignored them. Clearly under FDR the Jim Crow South now following Democratic Party rules, ruled the North as well . . .

By 1955 this pattern of thought had not changed. But again America had changed this time by WWII and the motion picture camera. If a picture is worth a thousand words, then how much is a moving picture with sound worth? Otherwise except for another doubling of our per capita wealth since 1900 to eight times our 1700 per person income little had changed.

Throughout the 1930's and 40's America had watched Hitler yelling hatred in Europe and Tojo screaming hatred in Asia. America had also listened and watched Americans hollering hatred here in America as well: Blacks, Catholics, Jews, Chinese, Latinos and Japanese were contaminating America's purity! In WWII we imprisoned the Japanese for the crime of being Japanese! Never mind that they had come to America "the promised land" in the 1800's before we passed the "Yellow Laws" forbidding any more "yellow" people from entry.

In 1942 the Democrat Franklin Roosevelt responded to the needs of WWII and pressure from his wife Eleanor, the NAACP*, the Black press and the many demonstrations of blacks demanding their right to fight for freedom in their own way, re-instated blacks into segregated combat units of the U.S. Army. The previous Democrat Woodrow Wilson had eliminated the Buffalo (black only) Regiments from combat in WWI.

Among these demonstrations demanding the right to fight for freedom, was the honored E.D. Nixon of Montgomery, Alabama. They too in WWII would die with equal bravery as all others—though they would receive no Medals of Honor until the 1990's.

In 1945 we uncovered the Nazi death camps where millions of men, women and even children had been murdered. We also freed our surviving starved soldiers and sailors from Japanese imprison camps. At the same time we watched blacks hung in America for crimes unknown; and Japanese men, women and yes, even children freed from America's prison camps. Many, many people saw the connections even if they did not want to. The picture camera does not lie. To these people America was in great need of reform.

In 1947 President Harry Truman matched Baseball and ordered the desegregation of the U.S. military by executive order. In 1948 Strom Thurmond launched his Dixiecrat Rebellion. In reality our Modern Civil Rights War had begun. Truman had done what he could and barely survive politically. What was now needed was a leader who would push hard upon that door of change, here in America . . .

The Life of Dr. Martin Luther King, Jr.:

The young Martin growing up in the shadow of his father (Daddy King) would sometimes accompany him in his travels outside Atlanta and of course his father would have encounters with the law. Daddy King dressed always in a suit and tie, would step off the church bus and talk with the officer and the police man would soon drive away. The young Martin never comprehending the true nature of the conversation. For Daddy King would step back on the bus and joke about our good law enforcement keeping the peace, ha, ha. Only as an adult would Martin learn the true nature of these many conversations . . .

In June 1953 at the age of 24, Martin Luther King, Jr. marries Coretta Scott in Marion, Alabama. Returning to Boston University they are forced to spend the night in their car after repeatedly being turned away by White Only motels. For Martin growing up in the shadow of his well respected father in the large black Atlanta community, this was largely a new bad experience. But for Coretta, it was nothing new.

Coretta Scott growing up in the Alabama countryside, her life experiences had been much harsher. Her father owned a truck and hauled timber mostly for whites. Poor whites not owning trucks were resentful and constantly threatened his life. Coretta grew up knowing that every day her father might not return. Eventually he bought a small saw mill. Soon after he was told to sell it, he refused, that night it burned down.

On October 31st, 1954 Martin Luther King, Jr. is installed as the 20th pastor of Dexter Avenue Church in Montgomery, Alabama. There he quickly gains the attention of the other black preachers and their admiration in Montgomery for his speaking abilities and skills. On June 5th, 1955 King is awarded his Ph.D. in Systematic Theology from Boston University. On November 17th, 1955 Yolanda Denise is born the first child of four to Martin and Coretta. They are a happily married young couple starting out on what appears to be the course in life designed by his father—*Daddy King.*

In 1956 in response to the Supreme Court's call for school integration: "with all deliberate speed;" came the "Southern Manifesto" in response: A petition signed by over one hundred Southern politicians from the fifteen slave states of 1860. But three "slave Democrats" refused to sign it, Senator Albert Gore (father of the later V.P.) of Tennessee, Estes Kefauver of Kentucky and Lyndon Baines Johnson (LBJ) of Texas.

While the non Southerners were not asked to sign this "Southern Manifesto" reaction nationwide may be judged by the facts of 1968: At that time after twelve years of "all deliberate speed" only one percent of Southern blacks were in integrated schools and only eight percent of non Southern blacks were in integrated schools. Clearly we as a nation had endorsed the "Southern Manifesto" with our actions emulating General err President Jackson telling the Supreme Court to "defend them, if they dare!"

In 1954 school segregation may have been declared unconstitutional, but clearly far more action was needed, to desegregate schools, to say nothing about the work places.

Reverend Ralph Abernathy pastor of Montgomery's largest black Church and chairman of the Interdenominational Black Council engaged the young Martin in a recruiting drive for volunteers for the local NAACP action committee. Abernathy wins the challenge by bringing in 3500 volunteers, but Martin despite being new to Montgomery brings in another 1500—black Montgomery is preparing for war.

Rosa Parks a forty two year old seamstress and a long term member of the Women's Political Council of the NAACP after a long day at work pays her dime fare at the front of the bus, gets off and reenters in the back door into the Colored Only section and sits down. The bus rapidly fills and the driver gets up and moves the White Only sign behind Rosa Parks. She gets up and obeys the law and stands in the rear so a white man can sit in her former seat. Thinking about this, Rosa Parks decides she will not do so again, but tells no one.

For most blacks in Montgomery and across most of America, this is a stark daily reminder of the racist world they live in. This act both big (people had legally been shot and killed by bus drivers) and tiny happenings thousands of times daily was the most appalling reminder of racism preventing their children from getting a decent education, their fathers from a decent job and mothers from decent health care.

On Thursday, December 1st 1955 Rosa Parks is ordered to give up her seat. For daring to say no to racism, she is arrested and jailed. Word quickly spreads in the black community of Montgomery. Among the first alerted was the now elderly E.D. Nixon of the NAACP who called the Police and was told "it's none of your damn business." He then called Clifford Durr a retired white lawyer where Rosa Parks and the WPC had met occasionally at his home. Upon his calling the police, he called back to say that she had been arrested for breaking the Bus Segregation Law.

Durr drives Nixon—a railway porter, to the jail where he posts bail for Rosa Parks who is released to meet her husband just arriving. Nixon then thinks about a bus strike that evening and on Friday morning calls Reverend Ralph Abernathy about Parks case and says her case is worth fighting for. Abernathy agrees and calls for a meeting of City Reverends and the NAACP leaders for Friday evening. Abernathy picking up Martin and others for the meeting at Dexter Church, directly across the street from the State Capitol, informs Martin Luther King that he is to take charge of what ever action that is to take place.

They unanimously elect Dr. Martin Luther King Jr. as President of what now becomes the Montgomery Improvement Association and decide on a black patron boycott of Montgomery Bus Lines to begin Monday morning. The NAACP begins printing the leaflets, the volunteers begin distributing them and Martin begins organizing those with cars into carpools for both students and workers. On Sunday they preach non violent protest. **On Monday, December 5th 1955: Black Montgomery throws the tea into the water.** This act of defiance (as in the Boston Tea Party) quickly sends Montgomery Bus Lines (MBL) into a panic. For blacks are more than half—perhaps 75% of their customers, so they begin to instantly lose money, on Monday the boycott is over 95%, by Tuesday over 99%. White Montgomery is caught off guard, they had not prepared for war.

On Monday evening black Montgomery marches to City Hall demanding justice for Rosa Parks, the ending of bus segregation laws, access to city bus jobs as drivers, mechanics and when qualified as supervisors. On Friday MBL announces they will no longer serve black neighborhoods. The King residence is by now being inundated with calls of "your going to die, nigger" and "quit now and your family might live," etc.

After several ineffective meetings between the mayor, MBL and black ministers during the second meeting when King objects to a representative of the White Citizens Council "the local KKK in disguise" joining the meeting and the mayor suggests "fine both you and he can leave and Reverend Abernathy can speak for the Black Ministers." Reverend Abernathy objects: "Reverend King speaks for us."

December turns to January and the strike continues as the black churches buy fifteen station wagons, painting them in church colors and uses them to haul people to work and school. Nonetheless, one day Martin passing by an elderly lady struggling down the street and offers her a ride. She replies: "Thanks but I'm not walking for myself, I'm walking for my children and grandchildren."

On January 30th 1956 white Montgomery begins to strike back when a sudden explosion rocks black Montgomery. It's Martin's house, by the time Martin reaches his way to the house an angry crowd is yelling "let's kill a few whitties; that will let them know we mean business!" Another black is yelling at a Deputy keeping the crowd back "come on, you got your .38, I got mine, lets have it out right here!"

Martin finds Coretta and their infant Yoki okay and after a tearful reunion mounts the shattered door step of his now former house and yells out "Ours is a non-violent movement. We must love our white brothers. No matter what they do to us, we must make them know that we love them!" The angry crowd does not go away and so Martin must repeat this message of love over and again, about our message to the white community is about peace and justice for all, until reluctantly the angry blacks go home.

That Sunday, and many Sundays to come through out black Montgomery, Martin Luther King's message of following Gandhi's teachings of non-violent protest requires far more strength then violent protest does, is repeated though out the black community. All thru 1956 the strike continues until finally despite numerous trips to jail, many shots fired at passing church station wagons and finally the city seizing them for being "a public nuisance" and many miles of relentless thousands of daily walks by black Montgomery the day happens.

On the very day that Montgomery seized the station wagons for inciting riots, "God spoke" as a black woman said "from Washington:" on December 1st 1956 the U.S. Supreme Court ruled that following its earlier decision in 1954 to out law segregation in education ("equal segregation . . . is inherently unequal") that all segregation through out Alabama and its local governments was un-constitutional as well. Legally segregation was over. White reaction was "we will hang King and Supreme Court Justice Hugo Black from the apple tree as we earlier (in 1859) hung John Brown!"

For the next three weeks black Montgomery walks for freedom as they wait for the document to be enforced. On December 21st Martin, Abernathy, Nixon and a white preacher waited for the first bus of integrated bussing in Montgomery; when it arrived, the white driver said: "Are you the civil rights leader? Martin replies: "Yes I am," the driver says: "Take any seat you want." Desegregation in busing had arrived in Montgomery, the former 1st capital of the Confederacy; the Heart of Dixie.

Throughout 1956 interest rises throughout the black South in Montgomery's strike and calls for local action rises. While Martin and Abernathy are in Atlanta trying to organize the future Southern Christian Leadership Conference as an umbrella organization to coordinate anti-segregation efforts through-out the South the Klan strikes. On Thursday January 12th 1957, the unthinkable happens not one explosion not two or three or even four or five but at least eight bombs explode in Montgomery during the night. Five black churches, two black parsonages plus a bomb explodes in front of E. D. Nixon's house as well-known for keeping a shotgun at the ready.

Among the worst hit is Reverend Abernathy who loses first his house, then upon reaching his wife Juanita by phone and learning that her and their child are okay, hears his wife yell out that his church, the grand daddy of black churches in Montgomery and arguably the nation has been blown up as well. The First Baptist Church built in 1908 as the largest Black Church in the South at the time, now lies in near ruins.

All during the next few days, volunteers work to secure the walls and ceiling of the shattered church but the shattered floor is unsafe and so they hold services in the basement. Reverend Abernathy rises to give his sermon but can hardly speak, as he wonders about what his efforts have brought upon his church.

Finally, eighty year old Suzie Beasley breaks in and says: "This morning I have discovered that our pastor is disturbed, a leader can not lead if he is disturbed." Reverend Abernathy, let me tell you about this church: She then went into a history of how the blacks of Montgomery came together under Reverend Stokes to build a building that all black Montgomery could hold their heads high about. So in the 1890's we began to contribute each

Sunday to the fund to buy one brick at a time. Our men began to dredge a pond where the church stands today, our women brought them lunches.

The joke went around what is that great hole in the ground all about? Why, that is the First Baptist Church that was never built. But we did build this church, one brick at a time. "Reverend Abernathy under your leadership, we will rebuild this church and if it is bombed again, and again we will continue to rebuild this church!" Reverend Abernathy cried in relief.

That Sunday throughout Montgomery the white preachers denounced the church bombings as sacrilege against the Christian faith. The bombings stopped and on Jan. 30th seven whites were arrested in connection with the bombings.

Within a few days they were released in a general amnesty along with the 119 blacks charged with violating the segregation laws. Whether these seven whites crimes were equivalent causing some $70,000 in 1957 dollar damages and risking many lives equaled the "crimes" of breaking unconstitutional laws was obviously in the eyes of the beholders. Martin Luther King accepted the victory over segregation and moved onward.

Birmingham, Round One:

Throughout 1956 interest in the Montgomery bus strike was taken up throughout Alabama and the nation. In Mobile—Alabama's second largest city, blacks demanded an end to bus segregation, the city quickly yielded on all fronts. Birmingham, Alabama's largest city that once upon a time called itself the Pittsburg of the New South, facing hard times, would be far tougher to break.

What had been corn fields of grain in 1870 by the 1950's had mushroomed into a metro area of 600,000 people. With coal to stoke the fires, limestone to encase the buckets and rich iron ore to make steel in local abundance, steel production took off. Then came WWII and demand soared but the good iron ore ran out, and suddenly Birmingham was in financial trouble. Its reason for existing—cheap iron ore; had disappeared; it would have to re-invent itself. Over the next six decades it did; no longer a blue collar industrial center but today's sports medicine capital (arguably) of the world. A city of 1.1 million metro—2010 census and growing once again.

But what about all those blue collar workers? The steel workers do not easily transform themselves into doctors. People everywhere want jobs, good jobs and for the blue collar workers of Birmingham they are fast disappearing. This isn't Montgomery depending on lawyers, special interest groups and state legislators as the state capital for its reason for existing. This isn't Mobile depending on shipping and commerce through the port for its reason for existing. No, this is Birmingham based on the dying steel industry. People, black or white are not happy, not content with their jobs disappearing let alone the prospect of having to share the few remaining . . .

Welcome to Birmingham, Alabama the city where I, the author was born in 1951. My father, born in Florence, Alabama recalled to active service for the Korean War (1950-53) decided to stay in the army when offered full credit from 1943 toward retirement in twenty six years. I did grow up mainly in the South.

My mother, a native of Birmingham was however determined that her children would not be raised to be racists. My father respected that decision, so I was taught to love all God's children at both home and in the Church's my parents chose to join.

On the streets of America however, I was taught to hate: In Fayetteville, North Carolina I was taught:

"Grab a—censored by the author, some evils deserve to stay buried."

Hate, my friend, hatred of the highest order. Decipher the above and you see it is "okay" to rape a black woman. Imagine yourself as a black woman for a moment, how many times would you need to hear the above before you began to hate. Imagine yourself as a black man hearing the above about your mother or sisters or girl friend before you begin to hate.

That hatred is quickly returned at every opportunity. Hatred taught in the 1870's Reconstruction carried forward into the 1950's and 1960's and spread across America by people black and white looking for good jobs.

As an American of the 1950's and 60's believe me, I was raised on a steady diet of "King the communist agitator, he's got commies working for him, don't you know." In the 1930's communism and Nazism were the only thing working, which is why they were on the march. So if you were not a Nazi or a New Dealer that pretty much only left the communists and after our second Red Scare of McCarthyism 1947-1954 you were looking for some way to reform America which you had no doubt it needed desperately.

If you were a religious preacher who felt the love of God in your heart, you gladly accepted help where ever you could get it. In the post McCarthy era, help I'm sure, was damn hard to find! Try to keep them out of sight but never underestimate the hatred of J. Edgar Hoover and his F.B.I. Take my word for it in the white South; King was not "a good guy." Clearly the hatred for everything King stood for was hated throughout America. After all this was the pure hatred that Thomas Jefferson had so feared:

"*God damn America, for your racist tyranny.*"
—Reverend Wright, Chicago 2008.
Painful but deserved, so let's end it today.—TSW, 2009

The easy victories were over and obviously not everyone was listening to Martin's words of love thy opponents. Birmingham and white America were now prepared for war. America's second Civil War, the Civil Rights War had truly begun, but Martin Luther King's message remained true to him from the day he mounted his shattered porch:

"We must love our white brothers. No matter what they do to us, we must make them know that we love them!" For the next decade Martin Luther King would continue to shout these words above the mayhem, above the water cannons, and above the attack dogs and definitely above the many prison cells he would be placed in, for daring to break the peace of enslavement.

Soon leading the blacks of Birmingham, Martin was quickly arrested and thrown into an abandoned section of the jailhouse where as the only isolated prisoner in a cell that lacked a functioning toilet with a bed of steel and no mattress nor a blanket or change of clothing. This despite the soon overcrowded jails where Sheriff Connors quickly started using abandoned buildings chosen for their lack of toilet facilities as make do prisons. Blacks marched for freedom in the thousands while Sheriff Connors tried to arrest them by the tens of thousands. Fortunately not all whites were unsympathetic and a white guard slipped Martin paper and pen and then slipped his written words out: soon entitled:

"A Letter from the Birmingham jail."

In many words Dr. Martin Luther King, Jr. explained "Why now is the time for freedom, not some other time in the future when it will be more appropriate. Now is the time for freedom, not when those who have all the advantages say it will be, for to them it will never be the time for freedom."

In describing his jail conditions he wrote "You will never know the meaning of utter darkness until you have lain in such a dungeon."

With the release of this letter from the Birmingham jail, it was as if the whole "freedom loving world" were electrified. The Western World exploded at Washington, President Eisenhower, who had told King "Now is not the time" was forced to act for even in America people demanded he act now! Slowly, he did so. King was moved to a decent jail cell, the thousands of demonstrators were gradually released and white Birmingham could relax in victory. For black Birmingham's spirit had been broken.

Yes, the spirit of black Birmingham as a whole, had been broken. Picture yourself locked with others of both sexes in a jail room without toilet facilities for days, and yes maybe you can see why and how determination can be overcome. But for Martin and Reverend Shuttlesworth of Birmingham, the fight had only begun . . .

In 1955 the bus strike had gained the attention of black's throughout the South, but little else. By 1956 the world started following via that new gadget, the television. By 1957 with the battle moving to Birmingham and peaceful demonstrators led by King and Reverend Shuttlesworth of Birmingham fighting segregation in downtown stores, being assaulted with police dogs and water cannons the world liberated by America just a decade earlier watched in utter disbelief. Yes, in a world filled with hate, America had its share, but with King, America also displayed its love as well. Soon their determination to win victory would be on display as well . . .

For the motion picture camera does not lie, no matter the lies of the person covering the news. The love of the blacks calling for freedom now, shone thru the police dogs and water cannons no matter how many lies of the announcers. For gradually many whites started wondering: why not freedom for all Americans, now. Latinos, Chinese and Japanese, and yes the Native Americans they too deserved their freedoms too. Our 1776 Declaration of Independence does not say we the white people, no it proudly yells:

"We the People."

In 1959 Martin Luther King was charged by Alabama for tax evasion. But surprise, surprise an all white jury saw the charges as manufactured by a vindictive state and declared King innocent on all charges. Yes, even in Alabama there were whites who were not vindictive. That was the heart and soul of Martin Luther King's "we must make our white brothers know that we love them" to raise their numbers to the majority. Yes the impossible dream could happen, even in Alabama.

To lead these efforts a new organization was formed the Southern Christian Leadership Council (SCLC) was formed. Martin Luther King was elected President with out opposition, but in truth this would remain an amateur organization until 1960 when Wyatt Tee Walker was hired as the new Chief Operating Officer.

Martin Luther King was in demand everywhere from New York to Los Angeles but the money had not poured in. A trip to Houston to raise money raised $1,100 barely covering expenses. This would now change with fund raising trips choreographed ahead of time to gain donations and pledges ahead of King's arrival which now typically raised $10,000 per trip. This was important because King would no longer have to run himself into the ground desperately trying to keep the SCLC afloat. By 1960 he would be able to take the lead fighting for the end of segregation.

Despite defeats in Birmingham, Albany Georgia and St. Augustine Florida the movement pushed onward and in 1960 came victory in Atlanta. Their Mayor Hartsfield and the senior leaders of the black community agreed—without consulting others including Martin and the youths leading the marches; to end segregation in Atlanta at the start of the new school year, in nine months.

The youth of Atlanta were enraged as Daddy King announced this in triumph—the yell of "sell out, sell out!" dominated. When Daddy King said "I have been fighting for this for thirty years"—someone yelled out "that is the problem!" Daddy King was shattered. It was all Martin Luther King could do to keep the peace between the older and younger generations. Clearly King's window of opportunity to win peacefully was approaching its end. For 1960-18 years = born in 1942: The WWII window of experiencing 30,000 deaths daily was ending, but not quite yet.

Our Window of Opportunity:

To understand this "window of opportunity" one must try to understand WWII from the experience of witnessing that football crowd opposite you dying every day, for two thousand consecutive days of "hell on Earth"—WWII in person. No one knows how many died in WWII, the estimates range from 60 million to a 100 million. Certainly the toll was in the many tens of millions from the Pacific, China and Russia to Europe. For two thousand days (1939-1945) the world was washed in the blood of millions, dying violent deaths, men, women and children.

In America which had tried so hard to stay out of the slaughter, rewarded with Pearl Harbor for its efforts, this slaughter was felt from afar. Nonetheless it was felt, not just by the fifteen million in uniform, but by their loved ones as well.

These loved ones included their children watching their mothers despair at the approach of government vehicles to their door. With very few other vehicles on the road due to war time restrictions, these vehicles represented some one being reported killed in action—desperately the child's mother prayed for the vehicle to please, please keep going.

After Normandy thousands rolled across America daily to give the sad news in person. Even to children not old enough to understand the slaughter happening far away, the look of despair on their mother's faces was unmistakable as she prayed that the vehicle would keep going.

This was *the shadow of WWII*. To all who had these psychological experiences growing up, they would affect their thinking in ways unseen by all. This shadow of WWII was America's "window of opportunity" to change non-violently. For America armed to the teeth with weapons, does not change non-violently easily.

For all these survivors, both great grand parents and children alike this shadow of psychological terror of mass murder, was very real. They could not want a new mass murder, ever again. Extremely biased against mass murder, they were also biased against violence, for sooner or later violence for or against change would mean mass murder and they knew it deep down in their hearts. History does matter, even the unrecorded history.

Soon after Martin was arrested in late 1960 for driving 30 MPH in a 25 MPH zone and sent to Reidsville Georgia State Prison for parole violation—a jail perhaps the worst in America, known especially among blacks for going to and never returning from. President Eisenhower did nothing. Vice President Nixon did nothing. Candidate to be President John Kennedy called Coretta King to send his condolences . . . Robert Kennedy however called Judge Mitchell in Georgia to ask: "Could not a bond be placed for so minor an offence?" Judge Mitchell decided to change his mind. That very night King's attorney had a plane flown to Reidsville to fly Martin back to Atlanta and Coretta.

For the first time ever blacks swung to the Democratic Party. Kennedy won by less than 200,000 votes out of 68 million cast, while more than 2 million blacks voted. They might have carried a few Northern states, the Solid South as usual voted for the old party of slavery, the Democrats. The Democrat John Kennedy won. A changing of the guard at the White House was coming. Black expectations rose.

AUTHOR NOTES

Note*: NAACP: The National Association for the Advancement of Colored People, founded in 1909-10 in New York City by a group of white and black intellectuals united in their opposition to "Gradualism" preached by Booker T. Washington.

Booker T. Washington wanted "half a loaf" on the grounds that "it's all we going to get now." My quotation of his intents. The NAACP felt it was cheering on the "Oriole:" Half black, half white mentality. All black is good and we should never forget it. Again my quotations.

Which group in my opinion was right, no longer matters, for they would all fight for freedom now!

CHAPTER VII

M L K:
The Beginning of the End

1961 MARKED THE official beginning of the *Vietnam War in U.S. history*. It in reality had been raging off and on since the 1930's without the Americans. The Viet Minh or Vietnamese Freedom Fighters led by Ho Chi Minh had fought the French, the Japanese and then the French again after WWII, eventually driving them out.

In 1954 at the Geneva Convention ending the original war, Vietnam by French insistence was divided into two governments a Catholic Regime in the South run by the Diem family and a Communist Regime in the North. By Ho Chi Minh insistence, a nationwide election would follow in 1956 for a united regime under U.N. sponsorship, guaranteed by the U.S. as an official observer.

In 1956 the South Vietnamese regime not wanting Ho Chi Minh as their president but one of their own, cancelled the nationwide elections as they had agreed to in the 1954 Geneva Convention, just two years earlier. The U.S. as an official observer should have screamed foul. Unfortunately after the McCarthy hearings, our liberals in both political parties were as silent, as can be—while Eisenhower continued U.S. aide to South Vietnam despite no elections being held at all.

Since the Catholic Diem regime was very unpopular in a country 97% Buddhist, the war soon resumed. By 1961 with Buddhist Monks setting themselves afire in the cities and the country side ruled by the now Viet Cong—communists led by Ho Chi Minh, Saigon needed help. The Republicans under Eisenhower responded only mildly.

In November 1960, on Civil Rights both Republicans and Democrats were in unison, we are in favor, just not now. Democrat John Kennedy won the presidency by painting the Republican Nixon as "soft on communism." In this era of post McCarthyism, this was as horrible as any charge possible. Not surprisingly, in January 1961 Kennedy sent the U.S. Calvary—that is the modern version, the (movie: "John Wayne and the) Green Berets" to the rescue. By 1964 a few thousand

U.S. Special Force troops were clearly not enough to win this on going war . . .

Chicago and the nation:

In 1961 the Civil Rights War shifted to Chicago which had partly been built by southerners moving north looking for jobs, good jobs after the Civil War, and to Mississippi. In Chicago the hatred natural to Mississippi from Reconstruction had been brought northward, and both Illinois and Mississippi would be bitter battle grounds.

Chicago, ten times Birmingham in size where the skies were deep purple from the steel mills was facing hard times as well in these ever changing times. Here segregation was by forcing blacks to live in the urban ghettos built nearly a century earlier while whites could move into the sprawling suburbia's of new housing.

In Chicago Martin Luther King brought his fight by loving program to organize rent strikes to force slum owners to fix the slums while the people marched on the city's housing and Real Estate Boards demanding the ending of racial profiling in where people could live. Mayor Richard Daley and Co. would fight them daily without remorse. This war would soon spread across America.

Mississippi, where there are no big cities, is the cotton fields of yesterday. Here segregation was by murder as the KKK masquerading as police simply stopped you for speeding or going too slow and murdered the black occupants, any whites in the car, murdered with relish.

A new group CORE* was determined to integrate interstate travel in the South and with King's support chartered two busloads of mixed races to travel from Washington D.C. to New Orleans by different routes. Both groups met hostility at every stop in Virginia, the Carolina's, and in Georgia, then came:

Alabama.

At Anniston one group were met by the KKK which quickly pummeled them to a hospital. Reverend Shuttlesworth hearing of them on the radio led a fifteen car shotgun armed caravan from Birmingham to rescue them from the hospital, where the KKK was demanding they be turned back over to them. Fortunately the KKK this day, were only armed with pipes and chains.

The second group reaching Birmingham was similarly met. Reverend Shuttlesworth brought these to his house as well. They hadn't even reached Mississippi, clearly federal intervention was needed to enforce the laws that local governments ignored. Actually citing the integrators for causing trouble and therefore worth arresting but not worth protecting.

Birmingham, Another Round:

At this time responding to heavy pressure from Reverend Shuttlesworth, King decided that if the Civil Rights War was to be won, the soul of Birmingham must be conquered, for rightly or wrongly MLK realized his defeat in Birmingham had galvanized the opposition nationwide. For if the civil rights movement was to be won, it must be won in the very state that launched Dr. Martin Luther King, Jr. to the world's attention. That of course was Alabama and its largest city which had defeated King's best efforts so far.

So began the second battle of Birmingham: The NAACP was organized, volunteers mobilized and the reverends preached loving thy opponent is the hardest way but also the only way to fight to integrate downtown stores and restaurants. But the adult volunteers failed to show up in adequate numbers, their spirits were broken by their earlier incarcerations with-out toilets. Reluctantly the organizers accepted the High School and Junior High School students to fill up their reserve ranks.

In early 1963 they marched and were quickly arrested non-violently by Sheriff Connors showing that he too had learned from the previous fights now televised all across the world. Day after day he kept his cool until it was finally time for the school children to march. Now it was:

"The Children's Hour:"

When the teen age children were called to action, they formed their ranks with their little brothers and sisters, for they the five to twelve year olds had **"freedom now"** on their minds that they too wanted all over Birmingham.

Very reluctantly, King said: March! King and others leading the twenty thousand or so black children of Birmingham quickly proved too much for Sheriff Connors who soon yelled: "Get those little niggers!" The fire hoses, the deputy's batons and the attack dogs were unleashed upon the children of Birmingham in downtown before the cameras of the world once again . . .

It was America's darkest hour, in front of all the cameras of the world, of batons flying and water cannons blasting the peaceful young demonstrators for freedom now! Then there were the attack dogs attacking children! Soon the previously cowed adults responding to their children's distress began pouring into downtown Birmingham in the many tens of thousands. The carnage unleashed was too much for Birmingham, too much for a stunned nation and too much for a shocked world . . .

America which screams freedom to all: was clearly violently refusing freedom at home. Even with the state troopers and the Ku Klux Klan joining in, even they could not prevent Birmingham's surrender. For the world was watching, calling, even begging Washington, the Kennedy's to please do something, anything to stop it, now. Your making the whole Western World look awful, please do something, NOW . . . please . . .

Martin Luther King had been on the phone calling Washington, but John Kennedy proved no more interested then Eisenhower, replying "but, now is not the time." King now redoubled his calls for "it has always been the time." Receiving so little support from the Kennedy's he decides to take his movement on a:

March on Washington.

If 1963 was Martin Luther King's high point leading nearly 300,000 people demanding: "Now, is the time for our rights." If 1964 was King's high point with his winning the Noble Peace Prize and passages of the Civil Rights Acts of 1964 and now it is 1965 and blacks still are heavily discriminated against the right to vote. Many people had always objected to this most basic denial of human rights and were fighting to "overcome" this act of discrimination.

One such leader was Jimmy Lee Jackson, now murdered by the deputy sheriffs of Selma, Alabama in late February, 1965 after leaving a protest demonstration at a local church in preparing for a direct march on Montgomery to demand "the right to vote"—arguably, the most precious of all rights in a free country.

Dr. Martin Luther King, Jr. attending his funeral services, denounced the still fairly new President Johnson for sending thousands of troops to defend Vietnam but not one soldier to defend one black man in so obvious peril, right here in America!

Deciding to lead the protest march on Montgomery a few days later vowing "we shall overcome" all objections and appeal directly to the now, Governor George Wallace on what soon would be remembered as,

Bloody Sunday:

On March 7, 1965 as the marchers crossed the Edmund Pettus Bridge exiting Selma, Alabama; State Police attacked the marchers that Sunday morning. Fortunately this immediately received national exposure for the world now followed Dr. Martin Luther King's every step with T V cameras.

President Johnson the senator from Texas who had publicly rejected the "Southern Manifesto*" of 1956, immediately dispatched federal troops to guard the demonstrators of Selma from further harm. Soon after calling for a national press conference to address this voter rights issue:

President Johnson addressed the nation with the words: "I am sending to congress; The Voter Rights Act, to guarantee everyone the right to vote" and concluded his speech with the words:

"in this too, we shall overcome."

—Dr. Martin Luther King, Jr. cried as he listened to these words, for finally the presidency was bringing its full power to the civil rights issue. At last the power of the bully pulpit so eloquently espoused by Teddy Roosevelt was at last hammering away at civil rights for all!

Later in August the Voter's Right Act was passed. But, it is now 1965 and the beginning of the end. For 1965-18 ='s born in 1947, WWII is now ancient history, to the young of the world, something that must be read about. No longer felt first hand in any way to the young people fighting this racist war.

The true meaning of WWII:

Many people do not accept the true meaning of WWII. I aged 16, only began to realize how brutal the war truly was when visiting Belgium in December 1967. Our parents and children, stationed in Germany—courtesy of the U.S. Army, were visiting some Belgians, when sitting by their warm fireplace my father asked the Belgian parents if they might visit us in Munich on their vacation to Yugoslavia next summer. ***The look of utter horror that came across their faces was unmistakable.*** After a very, very long pause, the father finally whispered almost: "possibly."

The next day I asked their daughter "about that unmistakable look of horror upon their faces." She replied that *"while her generation did not feel the same way,"* for her parents, the idea of crossing into Germany for any reason was impossible. Their memories of the war were *far too real* to them," the genuine fear they share, makes any trip into Germany impossible for them.

She (Marie-Pohl Jacques) then went on to say: "My father, a Lieutenant, was badly wounded in the stomach as well as losing a few fingers in 1940.

Having recovered he eventually found work in a fish market and when walking home one day, a truck stopped beside him and the next thing he knew he was a slave, working on the Atlantic Wall—the coastal defenses against the anticipated Allied landings."

"My mother was . . . raped first by one German soldier and later by a group of them, no they would not be visiting Germany for any reason," . . . *"their fears are too great."*

This is the source of the generation gap of the 1960's. For those who lived through WWII and witnessed 30,000 plus people killed every day violently and still many, many more acts of extreme violence every day for six long bitter years: their fears are too great: *"Never, never again."*

Even from afar in America witnessing the thousands of: "We regret to inform you that your husband/son died in action" being delivered daily after Normandy was simply too great not to affect their friends and yes, even the children who watched their despairing mother's reactions. Yes, even the unrecorded history is important—for it happened to them, even if from afar.

For the returning white soldiers, peace in our time is what they hoped for. As for making the world a better place, just give me a job, a good job and let me be in peace for I've already served my time in hell.

For the returning black soldiers of WWII, peace in our time is what they wanted but not the racism they had been fighting. The vaunted Aryan Race and the Samurai Warriors they had help to defeat, but now they return to the racist America they had left behind totally unchanged as if racial superiority had never been apart of the war.

Yes, they too want peace and a job, a good job and freedom now. Hence to the WWII black generation; Martin Luther King's appeal of fighting non-violently had great appeal: Peace, a good job and freedom now.

By the 1960's this era was ending, for the children reaching adulthood now, had no first hand experience with the reality of massive killings daily—except by the U.S. Government in Vietnam. Reverend King soon denounced the war in 1965 as a still another example of the strong crushing the weak. President Johnson having sponsored the Civil Rights Acts of 1964 and 1965 took this as a personal betrayal.

The Generation Gap— A Western Phenomena!

What Johnson could not even begin to understand: This was the generation gap of the 1960's getting ready to explode. Blacks want their freedom, now! The generation of King both black and white having lived thru WWII are afraid of violence, for they have seen more than one generation should ever have too. The post war blacks want freedom now and they are not afraid for WWII is their parents memory, not there's.

This phenomena was happening throughout the Western World. Above the Belgian girl: Marie-Pohl Jacques "my generation feels differently" was reflecting on Belgium exploding over the Belgian Congo (modern Zaire) perhaps the worst of the en-slavers; yet her parents screamed at being en slaved themselves, while doing nothing to free their own Belgian Congo!

I remember asking German students in the 1960's; how could their parents ever have elected Adolph Hitler Chancellor? Their over whelming reply: "Our parents are liars! They knew. No one could transport tens of millions of their neighbors, executing millions of them without every-body knowing. They knew, and did nothing!!!"

Arguably this was a generation gap brewing in the western minds since the Priest Martin Luther objected to the Church practices of the 1500's. But WWII had given it new life:

France in the late 1960's exploded over French colonialism; driving de Gaul and his: "We must uphold the dignity of the French Empire" from power. Italy exploded over their parents support for Mussolini; an ally of Hitler! The French, again for the supporters of Hitler after 1940. Western Europe like America was exploding with the rise of the post war generations.

And in America, the young whites say to their parents you preach freedom to everyone, yet brutally deny it here, at home! To this their parents take refuge in "Hey, we fought WWII, we changed the world for the better! Don't bother me with all the remaining evils of the world!

To this the children of post WWII reply: "We want the world proposed by Tom Jefferson in our Declaration of Independence, fought for by both George Washington and by Abe Lincoln, proposed again to the world by Woodrow Wilson, fought for by Gandhi, and all nations along the long roads to both Berlin and Tokyo and finally enshrined in:

"The Atlantic Charter"
as a founding statement of the United Nations:

> **The world governed**
> **by we the people,**
> **for the people**
> **and of the people,**
> **of all nations!**

And we want it, NOW!!!

During the 1960's the young of the western world demanded that their elders deliver on the idealistic dreams of post WWI—in the words of Ho Chi Minh to Woodrow Wilson: "Does your right to self determinance apply to the colonial world?" To the dreamers of the young at heart it clearly applied to all—everywhere. For the young in 1919 were beginning to dream of a world without empires. Most of the elders thought baugh humbug, but not to the young at heart . . .

By the 1930's with Gandhi fighting for self determination in India peacefully and Ho Chi Minh by force of arms in French Indo-China, the young would have been demanding it worldwide, except for WWII imposing on all other events, but America promised the Philippines its freedom in ten years in 1935, so a tiny start was in progress.

On August 14th 1941 a giant leap was made when Winston Churchill, desperate for American help signed the Atlantic Charter at the virtual demand of FDR. Four months later, many in America forgot the dream after Pearl Harbor, but Eleanor Roosevelt having pushed it on to her husband, would not forget the dream of a world without empires.

Then came WWII and everybody died, or so it almost seemed to many. And at the end: The cold steel of American muscle vs the Iron Curtain of the Soviet Union and the dreams were forgotten in the nuclear world of the Cold War, except to a few who kept dreaming the impossible dream of a world without empires.

Besides Eleanor, Britain remembered, and after their elders of the Labour Party agonized on what their stunning July 1945 victory actually meant, in 1946 Britain promised freedom to India in 1947 and steps would be made to:

set all of the British Empire, free!!!
Meanwhile the little dreams like freedom to all,

In December 1955 Martin Luther King was elected leader of what would later become the Southern Christian Leadership Committee by his fellow Montgomery black reverends. He was 26 years old leading a cause by people born before 1940, born early enough to have fought in WWII or at least old enough to remember their mother's worry as announcers announced heavy casualties reported in taking Guadalcanal in the Pacific, or still more heavy casualties reported in our most recent failed assault on Monte Casino in Europe. These were people who had seen and heard of more than enough violence for a life time.

Many people might think our death toll in WWII of 405,399 is paltry compared to the millions of Jews, Poles, Germans and Russians and unknown millions killed in China, but after the 6th of June 1944 we knew they would mount as we fought our way to Berlin. Just think of a thousand Americans dying every day for 300 days, and we knew still more deaths were to come.

In August 1945, we knew as we awaited the arrival of an army group from Europe to fight our way those last painful miles to Tokyo far more American blood would flow for the Japanese Samurai Warriors did not know how to surrender, for Japan had never been conquered. Even Genghis Khan had failed; defeated by the "Devine Wind"—a typhoon.

But that was the price in American blood we had accepted at Pearl Harbor and no one in America doubted we were willing to pay it. Thank goodness technology gave the Japanese an excuse to surrender. For there is no honor in withstanding Atomic bombs.

Thereby saving what everybody expected to be millions of deaths in Japan. Even with that saving of lives after the Normandy invasion we suffered about a thousand deaths a day until April 1945. Ten months of a thousand Americans dying every day. All who lived thru those agonizing days of terror, would be psychologically impaired for life. A disease that never reported itself. Felt by all, even from afar.

But now it's 1965. 1965-18 ='s 1947. The young have no direct memory of WWII, it's their parents memories, not theirs. They are not psychologically impaired. These youngsters white or black, American or European are not afraid of mass killings except by their own governments whether it be in Vietnam or in Africa.

These are not the truths promised by Jefferson, or by the great truth of the French Revolution: **"If any are to be free, then all must be free!"** and fought by their blood by the anti Hitlerite's of the world. The young of the world want the world ruled by the people, of the people and for the people of all nations and they are prepared to fight for it—now!!!

Even in the late 1950's there were people who wanted to fight for their rights with gasoline and guns, but they were few. Martin was even stabbed near his heart by a black woman in Harlem "for causing all these problems." But now it's the early 1960's with King's march for Freedom Now, having spread across America, there were many. By 1965 the first of the baby boomers were now being drafted to go deny other colored people (Vietnamese) their right to decide who there leaders would be.

There remembrances are quite different: They have witnessed there parents cursed at, themselves cursed at, their parent's generation arrested after hit by bricks and bottles for disturbing the peace of racism. Their parents would not fight back, but they will. For WWII is ancient history to them, there parent's memories and fears, not theirs.

We are a people not accustomed to setting ourselves afire to protest as in Vietnamese Monks. We have been taught setting other people afire is the way Americans protest against injustice.

Having grown up watching on television their parents abused, beaten and arrested by the local police from Philadelphia to Birmingham to Chicago and Los Angeles, these were their memories.

Naturally they thought differently and now their being drafted to go fight in a war thousands of miles away in a country where they are not wanted, and for what: Democracy? How can it be democracy, when in fact a continuously revolving door of military dictatorships all refuse to allow the people of South Vietnam to chose who they might want: Ho Chi Minh as their president?

To all too many black Americans, if the white man wants war, we should give it to them. Soon Philly, Detroit, Los Angeles, Washington D.C., Chicago and many other cities erupt in flames, because these under thirty year olds, want a more perfect world, NOW! Amid all this rising violence Dr. Martin Luther King tries to keep his message of loving one's opponents, no matter how hard but he is increasingly drowned out.

Yet the day before his assassination in April, 1968 he says it all "yes we will overcome and make this country fulfill its dream for all Americans" and then pays that highest price for all soldiers in America's quest for freedom for all since 1776 and is killed by a bullet that he had been expecting since December, 1955.

> *But in those proud 12 years and 5 months of repeated beatings and jails he had almost single handedly transformed America by pushing so hard upon that door of change in America, the land of the free with his love for those "who know not, what they do."*

As always not everyone was or would listen. Not everyone listened to Jesus or Gandhi either for they clearly had their opponents; for Jesus angry Jews and an indifferent Roman Empire and for Gandhi a very hostile British Empire and a bitter Hindu who blamed Gandhi for all the remaining evils or to copy Harlem: "for causing all these problems."

It is never easy to love one's opponents, when two sides disagree bitterly for a thousand different reasons it is unfortunately easy to let hate dominate as both the black Harlem woman and the Hindu man did. Yes, I agree with them on one issue, this is not a perfect world. But I say, thank you, to Jesus, Gandhi and King for making this far from perfect world, a far better place.

On April 4th, 1968 a young black American Johnnie Marie Ross wrote about King's death:

"So rest in peace in the name of the father and son;
For your dream has not ended but in reality just begun."

What of course was Martin's dream?

"I have been to the mountain top; I have seen the green valley below, free at last, free at last."

Freedom:

Freedom is easily said or shouted by even those who gladly will deny it to everyone. Hitler shouted "lebensraum"—living room for Germans. As in America: "Manifest Destiny;" all the land to the Pacific. What was to become of the people living in Hitler's lebensraum; or in America's "Manifest Destiny?" Get out of the way, or die.

Stalin shouted freedom to all, any questions . . . a bullet to the back of your head will quickly prevent any further questions. The British Empire shouted "it is the white man's burden" to teach all non whites to obey or be crushed. The Spanish Queen Isabella decided the natives of America will exchange all of their freedoms for Christianity. Africans sold slaves to any would be buyers. King Leopold of Belgium, perhaps the worst enslaver in Africa, slaughtered the people of the Congo with indifference if not glee. Our own not so distant ancestors sold their children to factory owners for a drink and little more while promising to their wife's I'll vote yes in the A.M. and then voting against Women's Suffrage in the P.M.

Do not kid yourself, we are all guilty. All who have had power over others have abused that power. It is obviously part of our natural endowment to survive by abusing others. So when some one acts to free others, it is truly a moment to celebrate.

We white Americans freed ourselves in 1776—certainly a moment worth celebrating. The whites started doing the same in Europe in 1789 as declared in "the Rights of Man." In 1863 we tried to free the black man in the land of the free. We failed, but it was truly an effort worthy of praise. Even if it were my own ancestors who fought defending the evilness of man-slavery.

In 1920 we freed women to the vote and political power, one might argue by doing so we finally welcomed them to the human race as equals. This is why for a change to last it must be written into law, or preferably into constitutional law. For we are very human, rules that one generation think are so fundamental and can never be forgotten, soon are:

United we stand, divided we hang . . . By 1860 both North and South looked forward to war . . . In 1920 our politicians declared war on war itself . . . After Pearl Harbor to both Berlin and Tokyo; here we come! In the 1830's thanks to President Jackson we passed Usury Laws, requiring banks distant or local to be our friends . . .

In the 1970's our politicians tore up those laws and now banks (anywhere) can legally charge you and me a million percent on our credit cards! Yes, they can, read the fine print! And our politicians, both Democratic and Republican do nothing—why?

Because the rich scream louder than you and me, that is why and believe me, both parties listen to the rich. So if you don't like it . . . Scream a little! Maybe someday we can go back to those good old days of the 1830's to the 1860's . . . when "we the people ruled."

Then came the great leap:
On August 14, 1941 we,
America pledged with Britain in
"The Atlantic Charter" *to free the world.*

And every nation joining the United Nations since then has joined us in that pledge which passed by unanimous vote at the creation of the U N in 1945 San Francisco.

What a momentous pledge of faith that was. We are today seventy years later, making steady progress on so challenging a goal. With Gandhi fighting for freedom in India—actually, then in prison, we thought the onus to live up to this pledge was on Britain.

Perhaps because this was so obvious, Britain shocked the world by voting Churchill and his "maintaining the empire" policies out of power in 1945. This even stunning the opposition—for Churchill was acknowledged by almost everyone as the great hero of the Allies of WWII, even more so in Britain. To the aristocrats of Britain, even the opposition this was truly a breath taking event! It would take months for the shock waves to reach the elder opposition, but it would eventually soak in, even at the top in Britain . . .

Not so obvious because it was buried in centuries of racial disrespect to say nothing of hatred were the many minorities in America. In white America we easily talked about the liberation of the British Empire. After all the original "evil" empire, was by definition evil to America and had always been so since 1775.

Now that evil empire was about to cease to exist, for Churchill had most reluctantly signed its death warrant by signing the Atlantic Charter—acknowledged by Britain in July 1945, with his overwhelmingly shocking political defeat.

For to the young at heart in Britain:
the world had changed and Churchill, had not!

But as to our own blacks, Latino's, Native Americans and yellow peoples—Chinese, Koreans and Japanese, they knew their place in the back of the bus, and our society as well. In 1941 the Civil War and its dreams were all but forgotten; only the NAACP and the memory of Honest Abe Lincoln were around to remind us.

Love is an easy word for women, a much harder word for men. All too often love is treated by men as a word for reverends, pansies and little else. Yet love can conquer hate, love tied with determination liberated Eastern Europe:

An electrician in Poland; Lech Valesa, proved so determined to resist the Soviet Empire that he almost single handedly defeated the mighty Soviet Empire.

Jesus used love to change the hearts of millions in the Roman Empire. Gandhi conquered the hearts of millions in India and in Britain as well. And Dr. Martin Luther King Jr. conquered the hearts of many in America—mine in 1964. Hatred killed all three, but nonetheless from all with love in our hearts; thank you to all three, for making this a far better world.

In America too, shock was coming; it just took a little longer to be reflected in our polls of the 1960's:

The charts below are for president reflecting that tsunami of political change. In Alabama the limited black vote switched sides, as obviously so did the far more numerous white voters:

		* Winner.	
Alabama's change:	1960:	1964:	% Change:
Democratic vote:	324,050 *	209,848	-35 %
Republican vote:	237,981	479,085 *	+101 %
Total other vote:	8,154	105	-99 %

In Alabama and the South in general, the change was extreme. The once solid Democratic South voted Republican for first time since Reconstruction nearly a century earlier.

At the same time in the rest of America:

Meanwhile, the rest of the country shifted gears as well though not as profoundly, giving Johnson his victory.

Wisconsin's change:	1960:	1964:	% Change:
Democratic vote:	839,805	1, 050,424*	+26 %
Republican vote:	895,175*	638,495	-34 %
Total other vote:	3,102	2,896	-7 %

If the circumstances are right, one person can change history.
Thank you, Dr. Martin Luther King, Jr.
Your time well spent.

In 1960 America was politically little changed from 1860. By 1964 America reflected America of today. Dr. Martin Luther King Jr. by hammering on that door of change in the 1950's and 60's with all his might, despite all the threats, jails, stabbings and hatred threatening to engulf him transformed America with his lesson of love.

The 1960's would reflect that America engulfed with the flames of hatred that eventually resulted in the burning of American cities, the murders of President Kennedy and his brother Robert not to mention the hundreds in the Civil Rights War and the thousands, if not millions in Vietnam. The price of freedom is rarely cheap. America would have to pay the price of its racial tyranny for centuries of prejudice and hatred, do not simply disappear. *They must be fought in every heart.*

The many battles of the Civil Rights War, was what Tom Jefferson had feared so long ago. Gandhi's successful non-violent war of independence against the British Empire and Martin Luther King's incorporating these lessons into America's shadow of WWII, Jefferson did not foresee. How could he have? While Jefferson failed to for-see Gandhi and King's message of love conquering hatred in both Britain and America, King failed to for-see our shadow of opportunity, little understood by anyone in the

1960's. How could he have, the split between the generations was only then occurring.

To these two great Americans, America and the world owes a great deal. Jefferson's dream of freeing man to truly governing themselves (1776) would help cause the French Revolution (1789) to free Europe from its ancient aristocratic ruling past and free America to eventually overcome its blatant racial tyranny in the 1960's. For Martin Luther King pushing hard upon that door of change even at the eventual cost of his life, gratitude is insufficient. For like Jesus and Gandhi, who fought for non-violent reform in the hearts of their opponents, Martin Luther King paid with them the highest price for freedom, their lives.

What should be understood, Martin Luther King probably never expected to live for twelve plus years when he started on his crusade. In December, 1955 Montgomery, his home was inundated by **"I'm going to blow your brains out, were going to kill your whole family" type calls.**

Martin knew they were real, Coretta knew they were real. When the Klan blew up his house in January 1956 he had to know he was on borrowed time, yet he persisted without let up.

The End:

One should ask: What could cause a family man to put not just his own life at risk but his beloved family's as well? The answer is a man of true faith in God.

In December 1955 not surprisingly he received one threat too many and broke down and cried in his kitchen after midnight: "Why me, why me . . . *Lord, why me?*" Martin decided that God answered his question: "*—and I shall walk with you.*"

So like Moses, Dr. King led his people out of ancient Egypt into modern America of racial tolerance for all. It is no accident that during this same time period—the 1960's that America began to recognize its long debt to Native Americans and yes, even respect for Latino's working on our farms all across America since our farm boys went off to WWII and returned to the land of the G I Bill.

Martin knew this was not a promise of a long life for himself or even for his family, but Martin accepted that this path of freedom for his people was God's choice for his role. In Martin's mind he wasn't asked, he was chosen by God: Reverend Abernathy had simply been God's angel. Worship, it might be said, for their beliefs, regardless of your religion, is the world's greatest hope for tomorrow. Please everyone, love all God's children.

The End of History:

What a good place to put this, Europe has learned to love all God's children. Do you know why Strasbourg is the capital of the E.U.?

Because France has announced to the world; we are tired of war, Germans we are not Louis XIV or Napoleon trying to rule all Germans or the world for that matter . . .

Why don't you come on over . . . rather than fight World War III, we can break bread together . . . rather than fire nukes at each other.

Let us share some wine in friendship, rather than breaking bodies and blood.

And Germany replies . . . my God, there is hope for this world!
We will come and visit . . . maybe stay for dinner . . .

For we are not the Kaiser and Hitler . . . we too are tired of war . . . we also have bread to share and fine wine to share with our new friends.

Yes Europe has declared the end of history. At least the history of Europe continually killing other Europeans. Italy and Yugoslavia say let us be friends, Poland and Lithuania have declared let us too be friends. Spain has yelled at Britain come on over and tear that border between us and Gibraltar away for we have good bread and wine to share, for nukes we do not want. Yes Europe, has torn its borders of hate to shreds . . .

Love and friendship to share,
ain't life wonderful . . .
maybe we all could learn . . .

AUTHOR NOTES

*Southern Manifesto: The South's rejection of the Supreme Court's call for integration "at all deliberate speed." Fourteen years after declaring Segregation unconstitutional in

1954 only 1 percent of Southern blacks attended "white" schools and only 8 percent of non southern blacks by 1968.

* The Rights of Man: "If any are to be freed, all must be free." Believe it or not this fundamental truth of the French Revolution, I had to discover by accident in my later research. In high school in both North Carolina and in Oklahoma, I never encountered it. The same goes for my collegiate education at both Delgado Junior College and The University of New Orleans in Louisiana.

This is why regionalism persists. All of us are the products of all who have gone before us, and what they (our past) have decided to pass on to us.

* CORE: Congress of Racial Equality, founded at the University of Chicago in 1942. Primarily white and middle class it was determined to somehow spread the dream of freedom. In 1955 it sent a group south to Montgomery to aid and abet those communist agitators, ah hem, Reverend King in non-violent training. In 1960 they again encouraged sit-ins in restaurants demanding the right to be served and after James Farmer became its first black national director a few months later sent mixed groups to integrate interstate transportation.

Winston Churchill would return to power in the 1950's. For the Labour Party could not restore this island of ruins (Britain) to prosperity in the late 40's. Unfortunately neither could the Conservative Party of the 1950's. Britain had spent a century digging itself into the giant hole of markets which can only buy from Britain—it's empire, into. Now with those colonies being free to buy from anyone . . . It would take the harsh free trade policies of Margaret Thatcher in the 1980's to begin to restore the Great to Britain.

This book contains many quotations from the Holy Bible such as: "for those who know not what they do"; "and I shall walk with you." These I freely use as I base them on my interpretation of Dr. Martin Luther King Jr.'s mind—Which of course is the whole point of chapters VI and VII.

CHAPTER VIII

Vietnam and the Birth
of Today's America

YOU ARE BEING sworn in as President aboard Air Force One as something terrible has happened . . . You are playing baseball when a little girl runs up saying the impossible: "The President has been shot, the President has been shot!" You turn and yell at her "Nobody can shoot the President, now go away!" She turns and slowly walks away, quietly saying "The President has been shot . . ." The school air raid warning sounds off, announcing something truly horrible has happened . . .

You are now the President, giving some of your time telling a little story to youngsters at an elementary school in Florida. The Secret Service wants your attention . . . You finish your little story anyway . . . You are slowly getting ready for a dental appointment in San Francisco, but you are hearing dreadful noises from the T.V. what can it be . . . you check, you suddenly forget about your dental appointment . . . President Kennedy has been killed, 911 has happened . . .

Welcome to our World: Reality . . .

The America we know today began in 1963, partly because few of us can remember before 1963—unless you are at least 55. But mostly because our political parties as we know them today began to take shape with King's March on Washington (demanding in effect; at least one party shift from civil rights someday to NOW!) and the election of 1964. World War II or Pearl Harbor had abruptly changed America, the McCarthy hate mongering of 1947-1954 seemingly confirmed it as well, we would now find out just how much.

Meanwhile the "I like Ike" (Eisenhower) majority of the 1950's, to minorities here in America, would you please, just get lost with your silly ideas about civil rights now, but please vote for us rather than the slave democrats . . . I mean what choice do you have?

On November 22, 1963 Kennedy was assassinated, and Vice President Johnson became President aboard Air Force One, no one could know ahead of time how the election of 1964 would turn out. President Johnson inherited a few problems with the job, headed by Civil Rights at home and to him personally, with the routine mistreatment of Hispanics in Texas and a far away headache, called Vietnam:

In the climate of the post McCarthy years, our American idealism became subverted by our anti-communism. Now every president, congressman and senator had to prove "they were tough on communism." We now supported anyone who opposed communism whether they might be French colonialists or brutal dictators like the Shah of Iran. Thus when the French colonialists decided to pull out of Vietnam. President Eisenhower decided to stay and back the government of South Vietnam installed by the departing French.

Our decision to fully support South Vietnam's decision to cancel the 1956 elections that would have allowed Ho Chi Minh to run for president in both Vietnam's under U.N. direction that we had guaranteed only two years earlier, clearly fell victim to McCarthy's "tough on communism."

Clearly Eisenhower, the congress and the press were all very wrong in not denouncing this decision. But in this climate of hysteria, very few felt brave enough to scream foul . . .

In 1961 President Kennedy could have chosen to let South Vietnam fall, instead not wanting to be seen as "soft on communism," he chose to commit the Green Berets (Special Forces) in greater numbers to actually fight communism in South Vietnam. But with Buddhist Monks burning themselves in the cities and the Viet Cong (Communists) controlling most of the countryside still more help was in need. So in 1963 he approved the South Vietnamese military's proposed coup against the very unpopular Diem (Catholic) Regime but with the provision that they were not to be executed.

The South's Buddhist military virtually wiped the hated extended Catholic Diem family out in early November. What the Catholic Kennedy would do, was cut short by Lee Harvey Oswald. Now Vietnam was Johnson's problem and the South Vietnamese military were now constantly fighting each other over which general would rule in the aftermath. What a mess! But this is largely back page news, on the front pages of America:

In early 1963 the Ku Klux Klan murders four little girls attending a Sunday school in Birmingham, setting off race riots across the nation which Dr. Martin Luther King, Jr. tries desperately to stop but only quiets. In August MLK leads his March on Washington demanding the Federal government act on Civil Rights now!

With over 300,000 blacks and whites attending it clearly is a demanding call for action NOW. The western world prays that America will listen but President Kennedy sitting in the White House rather than attending King's March on Washington looks at the map of Southern states that elected him president in 1960 and ponders on what to do? As always push has come to shove, what shall he do?

In this country thirteen Southern states from Texas to Virginia—the old Solid South that only vote Democratic as in the slave party of 1860 still counts for a lot—especially if you're a Democrat wondering how to get re-elected. Lee Harvey Oswald made sure we would wonder about Kennedy's answer today.*

In 1964 President Johnson could have chosen to let South Vietnam fall, instead he saw away to combine his inherited Civil Rights problem with Vietnam. John F. Kennedy the son of a U.S. Senator and Lyndon B. Johnson were both professional politicians (Johnson had been in Washington since the 1930's) and both treated the Civil Rights movement with great political fear.

Officially they like Eisenhower backed the Civil Rights movement; unofficially they (like Eisenhower) did as little as possible to support it. The reason for the Democrats was simple; the thirteen ex-Confederate states had provided them with the victory margin in 1960. Plus their simply was no guarantee that the other thirty seven states would overwhelmingly vote for Johnson's Civil Rights proposals. So how do you get them to?

In December 1941 Johnson left congress to rejoin the Navy. He fought at the battle of Midway, before Texas insisted he return to Washington as a very minor national hero (he was their!). Thus he had plenty of contacts in the Navy. Exactly what happened we will never know, but in August 1964 the Navy reported it had been fired upon by the North Vietnamese tiny fleet of coastal gun boats resulting in:

Congress overwhelmingly passed the Gulf of Tonkin Resolution calling for President Johnson to punish North Vietnam. The Republican nominee Barry Goldwater was even more passionate to kick their communist butts.

Johnson was thrilled to win overwhelmingly, winning forty four states losing only Goldwater's Arizona and five deep Southern states. By firing up America's anti communism, patriotic America voted for Johnson's Great Society Bills and largely ignored that when our warships "engaged" in the Gulf of Tonkin returned to port **after** the election they replied; "what are you talking about? We were never fired on."

So Johnson won his election, the Voter Rights Bill, his Great Society bills and a little war in a place called Vietnam. Only that little war refused to go away, so the number of troops quickly doubled and gradually doubled again and as the years ever so slowly rolled by with 1964 becoming 1965 and then 1966 and still 1967 the pesky little people of Vietnam struggling to breathe free simply refused to go away. Johnson facing growing anti war sentiment at home led oddly enough to him by Dr. Martin Luther King, Jr. finally it became **1968** with over a half million U. S. troops in Vietnam.

Martin Luther King was an early opponent of the "war" mainly because he had been preaching "love thy neighbor, not war" his whole adult life. Very quickly he saw Johnson's anti poverty bills being slashed by the ever growing war funding. Still another reason for opposing the war in Vietnam was humanitarian reasons—it was their war not ours. Soon young people began to oppose the war, after all if you were born in the late 1940's you missed the anti-communist madness of the McCarthy years and you were being drafted to go fight them commies, why? Because their Communists on a different continent—that's why and its:

1968:
The most dangerous animal in the wild is?
Any mother fearing for her doe, cub or duckling.
For us humans: It's both parents protecting their children.

If there ever was a second Civil War in America, 1968 to 1973 was when. For beginning in 1968 a war would be fought here in America for the heart and soul of America. On Vietnam's New Year Jan. 30th 1968 the Viet Cong launched an all out assault in South Vietnam capturing most of Saigon and other cities. Both the V.C. and President Johnson would soon be destroyed. Our counterattacks largely destroyed the V.C.

It was a military disaster for the Viet Cong and a political disaster for President Johnson. *Neither would ever recover.* For our army and Johnson had reported in the previous years, time and again, and again that victory was just around the corner, just around the corner only we never seemed to find that very elusive corner. After this offensive, with fighting in downtown Saigon, Hue and other "safe" areas, few could believe our military or the U.S. president either.

From this point onwards the regular Army of North Vietnam would continue the fight in the South. For Johnson the New Hampshire primary a few weeks later in February, witnessed another virtually unknown young Senator Eugene McCarthy's anti-war movement almost beat Johnson in the primary.

This president had won 44 states in '64 and here-to-for was considered a shoe in for '68. Clearly his blood was in the water, Senator Eugene McCarthy was a (ain't he—the previous senator from Wisconsin . . . dead?) who? character. Sharks (other Democrats) quickly began to appear on the horizon, forming campaign staffs: In March Johnson announced he would not seek a second term to a stunned nation. Very quickly Robert Kennedy already an opponent of the war entered along with Hubert Humphrey, Johnson's Vice President and still others.

Martin Luther King assassinated on April 4th sparked national race riots across the nation—Watts II in L.A., the Detroit War etc. as the primaries continued a full blown war for control of the Democratic Party loomed now between Robert Kennedy leading the young anti war party and Humphrey leading the old party of WWII and F.D.R. era stalwarts—the people who directly or indirectly indorsed the old Slave Party of 1860.

For in America there have always only been two parties in politics. Like it or not the Republicans led by Lincoln fought slavery. The Democrats had fought to defend slavery and that was why thirteen Southern states still voted Democratic a hundred years later—some memories die hard.

Johnson—now desperate for peace, opened peace talks in Paris with North Vietnam. Robert Kennedy wins the California primary and apparently the Democratic nomination but is shot dead that night. Meanwhile the Supreme Court ordered bussing takes effect requiring black and white school districts to merge causing all kinds of local troubles from Boston to Seattle. At my high school in Fayetteville, N.C. it was hell on earth—everywhere else too I'm sure. Both whites and blacks use to running their own schools now thrust together—fight literally for control—as in every day.

The Generation Gap:

America's generation gap was now a mile wide and a thousand miles deep. You can't trust anyone over 30 was the saying. Here's why: In 1968 if you were 35 plus, you were born in 1933 or earlier. That means you were eight or older at the time of Pearl Harbor. If you didn't serve in WWII you watched your fathers and brothers and uncles go off to war. One could say by definition psychologically those older than 35 were a part of that WWII generation.

By 1947 they were fourteen plus at the start of the McCarthy hearings, by the time they ended in 1954 you were at least twenty one and well brainwashed in anti communism courtesy of your new T.V. which most Americans now owned if under fifty. Odds were if male you had fought in the good war—WWII where there was no doubt about who were the good guys—us and who were the bad guys—them or in Korea them the commies.

If in 1968 you were 25 or younger, then you were born since 1943 and missed the good war: WWII and eleven at max when the brainwashing McCarthy era was stopped by General Marshall. Your brain if it did listen to McCarthyism didn't understand that adult hate filled talk.

You had instead grown up watching Mickey Mouse and Martin Luther King preach "love thy neighbor no matter how hard, never let them take you so low that you might start to hate." and all the mayhem that simple statement of love received in Montgomery, Birmingham, Boston, Detroit, Chicago and Los Angeles—all across America.

The generation gap was real: a mile wide and a thousand miles deep. To the elders life was hard—growing up during the Great Depression, fighting in WWII and being brainwashed by the hatred of McCarthyism how could it not be. To the younger generation growing up on Captain Kangaroo why should it have to be—why not make love like Dr. Martin Luther King said and not war?

Now they were being drafted against their will to fight the commies in Vietnam. The "love thy neighbor" children "no matter how hard" to kill people ten thousand miles away. Little wonder the question was often asked "just what are we fighting for? A revolving door of military dictatorships in Vietnam—surely Thomas Jefferson would never have approved. All of our founding fathers would have cried.

To the over thirty crowd, or at least to most of them with their McCarthyist brainwashing a commie killed today was one less needing to be killed tomorrow, nuke the bastards if you must.

These were the two crowds descending upon Chicago for the Democratic Convention. The under thirty crowd who thought they and Robert Kennedy the anti war candidate, now deceased who should have won (their opinion) and against them Hubert H. Humphrey, Johnson's Vice President. Little wonder that Mayor Daley a most definite over thirty'er sent his storm troopers to roust those peace nicks away from the convention. The Chicago police riot plainly viewed on television. Not surprisingly Humphrey won the nomination and Nixon won the election though both wanted to end the war as soon as possible.

The Nixon years:

With the Republican Richard Nixon winning the election of 1968 with his slogan of "I have a secret plan to end the war, but if I tell you—it wouldn't be a secret anymore" our parties began to take their modern shape: the Democrats wanting out of Vietnam sooner, the Republicans later—with honor. Nixon's secret plan was Vietnamization. Hand our weapons to the South Vietnamese and let them fight it out, before the next Presidential election.

Ho Chi Minh who often told of his days attending the Sorbonne University in Paris of the time he approached President Wilson after World War I visiting the restaurant where he worked. Asking the President if his message of; the right of the people in Europe to decide their choice of government applied to the colonial world? To this most popular message in Europe, Ho Chi Minh was ushered quickly away before ever receiving his answer.

President Wilson (if this occurred) probably did not want to answer it, considering how much his First World War European Allies opposed it. They had promised each other many scraps of land, regardless of how the people on it might feel and Wilson was actually proposing, that we Britain, France and Italy the victors, **the arrogant we**, should listen . . .

Never, so here comes WWII!—
the price of not listening to "**We the people**" . . .

Ho Chi Minh, after graduating in France and living in the U.S. for several years in the 1920's, concluding that America would never go communist he returned to Vietnam. In Vietnam with its absentee land owners living it up in the cities and its landless peasants working without hope of a better life in the country side, he knew in Vietnam the people would support communism—land to the people.

Sadly, in 1970 he died, never receiving his answer except by more bombs than dropped in all of WWII on North Vietnam. The people of both North and South Vietnam went into deep morning upon learning of his death. Even the city people believing in capitalism, mourned his death, after all he had driven the French out—their George Washington. In Paris people talked, in Vietnam the killing continued even if everyone now knew how the war would end . . .

How Could We Have Gone So Wrong:

In 1945 America dominated the world even if Stalin's Soviet Empire disagreed. Remembering just how wrong our victory in the American Civil War and the Allied victory in WWI had resulted in hatred in both America and in Europe we reached a helping hand out to war shattered Germany and said grab on. We then took our other hand and reached out to starving Japan and said grab hold and together we will pull this world to the 21st century world of 'love thy neighbor.'
Germany led by Adenauer reached out a broken hand of friendship to the rest of Europe and said grab on and maybe we can all make it to the promised land of 'love thy neighbor.' Britain that isle of ruins, vowed we shall do what we can. France and Italy still literally at internal war with themselves said why not?

President Truman recognized that the will of the people of Japan was worth far more than a single life, therefore Emperor Hirohito who in theory led Japan to Pearl Harbor, was allowed to live out his life as emperor. For to the Japanese people he was their living god and we could not change that in 1945. So Asia would have to advance separately.

The will of the German people wasn't just Hitler and his legions, but also the spirit of that long ago Priest Martin Luther and the Mayor of Cologne (Adenauer) who dared to stand up to Hitler—when the rest of the world yelled "peace in our times"—Neville Chamberlain, Prime Minister of Britain. Had we the people of the world stood with Adenauer in 1938 how many lives would we have saved? We must all share that guilt.

Speaking of unfairness for all the goodness America has done for this world? When has anyone ever lifted so much as a finger to help America?

I can think of once, after the 1950's, the 60's and onward into the 1970's America with its cities burned out, from both the Civil Rights War and 59,000 Americans killed in Vietnam and countless shouts of you're a racist, and you're a traitor, here at home. The world sailed into New York harbor, literally sailed into New York harbor with sailing ships both big and small to celebrate our bicentennial in 1976 all around the Statute of Liberty.

Maybe that wasn't a lot, but thank you as an American who loves his country greatly, thank you from the bottom of my heart. For we truly needed that vote of appreciation after thirty years of self inflicted hatred—which started with Senator McCarthy's hate mongering of the late 1940's and 50's.

Please Europe, do not repeat the mistakes of the past and demand someone else pay and pay dearly for I want a good deal. Life will never be fair if we demand that others must pay more than me. Europe you have decided to have a common currency, like it or not that means everyone must pay for whatever benefits you decide to have.

So if a Greek Civil Servant can retire at age 47 because Greece gave us the world Democracy a few thousand years ago than all of you must agree that is fair. Otherwise if you like me, believe: 'Thanks, for your ideas of a few thousand years ago' is more than adequate payment. Now about 'our' retirement age . . . that as a continent you must decide as a Euro society; you must decide for all of you.

So be brave, step forward and deal with this most unfair world. Do what is right and welcome to the third millennium of truly loving thy neighbor in the words of Martin Luther King "no matter how hard" it may be.

Was it fair that a seven year old child should have to volunteer to step in front of the batons, fire hoses and attack dogs of hatred in 1963 Birmingham, Alabama? Of course not, but thanks to him and all of them, his little sisters too, America finally lived up to its proud boast as the land of the free! "We the people, all the people, free at last!"—MLK

It takes guts to do what is right. It took courage and supreme confidence for Washington to cross the Delaware in 1776 and for Dr. Martin Luther King Jr. to lead the children of Birmingham into the future. I salute them both and all who had the guts to step forward with them, I only wish I could have had the guts to step with them.

America came out of W.W.II having beaten Germany with one arm and Japan with the other thinking we could bend and twist the whole world into what ever shape we wished it to be. Yes we were overconfident—and very arrogant. Yes we are very prone to being the "Omnipotent Americans." The ones who think they can bend and twist the whole world into whatever shape we wish it to be. For better . . . most of the world is in great need of reform, and for worse . . . while we may have the might, 5% of the world's population dictating to the other 95% can never be right.

We all too often forget that our victories won over both Nazi Germany and Imperial Japan were won in large part because of the support both big and small from virtually the entire world. The Soviet Union, Britain, China, India, Canada, Australia, New Zealand, Brazil, and yes even the Ethiopia's of the world contributed to "our" victories. This is not to even mention the sacrifices made by those countries overrun by Germany and Japan. This would include still another long list of countries from the Philippines to Burma and from Greece to Norway, by way of France. In short, we can be omnipotent, but only if the world supports us.

So, how did we get into the quagmire of Vietnam, and how did:

We go so wrong—if so?

Before I get started here, let me add the communists of Vietnam were not the good guys. They literally believed in winning, no matter how dirty you must get: So beating a child half to death, strapping grenades onto his/her back, and letting them escape, to run to the Americans, and exploding the child and Americans nearby, was all too often the reality of Vietnam. You as an American were quickly presented the real choice of the child's life or yours . . . The reality of infantry fighting in Vietnam. The only truly relevant question here, however was it our fight or not?

Clearly anyone surveying the reality of South Vietnam in 1956, would have to know Ho Chi Minh was going to win any popularity contest of any kind. In 1970 when he died almost everyone in Vietnam mourned his death after fourteen years of fighting . . .

Much like that slave owner in the U.S. in 1799—George Washington, who many, many people today would consider as despicable a person as you could get. Since the will of the people should always be respected by people who truly believe in democracy, Ho Chi Minh was their choice just as that slave owner was ours to make in 1789.

So, back to how did we get into the quagmire of Vietnam?

A good place to start is with that question asked long ago: Ho Chi Minh at a fancy restaurant while attending the Sorbonne University while the Allied leaders were debating the terms of the Versailles Treaty ending the First World War.

Whether this story is true or not I do not know, we only do know that Ho Chi Minh would repeat it several times. In any case true or not it certainly deserves an answer:

If we truly believe we are "a nation dedicated to the proposition of liberty and justice for all"—Abe Lincoln.

Then while many of us may feel that we are intellectually superior, I think we all would agree that every people should be entitled to self-determination to the extent possible. Therefore the answer must be: Yes.

This of course should mean that if a people freely chose a government not to our liking, that decision is their business, not ours. This does not mean that we should not try to influence them to do what we think is right, but the choice must always, be theirs.

With these principles in mind let us now re-trace our steps into our Vietnam Nightmare . . .

In W.W.II President Roosevelt ignored both Free and Vichy French opposition and supplied the Viet-Minh with arms and ammunition. I believe he did this because he had no interest in restoring French colonial rule after the war and in the meantime the Viet-Minh were fighting the Japanese and every Japanese killed by the Viet-Minh was one less that we ourselves might have to kill.

After W.W.II, President Truman made the decision to "switch sides" in French Indo-China (Vietnam, Cambodia and Laos). We may think this was a wrong decision, but his reason for doing so—to help prevent the communists from winning the 1947 French elections; certainly too some extent justified his actions.

Most un-fortunately after the French elections, he elected to continue American support for French colonial rule, on the grounds that the Viet-Minh was communist. This was only partly true, but they were largely communist led. They were also all "freedom fighters."

To support French colonial rule, no not that! To fight the freedom fighters, yearning to breathe free, no not them either. To help fight the "communists" in Indo-China, President Truman dispatched a few hundred U.S. Army technical and support troops to Vietnam. In reality this is when our "nightmare" began, in 1947.

At the 1939 New York World's Fair all kinds of dreamy futuristic devices like flying cars were presented to the world as the future to come. Unfortunately the world chose that same year to make war the future to come ending with two atomic bombs exploding over Japan—a very nightmarish futuristic device not at the world's fair. However one dreamy device on display at New York would explode almost immediately after the war—television.

In 1947 the first television station went "on the air." Very, very quickly everyone had to have one as you can imagine. Thus television arrived just in time for:

The McCarthy hearings to pour his hate into our living rooms destroying many good Americans in both government and the private sector for daring to think out of main-stream America or sometimes just knowing someone who allegedly did. For year after year his hate and the fear his accusations instilled in others of communists among us poured into our hearts. The impact of this hate mongering and that of many others of both political parties trying to yell their accusations even louder, so as to capture the camera lime light from him can not be understated. In this feeding frenzy of political ambitions, America the home of the brave quickly became the home of the afraid.

Though the hearings of the Anti-American Activities Investigations never produced a shred of evidence against most of the accused their careers were still ruined. People literally fled the country rather then be led before the cameras and be so publicly repeatedly accused of thinking "un-American" thoughts.

How could you defend yourself against the accusation that: You were a friend of the previously accused were you not? Any yes answer was effectively saying yes I was a cohort of that communist sympathizer. If you answered no, evidence of your repeated contacts with the previously convicted by accusations only would "prove" your guilt of sharing their alleged beliefs before the public's eyes.

Soon our elites of both the press and politics were afraid that if they dissented in any way, they too would be accused and ruined in the court of public opinion. Because now with television pouring all this hate and fear into the public's heart—we the people were so afraid of communists everywhere amongst us, the accusations would be believed by many just as Herr Goebbels said about any lie repeated often enough.

When the investigations proceeded to the Army-McCarthy hearings my older brother tells me our mother said: "Now that man is going to try to destroy the Army." If she did say that, it was extremely prophetic. While Sen. Joe McCarthy (Rep. of Wis.) failed to destroy the Army in the 1950's he did set the climate for its destruction twenty years later . . .

When General Marshall, commander of the entire army during WW II rose to the defense of the Army in 1954, at last the witch hunt after lasting seven years was ended. One should ask why this witch hunt was allowed to last for so long, doing so much harm.

The conservatives in both political parties benefited initially, so why not . . . The Press was un-aware in the beginning of the true power of televised accusations . . . The Liberals were its many intended victims . . . many including John F. Kennedy in reaction out of fear joined in!

Yes, Sen. John F. Kennedy, Democrat did his best to out yell Sen. McCarthy, in this feeding frenzy to gain a head start on his presidential ambitions. In my opinion he was a politician feeling for which way the wind is blowing and like a good politician jumping to the head of the crowd, led the charge. In 1960, he won the nomination . . .

We the people were in fact its many victims, both conservatives and liberals alike, because we were now all, so, so afraid. Hence the saying:

The American people cannot stand the truth.

In the climate of the post McCarthy years, our American idealism became subverted by our anti-communism. Now every president, congressman and senator had to prove "they were tough on communism."

Perhaps, now you can understand why I am not a big fan of JFK. He like McCarthy must share this guilt.

Thus when the French colonialists decided to pull out, President Eisenhower (having written a speech denouncing McCarthyism—but chickening out—his own admission) decided to stay and back the government of South Vietnam installed by the departing French. With our decision to fully support South Vietnam's decision to cancel the 1956 nation-wide elections that we had guaranteed only two years earlier by Eisenhower; the congress and the press were all very wrong in not denouncing this decision. Clearly our idealism had fallen victim to McCarthy's "tough on communism." In this climate of hysteria, very few in the home of the brave felt brave enough to scream foul.

For we as a nation had chickened out and this was the nation MLK was determined to reform. We as a nation had reversed everything honest old Abe Lincoln had stood up and fought for—a new Civil War was coming . . .

In 1961 President Kennedy could have chosen to let South Vietnam fall, instead not wanting to be seen as "soft on communism," he chose to commit the Green Berets (Special Forces) in greater numbers to actually fight communism in South Vietnam. Thus 1961 became the official start of Vietnam—U.S. combat officially begins.

In 1964 President Johnson could have chosen to let South Vietnam fall, instead willing to pay any price to win the election so **President Johnson chose to completely betray America's idealism.** So rather then tell us the truth he opted to tell us a lie:

He and the Navy made up the Gulf of Tonkin incidents. It was what the adults (over 30's crowd) of America wanted to hear: Let us go kill some commies. After all, this was the post McCarthy years and anyone not wanting to kill commies was un-American. The generation gap was building to record heights. Just as a century earlier the gap between North and South was building to record heights.

In 1968 President Nixon could have chosen to tell the American people the truth, the whole bitter truth. Coming from him, a proven anti-communist from the McCarthy Hearings era—he had led the House Anti-American Activities investigations, he could have just pulled our troops out. Instead he went to China, as if the Red Chinese were going to help us.

Please do not blame our troops for answering the call, even I sensing the truth thru the lies of several presidents, could not believe the truth staring at me, square in the face. After deciphering my brother's letters from Vietnam, I elected to join the Navy . . . We are all human, the very idea that our own government could be lying to us, was so hard to believe. **Both parties were lying, how could they** . . .

In acknowledging that we had failed to win militarily, he now tried to win diplomatically, while leaving our army still in combat. In doing so, **Nixon betrayed our fighting men,** by in effect telling them: I have no confidence in you winning, but I want you to keep dying anyway. They died in 1969, 1970, and still more in 1971 and in 1972. The U.S. Army virtually died itself as the number of "fragging" incidents soared—named after the fragmentation grenades often used to kill someone trying to get you killed, like officers who obey their orders.

In 1972 after using trickery to get the opponent he wanted (substituting the wrong speeches to Edmond Muskie, so he would talk about retirement problems to farmers (who do not retire, they just do less, and less) and so on so Nixon won easily against his choice of opponents:

George McGovern, but tripped over his greed at Watergate and was forced to resign in disgrace in 1974. The U.S. pulled out of Vietnam in 1973 and Saigon fell in April 1975.

So, who do we blame for this fiasco which killed 59,000 Americans and millions of Vietnamese?

You can take your pick; you have the Democrats Truman, Kennedy and Johnson, and the Republican presidents Eisenhower and Nixon plus Sen. McCarthy. Fact is they were all guilty of betraying our fundamental belief that all people should have the right to the government of their choice no matter how wrong they might be. We fundamentally disagree with each other every four years.

This is the truth that our politicians have lied to us all these years; both parties are guilty—which is more guilty is clearly in the eye of the beholder. Rather than face the truth and admit their own guilt; we actually hear blame those other traitors. Unfortunately that is politics as usual.

Rarely do we get those brave enough to agree with Hamilton who declared "elect Jefferson, the peoples choice" to his defeated fellow Federalists, who literally feared for their lives by voting for that supporter of the French guillotining their opponents. They in 1801 overcame their fears, but after the McCarthyism of 1947-1954 we could not stand the truth, for we were all so, afraid. Leaving all of us in the 1970's both Republicans and

Democrats only with that bitter feeling that we had been betrayed—but by whom?

Ourselves or to be more precise by the congress of our so called "greatest generation" who having survived the Great Depression, commanded the greatest generation in WWII to victory then betrayed them by allowing their fears of communism to brainwash their children with McCarthyism.

In this we are not alone, the French in the 1940's to 1960's were in the same boat of we have been betrayed but by whom? The communists betrayed France when they refused to recognize the Nazi threat arising next to them and when losing the election to the right wingers told the troops not to fight. The right wingers having lost to the Nazi blitzkrieg in 1940; then crawled into bed with the Nazi's as the Vichy government. Only then did the communists choose to fight in the underground. In 1944 when the Allies including the Free French liberated France this war continued as both sides the right and the left recognized the betrayal of the others but not their own.

We today might think America going communist was a nightmare not going to happen as Ho Chi Minh concluded in the 1920's. While he was correct it wasn't his property at risk. Just as the Slave Democrats voted for succession in 1861 to *those who's property is being threatened any risk will be greatly heightened.*

In 1917 Russia fell to communism. In 1918-1919 both Hungary and briefly Germany were threatened by a communist takeover. In 1918 America with many people looking for a third party after both Democrats and Republicans voted for the most unpopular war in American history: World War One, the Socialist Party rallied to the anti war cause.

With both Republicans and Democrats facing the sudden uphill battle for re-election in 1918 the Red Scare began. Any Socialist was very quickly declared a Communist and a criminal anti war rioter and quickly sent to jail—crises over—except for the fear. The fear was of communism, because all people tend to believe their own lies especially when they hear others repeat them and the rich who supported the vote for war repeated the lies often. After all by making the Socialists into communist anti war protesters justified putting them in jail and to the rich and ultra religious that is the only place a communist should ever be. Lesson learned.

In 1929 came the Great Depression where capitalism seemingly failed to work. The Republicans tried and failed as the economy continued to sink into oblivion. The Democrats winning the elections of 1932 and 1936 tried radical solutions for a very conservative country (we are a very capitalist nation) only achieving stability at depression levels with 25% unemployment.

Reality was Hitler ended the Great Depression by killing millions of people. Out of our fear of being next we spent money by the ton in a hurry. After Pearl Harbor that record spending was chicken feed.

In surviving the Great Depression we had tried "radical" solutions some good like Social Security others bad but conservatives and especially the rich never like radical solutions—not even Social Security. To them the elderly should do us all a favor and just hurry up and die. For why should the rich pay taxes to feed the poor. Because we the people insist they should do so, no matter, whether they like it or not! That is why!

During WWII Communist Russia—good ole Joseph Stalin was our ally against Nazi Germany. Conservatives and the rich were never happy with that. The conservatives and the rich of both parties were very ready for a new Red Scare; in McCarthyism they found their cause. Thus out of our fears of communists among us, we lost our ideals.

By the 1970's all we had was the bitterness of betrayal by those other horrible people after all, it could never be us.

For the next twenty eight years (1976-2004) we would continuously call our political opponents traitors. Yes, Democrats you yellow bellied liberals stabbing our soldiers fighting for your freedoms in the back! Yes, you Republicans too, for betraying Honest Old Abe Lincoln's truths. For 28 years you yelled traitor to those fighting for the truth!

We were all betrayed by five presidents in a row from Truman to Nixon. Three Democrats and two Republicans; all determined to deny us the truth:

That we are a nation dedicated to the proposition
of Justice and Liberty for all—Abe Lincoln.

Therefore we should have done what Lincoln would have done, it's your country, you make the best of it.

Remember this lesson of history: **Japan:**

The ancient aristocrats of Japan were afraid that Japan was about to be humiliated like China, or worse, a colony like India in the 1800's. Out of their desperation, in 1867 they declared Japan a democracy. Declaring a country a democracy, does not make it one. Only we the people of any country can make it one. The people of Japan in 1867 had no idea what a democracy was . . .

So they in effect elected the same aristocrats that had always ruled them, to "rule them in the name of democracy." Gradually however, the Army realized they had the guns, so quickly the Army decided, what the Emperor thought . . . and in ancient Japan, the emperor is always right. Thus in the 1930's, the Army decided China should solve Japan's Great Depression woes . . . China refused, but the Emperor cannot be wrong . . . thus the Army decided the Navy must supply the weak Americans to solve Japan's ailments . . .

In 1945 the Japanese Army surrendered and General Douglas McArthur of the U S Army became the de-facto Emperor of Japan. The people of Japan obeyed. Culturally despite modern education, Japan was still in the Middle Ages . . .

In 1954 we granted Japan its independence. In my opinion it still wasn't a democracy because the majority did not truly believe in one. But the majority of Japanese did know democracy had won WWII . . . So they were confused . . . given enough time . . .

In the 2007 the Liberal Democratic Party, that had ruled Japan since the 1946 elections finally lost. Japan, welcome to your own version of democracy at last!

Only when the people are ready,
does Democracy begin.
Not, when someone declares *it to be.*

AUTHOR NOTES

Note: The Kennedy staffs were no doubt leaning to the left, but as to Kennedy the consummate politician, I must wonder.

CHAPTER IX

INTEGRATION !
and it's all out war here in America

BY ORDER OF the Supreme Court in 1968: America fourteen years after the Supreme Court ruled segregation was inherently unequal in Brown vs. Topeka and delay after delay and repeated delay, the Court ruled:

People of America, thou shall integrate today!

For the vast majority of America had delayed and delayed and it was now war, all out war, with-in our own schools and our minds. Integration of our schools meant war, and everybody knew it. That was why it had been delayed and delayed almost everywhere!

From 1619 when the first unhappy slave was sold in America to 1968 is 349 years of slavery and Jim Crowness—slavery by a different name. Some call it four centuries of bitterness and disrespect and hatred. Yes, lots of hatred, four hundred years of hate do not go quietly into the night. Dr. Martin Luther King, Jr. our spiritual guide to the promised land of respect for all is dead and so is Robert Kennedy, all we have is both hatred and determination to somehow find our way to:

Our own promised land of Love for all, Nirvana.

The American Indian is at war with us having seized Alcatraz as still another broken promise—we had once promised its return and now we white people who speak with forked tongues are now telling American Indians to lose our promises now that Alcatraz the prison is closed, because we think it should be a park. San Francisco State University (SFSU) dares to hold rallies demanding we (white people) actually should honor our promises of the past—how dare they!

Our cities vying for attention are going up in flames for blacks want justice today, not more broken promises about someday in the future. And our Vietnam Vets are preyed upon as if they are the traitors for having answered Uncle Sam's call to arms, they too, we want them to get lost as well. The only thing we seem able to find how to do is cry for America, once a great country, now thoroughly humbled by our own disrespect.

The Re-Segregation of America:

In 1946 with all that money spent in WWII sitting in required WWII savings accounts; now just awaiting cars and new homes to be built our post war economic boom took off to every one's great relief, by 1947 it was the roaring 1920's again! Only now for we the people, not just the rich, because WWII had primarily been paid for with deficit spending so taxes remained high to pay off the staggering debt plus the cost of rebuilding Europe and Japan.

Do note: Our tax rates were kept high for everyone's benefit!

Having learned the hard lessons of the Great Depression we were all determined to spend some of our wealth in rebuilding the world so marginal tax rates remained at 70% though some added loopholes were granted. Thus our economy grew for all, not just the richie rich as in the 1920's.

The Marshall Plan to rebuild Europe and besides feeding a starving Japan; facial reconstructions for the hundreds of living young female survivors of Hiroshima and Nagasaki: Sadly these young ladies would soon die; victims of radiation poisoning—sudden outbreaks of fatal Leukemia which we were all just learning to deal with . . .

Nonetheless we were still determined to help rebuild the world; so they could buy our products and world trade would grow into our world of today. Few understood all this then, but repeating post WWI (high trade barriers), the Great Depression and still another even deadlier world war we were determined somehow not to repeat the mistakes of the past.

With all that growth of new cars and new homes suburbia was born. In 1947 it was largely by choice even allowing for blacks not allowed to join in the celebration; in 1968 and the Supreme Court's decision to enforce desegregation nationwide it became by fear. Fear is hard to grasp, harder to understand but from Boston to Los Angeles and a thousand places in between when whites moved to suburbia blacks moved in to their former neighborhoods.

Thus in my neighborhood of Mid City in New Orleans where I moved into in the late 70's was 85% white, as blacks poured in and whites fled, blacks moved into the majority in the city. When New Orleans fell to the conquering hordes of blacks—so it seemed to many, many whites the world did not end. The new black Mayor Marc Morial tried to minimize the change. Doing so, he proved to be one of us.

The city continued to get worse as revenues continued to fall the same as they had fallen when whites had ruled. Yet when I too joined the exodus in '97 my old neighborhood was 85% black. Of course Katrina wiped all of my old neighborhood and our neighbor's out as well, regardless of color. My sister and her husband were among the hundreds of thousands of refugees. For flood waters do not care about the color of our skin, so let us find another example to continue.

So let us take the city built by Henry Ford and the automobile: Detroit to try understanding fear. In 1950 Detroit had 1.9 million people most I am sure were white. By 2010 the 1.9 million had fallen to .9 million over 80% black which works out to over 700,000 blacks with-in the city. Meanwhile metro Detroit which includes the city and suburbs had gradually grown to 5.5 million which is 21% black which works out to perhaps 1.2 million blacks.

Thus 42 years after "desegregation" was ordered by the Supreme Court, Detroit has re-segregated itself, by both fear and choice. Suburban Detroit less the city is 4.6 million people which includes 0.5 million blacks or 11% black and I'm sure there not evenly spread out—Flint, Michigan has a majority of 80,000 blacks alone.

In 1997 I moved to the ultra liberal city of San Francisco and befriended a young coworker, whose mother, was slightly my elder and was retiring. Like many people she was looking for an affordable place to retire and the French Quarter prices are reasonable compared to San Francisco's.

Yet everywhere she went in the French Quarter she received "I'm sorry this property isn't actually for sale" or the equivalent. Do you think the fact that she was black had anything to do with this recurring answer?

Some things Dr. Martin Luther King, Jr. fought against in Chicago he did not change. For fear is a whole different mountain. The mountains of legal racism and disrespect he climbed but fear even he could not make that go away.

The mountain of blatant racism we have conquered with Political Correctness and our decision as a nation in 1965 to extend the vote to all Americans. Our mountain of racist insults we conquered with the election of Barrack Hussein Obama as president. But the mountain of fear remains—it has yet to be conquered.

Think for a moment about all the insults and charges against Obama, yes he has been accused of not being born here, when even by the testimony of the Republican Governor of Hawaii he has been declared "a natural born U.S. citizen." This even while his opponent John McCain was only a citizen of the U.S. by law. For McCain was born in a foreign country: Panama of U.S. military parents.

The point is, I have never heard Obama called a n—. Believe me, that is a ton of progress! Granted I am positive he has been called a n—in many places, I no longer choose to attend, but by comparison: When I was a child, blacks could not be elected dog catcher. Please remember, Abe Lincoln could not even get on the ballot in the South! Granted I live in a liberal rock—San Francisco, but at least Obama was on the ballot in Alabama where I was born. That is a ton of social progress, just by itself!

If you are not satisfied with the state of our nation, I applaud you. For we are far, far from perfection, but please also understand that in this far from perfect world we will never be perfect. Take hope in the progress made, and continue to fight for getting nearer to the promised land, when all of us, and I do mean "all" of us can say, come on over, let us share some good wine and food, and maybe stay for dinner too.

Choosing to work with others is a personal choice. Choosing to allow your children to associate with others requires a far higher level of trust. Bears are usually friendly, but don't get too close to its cub . . . If all you hear about is anger and riots from all around; you say sell, sell and take your children to where you feel it will be safe for them—many did this in 1861. The house used for General Lee's surrender at Appomattox, Virginia in 1865, was owned by a new tenant. His previous house had been smack in the middle of the 1st Battle of Manassas in 1861. You can run and hide, but life soon catches up.

That is reality. From 1968 with court ordered desegregation in force though out America there was plenty of yelling and screaming from schools throughout our country. Thus America re-segregated itself in the rush to (run and hide our children in) suburbia. Any question about this can be answered by looking at who belongs to your church. For they too have been re-segregated.

In Fayetteville, NC a black family asked to join our church in the 1960's. They were welcomed. About two Sunday's later their car was keyed (scratched up) while they attended church. They unfortunately soon left.

To some people, nothing not even church matters over race. In downtown San Francisco there is a (Glide Memorial United Methodist) Church known for its toleration—ain't that a shame on all of us and do note few drive to it. If our churches are racist, what does that say about the rest of us? The mountain of fear clearly has yet to be climbed.

Our other divides:

While this book has been mainly about the black/white divide the brown people and red people and yellow people divides needs to be addressed as well. While that should require another book, I must touch upon them in this book as well:

The yellow divide is truly only felt by the Japanese descendents—those imprisoned for where their ancestors were born in WWII. At last they were forgiven for this non-crime in the 1990's. A full century after the "yellow laws" for bitted further entry by immigrants from China, Korea and Japan.

Another more accurate way of stating this truth: Us white people admitted that we the people were the Romans and Jews of the Bible crucifying Jesus for the non-crime of espousing love thy neighbor. Absolute heresy in a kill or be killed world. Hopefully some day soon Chinese, Koreans and Japanese Americans will welcome all their neighbors into their homes with open hearts including each other.

For that switch from the kill or be killed world of "all" of our ancestors to the love thy neighbor world of today must and must remain our goal in this far from perfect world. Of course I am not Chinese or Korean so if you disagree with my opening line: The yellow divide . . . by Japanese—please forgive me—but they truly feel betrayed.

The red divide of broken promises and still more broken promises to Native Americans goes probably back to every colony or nation that ever dealt with them. Reality is always a hard lesson. A hard lesson of deal making between countries is—it's only valid as long as the deal benefits both parties. When circumstances change the agreement will soon change or declared invalid by whom it no longer benefits. That is why history is so filled with war.

The only way to avoid war with thy neighbor is to welcome them into your own home and tear that border between us down. Thus the Tuscarora's and Cherokee's become one nation and all can hopefully survive into the future as both Germany and France have done.

Thus when General err President Jackson told the Supreme Court "defend them (Native Americans) if they dare," he too was all but declaring war on the Supreme Court. The Native Americans had land and we the people wanted it. Not surprisingly his quotation was warmly received North and South. Killing Indians and a few lawyers was but a small price for their soon to be ex lands.

Yes our fear of Native Americans vanished with the buffalo or with the slaughter at Wounded Knee soon after in the 1890's and a few of you have grown rich on Indian Casino's—and as usual those who speak with forked tongues.

While your majorities still find the leap from the Stone Age to our modern world a bit too far. All of us must stand with you and to the extent possible help your peoples make that leap.

The brown (Hispanics) divide of rejection by many is nothing new. In colonial Pennsylvania Ben Franklin wondered about the Germans. In the 1830's it was the Irish pouring in, later it were the Italians, Poles and Russians. In the 1890's we passed the yellow laws as a prelude to anti immigrant laws of everyone in the 1920's.

I sympathize with your impoverishment for my ancestors came here before the steam engine greatly cheapened the cost of the journey. To pay for the three month journey by sail they were greeted with "sold for eight years hard labor for a thousand pounds of tobacco—In Pitt's Landing or modern Portsmouth, Va., in New Amsterdam (modern New York) it might have been a thousand pounds of wheat. In colonial America cash was always in short supply as was labor.

Yes, for eight years, sold for about $500 in our money, now that is true poverty. That is the poverty of the poor in the Old World of Scotland which would help launch the French Revolution to make this poor old world greatly better.

Granted a few of our ancestors were middle class—a few arrived on the Mayflower or in colonial Virginia—or one my other ancestor's the Gerard's of Mobile, then French. But the majority of us came for the money. This would include Walturs pronounced Valters and respelled as Walters of my great, great grandfather in the late 1800's.

How poor would you have to be to willingly sell yourself for eight years hard labor? Just to have a chance of survival in a new land willing to pay very high wages in this New World. The terms of payment have changed but to a Turkish student here to learn English—our wages are super high as he was astonished to learn in San Francisco a few years ago. So never be embarrassed by your impoverishment for all of us have been there.

Admittedly we must close the doors, for a variety of reasons. For one thing the 2010 census will reveal we have reached 100 people per square mile (PSM) in density of people. Excluding Alaska, 100 PSM may seem scattered compared to the 600 PSM in Britain or the 1100 in Holland but we are starting to rival the 200 to 300 in France and Spain, and rivaling Europe has never been our goal. So know too that you are welcome if we can only figure out how to not be swamped by your numbers.

Now Arizona (today's motto: The Grand Canyon State) has declared war on Hispanics. Try to take comfort in the following: Arizona declared war on the Grand Canyon a century ago. Teddy Roosevelt fighting to save the canyon losing to greed in congress declared it a National Monument and pledged to fight Arizona in the courts. We won that fight and we will win this fight for your rights as well.

For your rights, are my rights, and my deceased mother's right to adopt a yellow child—a Korean baby girl. Her great, great . . . grand father paid dearly for the right to come here in 1703. Sold for eight years hard labor to the highest bidder in payment for the three month trip aboard a sailing ship of the world of three centuries ago, she inherited that right paid by him. Having paid dearly for that right, if anyone dare's to challenge my sister's right to be here—I'll declare war on Arizona.

These are fighting words on her behalf and on your behalf and every other immigrant's behalf as well. No one should ever single out someone and say you must carry ID papers at all times. The Nazi's did that,—that alone should be fighting words. For in America we are all immigrants, paid dearly by all in many different ways even if some forget their own past.

The Arizona Law 1070 may be a big ado about nothing for like all laws much depends upon how it is enforced. But, let it be enforced once against a legal immigrant like me, my sister or a brown skin American and it shall be war.

Most of the people who passed this law shot down President's Bush's Immigrant Bill of 2007 sponsored by Senators McCain (of Arizona) and Kennedy—and now in defense they yell Washington does nothing! Nobody loved that bill; both liberals and conservatives had to give much. But declaring war on 10 million people in the U.S. is hardly the best answer either. There are at least 20 million U.S. citizens who are indistinguishable from these 10 million illegal's. Plus millions more of other nationalities of other divides besides Mexican-Americans.

For those many other divides and there are many both the high and comparative to their numbers the mighty Jews of America who first began to arrive in the 1600's I quite often resent your hold over our politicians, but none the less, you too I welcome.

I could keep going for there are many: Philippine's, Vietnamese, Thai's, Bangladeshi's, Indian's, Pakistani's, Iranian's, Lebanese (Danny Thomas of the 1950's—Muzyad Yakhoob and his daughter Marlo Thomas—"That Girl"—one of my first loves), Egyptian's, and how many other nations have I missed. Buddhist's, Hindu's and Muslim's and even those of other religions and even those who chose to have no religion, you too are all welcome. I am a Baptist because I choose to be so. As an American, that too is my individual right. My rights are worth fighting for and so are yours. Welcome!

At last, Barrack Hussein Obama!

Finally electing a black man president in 2008 we have as a nation conquered the mountains of hatred and disrespect, for even if we add all our minorities excluding white Catholics, Jews, Quakers and others we get perhaps 30% of the vote. Believe it or not some of them didn't vote and some voted for McCain or others. So if we assume on the high side that 25% of those 30% voted for Obama—that means at least 28% of the 70% of the white vote went to Obama. For 25%, the minority (Hispanics, African, and Asiatic) vote plus 28% of the white vote ='s 53% the total Obama vote. Granted 28% of 70% is 40% of the white vote, but in our far from perfect world 40% of the white vote was probably enough to push Obama to victory.

After all honest Abe Lincoln won with 39.8% of the total vote. Hopefully this time we will not have to fight a Civil War over it. At least

Obama was on the voter's ballot in all the states unlike Abe Lincoln. That alone is both a giant improvement and unthinkable then. Think about that, perhaps you can now understand why so many people wonder what happened to the country they were born into? Not every one finds the leap into the future easy . . .

So in this world 40% of the white vote qualifies for enough of the remaining 70% to have at least considered i.e. thought about voting for Obama and doing so. For I am confident at least one in five of those 70% of whites voting for McCain thought for at least one moment about voting for Obama. One in five of 70% is 14% plus the 40% actually voting for Obama means at least 54% of whites thought about voting for a black man. That is respect. Unthinkable, when I was child.

Our hatred is all but buried, we as a nation began burying our hatred on August 14th 1941, even if no one knew it when FDR signed the Atlantic Charter recognizing all peoples right to self determination.

It is a bit of a stretch, but people in the USA are people and thus American Indians, and those of Japanese, Chinese and every other color under the sun are people! They too are included as Dr. Martin Luther King, Jr. would soon remind us:

At Last, our Modern World takes over.

It must seem strange but the shift from the **ancient 'world of kill or be killed' to Martin Luther King's 'world of today's love thy neighbor'** requires a whole change in the way all of us think. Even Churchill and FDR (the very ones who signed the original document) failed to understand just how big a leap it was when they signed The Atlantic Charter. A Sea Change in thought was coming as the dreamers of 1919 were at last beginning to rise to power.

This Sea Change in thought would not even begin to take over until the 1960's explosion forced the adult world to acknowledge a rebellion was in progress. A great view of this in hindsight is reruns of The Archie Bunker Show." Our WWII generation suddenly found themselves being held to far higher standards of conduct then the kill or be killed world ever expected of them.

Our conduct in Africa, Asia and the world were now being judged by the world court of public opinion even if "The World Court" was held in absolute contempt by our WWII generation who still yelled bah humbug to its findings.

The scene from the Civil Rights War that hit home with me personally was when a group of black men wearing raincoats braced themselves against a brick wall as they were being hosed down in Birmingham turned their backs and clearly printed were the words "I am a Man." I struggling to be a man clearly understood their message.

When the Supreme Court ordered us, we the people, to desegregate in 1954—that was just the Supreme Court, not we the people. Ten years later after Martin had marched on Washington, we passed Kennedy's Civil Rights Bill and in 1965 **we the people** passed the Voter Rights Act after Bloody Sunday in Selma, Alabama.

In 1968 the Supreme Court ordered we the people to desegregate. We could have elected some one who like, Andrew Jackson who would have challenged the Court to "defend them, if they dare."

We the people did not challenge the Supreme Court to **step in front of a firing squad** of Americans who disagreed with their decision. Instead both Republicans and Democrats declared war on our hatreds.

Many dammed the Courts but we instead chose to conquer our hatreds. But 400 years of slavery, Jim Croeness, and the only good Indian is a dead Indian and imprisoning Japanese for the crime of being Japanese do not go easily, in climbing these mountains of hatred and disrespect we built even higher:

The Mountain of . . . FEAR:

In 1968 we integrated—it was war, absolute hell in our schools as blacks and whites fought the Civil Rights War from Boston to L.A. and thousands of schools in between. In my high school the 1968-69 school year was hell on earth. The Highway Patrol was called almost daily until they set up camp at the high school. At 71st Senior High outside of Fayetteville, North Carolina it was my Junior Year. The school board in recognizing the Supreme Courts decision to require integration throughout the nation after years and years of delay since its 1954 ruling outlawing segregation for any reason chose to make the black high school our junior high and the white high school the senior high for all. So, 71st High became 71st Senior High.*

Both blacks and whites were both use to running our schools, both wanted to run their school, period. It was hell. Welcome to America at war with itself over Civil Rights at home and oh yeah, that war overseas called Vietnam. When I was a child, a friend and I dug up a black ant pile and dumped it on a red ant pile. Ants have no eyes but they quickly realized them ants, ain't us. Fascinating it was. That's how 1968 was but if you were getting beat up, fascinating was not how you would have described it. War is hell. Yeah that's 1968, both in Vietnam and here in America.

All across America war at school was hell in America. Fortunately in my high school many of us were Army/Air Force brats who had gone to school with each other in far off places like Germany and Japan. These battles of 1968 were probably fought long ago when Truman ordered our military to desegregate.

Thus both Germany and Japan came to America's rescue. Or at least us kids who having gone to school peaceably in far away places recognized them others as us, no matter the color of our skin. Thus in my senior year (1969-1970) we elected the ex black high school's Sophomore President (Ronnie Newkirk) our Senior Class High President, and our ex Junior President our High School President.

Peace at last—you can not imagine the shock of racist in both races. Most schools across America were not so lucky, so the war continued. In Boston a most liberal city war spread to the streets as America faced up to its racism, squarely in the face, and MLK was no longer with us to lead us to the promised land of love for all.

While our politicians screamed bloody murder about what the Supreme Court was doing to us; few were willing to actually fire bullets for our politicians of both parties had already decided not to kill one another for it was not their personal property at risk as in 1860. Our politicians gave themselves a pay raise and moved their kids to private schools.

Our politicians of both liberals and conservatives of all stripes yelled and screamed which you have heard many, many times since while leaving us the people to sort things out for ourselves. For the past forty years we have been doing so. After fighting these all out polite wars in our schools we moved them as fast as possible to suburbia and left the wars to our cities.

Now to Write the Unspeakable:

While many cities like St. Louis, Birmingham and Detroit have been taken over by blacks—the view of many whites. If you live in a liberal rock like San Francisco these are called all out polite wars; we decided in the 1960's not to shoot one another but disagree—that, we can still agree on. The level of anger between the races, varies widely by locale but make no exception; it still exists. "Four hundred years of slavery and Jim Crowness is a very heavy burden to carry and whittie knows this" (and he still has guns) to quote Dean Kenneth Monteiro of SFSU (with my commentary).

In New Orleans historically a liberal Catholic French city bus segregation ended when the bus service simply decided to remove the signs without a fight in the 1960's. The blacks had moved into the majority in the 1980's and elected several black mayors, then came Katrina and the battle of the races suddenly began anew.

For like the plaques of the past the flood of Katrina affected the poorest more severely than the wealthy. While the flood did not care about the color of our skin, we apparently did. Wealthy people were willing to pay extra to live on the high ground which rarely flooded. Shockingly white people were the majority of the wealthy who gladly paid extra to live in the French Quarter which was built there because when the French arrived before dikes called levees locally were built; it was the only high and dry ground.

Five years after Katrina this war continues over which neighborhoods get rebuilt. The participants will call it many different things but it still comes down to white vs. black. Or if you prefer black vs. white but race is what it is all about.

Many cities have merged with the county (as in Jacksonville, Fla. and Indianapolis, Ind.) to prevent blacks from taking political power. In North Carolina the state passed laws enable ling cities to aggressively annex areas even against the will of the people.

Thus Fayetteville a very old city going back to colonial Cross Creek lumber cutting mills at the Piedmont rapids of the Cape Fear River to the coastal lowlands suddenly became one of the fastest growing cities in America in the 1990's growing from 76,000 to 121,000 a 60% jump in a decade. The county grew 10% from 275,000 to 303,000. The percentage black population is 42% in the city and 35% in the county, so the war err race of the races continues unabated. They might call it many things but race matters—a lot.

Cross Creek renamed Fayetteville after the Marquis de La Fayette (of Revolutionary War fame) visited the U.S. after the French Revolution and the creeks no longer crossed each other in the town rose to a small city as one of the southern terminuses of "Tobacco Road" north to Richmond, Virginia. Yes by the Civil War, Fayetteville had grown to wealth on the backs of slavery enforced with the whip and when needed the guns of hatred.

Modified by the opening of Ft. Bragg in WWI which is now the home of the Airborne this is a city of great hatreds with many, many hatreds since. My brother still recalls the welcome sign to new arrivals in the 1960's as: "Welcome to Fayetteville, the home of the Ku Klux Klan." New Orleans, this was not. San Francisco, . . . but a distant dream.

This is a war of fear about fear that is still ongoing throughout America that I can write little more about for its outcome lies in your future and not in my past. I can only hope that we will welcome our neighbors regardless of color or religion as neighbors and continue to discover one heart at a time that they are in fact us, so that we need not to repeat the errors of the past.

We should remember that all lands inhabited by all peoples are full of tales of Tuscarawas hunting down the last of the Cherokees to extinction but rarely the arrival of a third party to exterminate the Tuscarawas instead. All of us have been guilty of mass murder, for the Neanderthals are no more anywhere.

Just how far do we need to go?

If you want a measuring stick of how far we need to go: I suggest we rename all U.S. counties after that honored person of the Western World: 'Obama' as the winner of the Nobel Peace Prize for giving us hope—that are now named Jeff Davis or Jefferson Davis—the President of the Confederate States of America. When Georgia, Louisiana, Mississippi and Texas do that, the nation of fear will have been won—please, do not hold your breath.

And note for the record these same four ex Confederate states all led the nation in the number of illegal lynching's murdering over 300 blacks—each between 1877 and 1939.

I'd be happy if they rename them Lincoln—after all they are all but solid Republican states now. For now how about the land of Lincoln welcoming each other as both friend and neighbor:

In 1919 Chicago exploded in five days of war between the races. Blacks entered into an unmarked white only beach—they were not welcome, soon driven off that might have been the end, but it wasn't.

Meanwhile on the water a group of blacks were playing on a raft, it too had drifted over into the front of this un-marked white-only beach. One white threw rocks at them eventually one struck home—killing a black having fun. It was fun no longer. The other blacks on the raft charge ashore, a policeman arrives and arrests one of the blacks, not the white who threw the killing rock. Now it was war. Five days later, 23 blacks and 15 whites laid dead and white only signs were now everywhere.

Dr. Martin Luther King, Jr. tried to remove those signs of fear. Even he could not do so. Today in the aftermath of the riotous 1960's for the most part they have disappeared. But make no mistake they still exist in the hearts of millions of Chicagoans and many more millions across America.

I'll never forget returning to the U.S.A. in 1968 and discovering "white only" signs just across the street north of Washington D.C. Until then I had always lived in the South, Hawaii or Germany. In the South—I as a white had basically thought nothing of it.

Not seeing any such signs in either Hawaii or Germany and knowing America had been torn by race riots I simply had no idea that in Maryland—a Northern (slave) state was almost as bad as the South. I too needed an education—like Martin Luther King, Jr. it just took me a life time. He of course learned enough on his wedding night.

In the mean time while we wait for those abominations to end we might ask what is our own school, church, synagogue, or mosque doing to end the fear in our hearts. After all even in the 1950's a few good people had the guts to stand with Martin and fight for justice non-violently in Montgomery, Alabama—and yes a few of them were white.

* How did 71ˢᵗ High School get its numerical name? There are two stories:

AUTHOR NOTES

1—After the British surrender at Yorktown, the 71ˢᵗ Highland Regiment POW's were planted here awaiting the end of the war in two years. So many POW's decided to stay, they eventually decided to name their elementary (which I attended for one year before it literally fell down under the weight of us baby boomers) and later high school after their old regiment.

2—The less colorful reason: Once upon a long time ago the state was plotting out the future school districts and #71 was along Raeford Road and went unnamed and like Nome, Alaska was stuck with it. Nome is 'no' (fold in the map) 'me' with the 'na' as in name i.e. 'no name' for the tiny town. So #71 became 71ˢᵗ and No-me became Nome.

CHAPTER X:

Making Capitalism Work for Everyone

HOW CAN WE make capitalism work, for every one? By making everyone a capitalist! Now, how do we make everyone a capitalist, with-out destroying everyone's incentives for working, you might ask? After all, if everyone is a capitalist, why should anyone work? That is the question that has doomed every scheme before. We certainly do not want to create a system that relies heavily upon fear, as the motivation for working. My proposal avoids that, by increasing the rewards, for working!

The minimum wage conundrum:

The easiest way to increase the rewards for working, many people will argue, is by increasing the minimum wage. This has two very real drawbacks: In the first place, the minimum wage only affects our poorest workers, unless we want to raise the minimum very high, to say $20.00, or even $30.00 per hour. This however, has a very big drawback: Every time you raise the minimum wage, you eliminate jobs.

This is because whether we like it or not, every one of us, are competing with both automation, and $1.00 per hour workers in Mexico and as we have recently discovered, with 25 cent per hour workers in China and Bangladesh. Some people might argue, nonsense, how would you replace workers at say, fast food restaurants?

My answer is: not as hard as you might think. If the minimum wage were raised to say $20.00 or $30.00 per hour, I guarantee, you would see more "make your own" sandwich shops. Much as you already see, make your own salads, today.

What about corner groceries? There would be fewer of them, and most of them would be family run enterprises, where the minimum wage would not apply. What about hotel/motel housekeepers? You would see again more family run facilities where the minimum wage would not apply. In short, we are all replaceable, to at least some degree, whether we like it or not.

Fulfilling Jefferson's Dream:

Some two hundred years ago, Thomas Jefferson said his dream of America's future was, that "America should become a nation of yeoman farmers." For all my adult life, I mistakenly belittled that statement, as thinking poorly on his part. I mean really, his dream was that we should be a nation of farmers!

In his time, clearly there was a need for industrial growth. Farmers, both big and small we had plenty of, while we were almost totally dependent on imports for manufactured goods.

His political opponents led by Washington and Hamilton, advocated the development of manufactures, which was destined to be our future. To me Jefferson, the supposed revolutionary was being regressive in advocating we should make our future "a nation of small farmers." As in so many other things, I was so wrong!

Another translation into modern words for "yeoman farmers" is: small "independent" farmers. This is now what I think, he was thinking then. The small farmer of his day, owned his own land, though they tended to be dominated by slave plantations in the South, and non-slave plantations in New York.

Jefferson's dream was that the small independent farmer would become the backbone of our republic, both in the North and South. Please forgive him of his ignorance, in the world he lived in, incomes had never doubled. Our modern world of incomes doubling every fifty years, he could not for-see.

The great strengths of the yeoman farmer were that he was both a worker on the land that he owned and a business man who had to sell his produce. We could also say that he was both a worker and a capitalist with his farm being his capital.

Thus is what he meant by his dream of us becoming "a nation of yeoman farmers," was "a nation of worker capitalists," or middle class capitalists if you prefer.

Having lived in 18th century France and visiting industrial Britain with their stark class structures between the rich and poor, Jefferson probably was dreaming that we would stay a middle class dominated society. We now know what his dream was and therefore what needs to be done to fulfill his dream. The only remaining question is, how?

Ever since the rise of modern industrial capitalism about 1800, many caring people have tried in many ways to either improve or replace capitalism entirely. This is because capitalism "in the raw" only works for the rich and powerful. All efforts to replace capitalism, have failed miserably. All efforts to modify or tame capitalism have only partly succeeded. The fact is, almost everyone would agree on "every form of modified capitalism in use today, needs improving on." Whether it is the American, European, Japanese or Latin American variants, there seems to be either too much "modification," or too much "capitalism." Your view basically defines whether you are a liberal, or a conservative. In America, it largely defines Democrats and Republicans as well.

The reason all these efforts have failed, is because people lose sight of, or just don't realize that people only work for two reasons: They want—to gain the benefits of working, and/or they fear—the consequences of not working. If you destroy the benefits of working—communism, you only have their fears, to force people to work—Stalinism.

If you destroy or eliminate their fears of not working—socialism, selling the benefits of working, becomes near impossible, because they get nearly the same benefits for not working. So, once again how can we make capitalism work, for everyone?

Having been a worker for peanuts all my life, I know all too well the despair of our poor. The despair is very real; it permeates their lives almost every living moment. To the wealthy or even middle class it is difficult to understand what it means to go through life, with-out hope for a better life.

With-out hope; what an awful thing not to have, yet tens of millions of Americans have just that, no hope for a better life. Having worked in hotels most of my life, I have always been impressed with the hard working housekeeping staffs. For all too many of these people, they know their lives will never get better. Yet, they struggle on, because somehow they know, it's the right thing to do. They know it is right full to earn one's living no matter how meager and wrong to live off of welfare. They usually are either immigrants, or most despairingly of all, members of what has become our all too largely permanent underclass. It is these, the hard working poor Americans who are long overdue some real help.

During the Civil War, General Sherman promised the freed slaves, forty acres and a mule. A promise never kept, for a variety of reasons. I'll be charitable and mention one, people began to realize that the freed slaves were so horribly educated, many not even knowing how to count money, that they would quickly be cheated out of their forty acres and a mule, so that it would be largely, pointless.

We should remember that this level of criminal education imposed by the slave owners, is where our majority black population, has had to claw their way up from. When one realizes the importance of our parents' education or lack of in our own development into who we are, perhaps you can see why it is such a tall mountain for so many to climb. This tall mountain is made even taller by our segregationist societies of both yesterday and today. It should be little wonder that so many slip, lose their footing, and fall into the traps of despair, alcohol, drugs and crime.

While there are many causes for crime, almost everyone can see its connection with poverty. But the connection is not with poverty, otherwise crime would have soared during the depression years when it did not. The connection is with the despair of having lost hope. Get rich quick schemes, always appeal, to those who know they have no chance of getting rich or living the good life, any other way. My proposal will not make the poor rich, it will however empower them to acquire property, and above all, to hope for a better life, by honest work, even at the lowest wages.

The idea of being propertied is so important to any society, because anyone who has property has a permanent stake, in the well-being of that society. Our permanent under class have climbed as a society, a good part up that tall mountain, don't you think it's time we deliver on that promise of forty acres and a mule—in an updated form. With the proper safeguards, we could revolutionize our society for the better.

The facts of our criminally colossal crime rates despite over two million Americans in prison today, is a monstrous indictment of our failure as a society, to give hope to what has become our permanent underclass. Building more prisons is like building more work houses as in 19th century Britain, to sweep our un-wanted American citizens off the streets and out of sight! Surely building more prisons is no worthy solution. Thomas Jefferson and our other founding fathers would be ashamed.

I do not want to either build more work houses or give our poor another welfare program. My experiences in talking with them, convinces me that regardless of their good intentions, welfare programs simply do not work. While they do provide humanitarian help, they also destroy a person's desire to help themselves.

About twenty (now thirty!) years ago, I was working for H. & R. Block, in New Orleans, when two young black girls sat down in front of me. As I was doing the tax form, one answered: Single, no children. The other exclaimed: "What, you mean you don't have a baby! Don't you know all the money you get from having a baby!"

Now there are many great reasons for having children, but if the biggest one is welfare programs, of any type, something is really rotten somewhere.

My proposal is an I.R.A. program for every worker tilted toward those who need them the most who currently do not have them, the working poor. Instead of welfare or more prisons, a helping hand is what I propose. The working poor simply must earn these benefits, for their own "earned" self esteem welfare. The worker must feel that they themselves have earned the benefits of their work which they will have, at least partly. That is why the worker must make a major contribution.

The employer must make a major contribution, in order to give that helping hand substance. The government must give a flat amount, in order to tilt the benefits toward those who need them the most, the working poor who will now be able, to have genuine hope for a better life, by good old honest work.

The exact amounts of income and matching employer's contributions are not important. The exact government contribution, of so many cents or even dollars per hour worked, is not important. If you want to cap the mandatory contribution levels, at any income level above say $50,000 incomes per year that too is fine.

What is important is the concept, of:
Empowering the working poor, to lift themselves, out of their
present hopeless despair, by *earning their way out.*

It is my belief that this plan will do just that, with-in five years of its enactment every working person should be able to see their rapidly rising personal account balances. They will be dreamily talking to their co-workers and their children about what they are going to do with their money. Think how that could truly revolutionize our current permanent under class. Think about what this could do to our current atrocious crime rate—by giving hope to the hopeless.

This would also energize all our working class people to work harder for all Americans would benefit from this savings plan. It would further effectively solve our future Social Security problems by helping each worker to build their own retirement program.

Yes, Thomas Jefferson you were right two hundred years ago, our future should be a nation of yeoman farmers. By updating "yeoman farmers," with the 21st century "worker capitalists" Jefferson's 19th century dream can be our future. Together, we can empower our hopeless, to dream, the impossible dreams, that no longer, need to be impossible. The only remaining question is: Do we have the guts to seize the bull by the horns, and tame the capitalist beast into working, for everyone.

Yes, we need to seize our economy by the horns and re-design it for "we the people's" interest, not Wall Streets. If we do it right we can all be capitalists and workers at the same time! That would make many enlightened Wall Street-ers happy. This plan should be implemented once the economy gets growing, for initially it will take some money out of spending. Later monies could be released to stimulate the economy.

My proposal: Every Worker a Capitalist:

1—The minimum wage is to be raised to $7.00 per hour over 2 years.
2—Every worker or salaried person have a company run, government monitored, Individual Retirement Account (I.R.A.) available. That goes with them from job to job. Current company I.R.A.'s could apply.
3—Every worker or salaried person, be allowed to contribute up to five percent, with a required matching amount, by their employer.

4—The government contributes fifty cents per hour, for every hour worked per year, up to a maximum contribution of $1,000.00 per year.
5—While this might be called a "retirement" program, some of this money would also be available for home purchases, education, and even some for a trip to Maui if that is what the individual wants. After all this will be their money.

This would mean a single full time worker, at the minimum wage (now $7.00 per hour) earning $14,000 per year would contribute $700.00, matched by their employer, plus (50 cents x 2000 hours =) $1,000 from the government for a total annual investment of $2,400 per year. Our working poor would then be investing 17% of their income in building a better America for themselves and you. Yes, this is revolutionary.

Let's examine these proposals: To properly do so, we must look at the cost/ benefit ratio. Let's start with the costs: First of all, the cost would be high but considering most middle class people already have IRA's that would be applicable, the expense would be primarily for our poor who do not have them.

To business, about $100 billion total in new expenditures, ouch! On the other hand, that's less then one percent of our $14 trillion economy. Over a two year phase-in period, that's less than half of half a percent per year. They may not like it, but they can easily handle that cost.

To the individual workers and salaried people, another $100 billion total, again ouch. Remember however, this plan is for their benefit and voluntary, so before you scream no way, please wait until you see the benefit side.

To the taxpayer's, about $150 billion total, (another) ouch. This is not a cheap proposal, revolutionizing society never is. The question that must be answered in the affirmative is: Would the benefits outweigh these large costs? Let's take a look at the benefits:

The direct benefits of my proposal:

Real People:	Annual Earned Income:	What they would have, After 5 years:	After 10 years:
Single working mom, currently, with no hope:	$14,000	$12,000	$24,000
Poor working family, currently, with little hope:	$28,000	$24,000	$48,000
Lower middle class working couple:	$40,000	$30,000	$60,000
Upper middle class single worker family:	$80,000	$50,000	$100,000
Upper middle class two worker family:	$100,000	$70,000	$140,000

The above table is based on each person working (40 hours x 50 weeks=) 2,000 hours per year. With no inflation, compounded interest, or capital gains included.

Focus on the single working mom, currently with no hope. Under this plan, in just 5 years, she has $12,000. That's enough for a down payment on a modest house! In 10 years, she would have $24,000! That's a big down payment, to get the monthly bill down to an affordable level, in most of the U.S.A.

Even if she did the above, 5 years later she would have another $12,000 to help put her children in college or trade school, so they would have a better future. Now that is empowerment. That is what every working person in America should earn, at the minimum! We can do this, at an affordable cost. If we take into account interest and capital gains, the benefits would of course be even greater, even after discounting for inflation.

Now look at the other people on this simple chart. Their benefits are even greater, because the benefits are earned by working! This allows every working American to be a capitalist, without destroying the incentive to work.

With this plan, the more you earn, the more you gain! If this plan is enacted, America would be transformed or even revolutionized into the nation we should be, the nation Thomas Jefferson dreamed of.

How can I say that, you might ask? Think about it this way, When America was founded back in 1789, we were founded by an overwhelmingly capitalist people, for the majorities of each state were independent small capitalists, their capital being their farms and small stores that they owned.

To paraphrase Thomas Jefferson, we can once again, be a nation of yeoman capitalists. That was his vision, of what America's future should be and we can make it happen!

What do you mean by yeomen capitalists? Well, if we take all those annual contributions over time, keeping inflation adjusted out because no one can accurately predict inflation, and it also clutters, but factoring in a conservative net 3 percent real growth, and a braver 5 percent real growth we can see how these monies can really grow by "working into genuine capital" (my definition of yeoman capitalist), with no withdrawals:

Real People:	Single minimum wage worker	Poor working: family:
Annual Earned Income:	$14,000	$28,000
Their contribution:	$ 700	$ 1,400
Employer' matching:	$ 700 $	1,400
Government's:	$ 1,000	$ 2,000
Total annual contributions:	$ 2,400	$ 4,800
At a real return of:	@3% or @5%	@3% or @5%
after 10 years:	$ 27,510 $ 30,103	$ 55,020 $ 60,206
After 20 years:	$ 64,479 $ 79,220	$128,958 $158,440
After 30 years:	$114,162 $158,014	$228,324 $316,028
After 40 years:	$179,935 $287,071	$359,870 $574,142

The benefits or individual account balances for lower middle class and upper income people would be obviously, even greater: In direct proportion to their combined contributions:

After 40 years they would have according to the above table rules:

The Lower Middle Class family:	@3%:	$ 448,343
	@5%:	$ 717,051

The upper middle class single worker family: $1,183,085 @ 5%. The upper middle class two worker family: $1,656,319 @ 5% and these are the minimums, you could save even more producing even greater returns!

These dollar amounts are in today's money. So were talking real money, what I call yeoman capital. Even the poorest of our poor workers would be empowered to become a minor capitalist ($287,071 @ 5%)! To Bill Gates a quarter million dollars might be chump change, but to the single working mom, it's a pipe dream, and we can make it happen!

Yes, even she could take a well deserved trip to Maui.
The real benefit would be too all of us:

There are other benefits to this program, besides the obvious above: By empowering our current permanent hopeless poor to realize there is genuine hope for them to have a better life by working, they will want to earn their way to that realization. The get rich schemes of crime will have far less appeal to them, because they will know they can attain everyone's goal of a better life by good old honest work.

Our whole society will then benefit from this plan far out weighing its costs. **Building homes for the poor is far cheaper in the long run then more prisons**—our founding fathers would be proud of us.

So too would Dr. Martin Luther King, Jr. after all if our permanent underclass joined our middle class would you not be glad to have them as a neighbor? This would of course fulfill his dream of accepting his children for the content of their hearts.

This we can do, at minimal cost. We can turn our capitalist world upside down! Do not listen to the detractors, after all it is their power over us; the peons of olde that we want to reverse! Granted not everyone will want this, even those at the bottom, who would demand their money NOW!

Pay them.

Let them realize their error over time. But, do not let the majority go down the sink hole of our past Gilded Age!

Let us make America the home of the middle class again, Teddy Roosevelt and Tom Jefferson would sing in our joy!

Plus remember the side benefits of people realizing that good ole honest work even sweeping streets and sidewalks at the morgue would provide them with:

Empowerment!

Please you the little guy, tell me what's wrong with that?

Absolutely nothing.

I say let the rich scream! Let the poor rejoice!

Heck, someday we might even invite the ex poor to come over and share some fine wine together.

Hey, why not stay for dinner?

That my friends is how to treat the downtrodden. Do this and once again we would lead the world in how to raise everyone to the middle class again.

Once upon a time my ancestors flocked to America because just doing so meant—if you survived—joining the middle class.

With this program in place everyone just by working—no surviving required—just more work and you too would be a member of the middle class no matter what you worked as.

Yet the greatest benefit is, the more you make the greater the benefits so you get rewarded for staying in school and acquiring greater knowledge for greater rewards!

In essence:

It's a win, baby, just win solution!

CHAPTER XI

Where do we go from here?
Is it all downhill from here?

No, its uphill, all we got to do is climb.
So, let's start climbing:

THE MAIN REASON our best days are still ahead of us, is we are a democracy, and like it or not that means we have the power to re-invent ourselves. I don't think we have to re-create our constitution either.

Franklin (died 1791), Washington (died 1799), Hamilton (shot dead 1805), Jefferson (AM 4 July, 1826) Adams (a few hours later) and all the other founders knew we were a big country and would hopefully grow even bigger. North and South disagreed and New York vs. New England goes way, back even before 1789. Heck even 1776 was war for ever between them.

Fortunately, when Burgoyne invaded New York from Canada he just had to send Indians to raid New England, scaring the hell out of areas just recovering from the French and Indian War.

Thank you very much, Burgoyne. Only then did New England come to Albany's defense. Us agreeing has been rare, without a fight, first. Usually the U must fight the S. Then we compromise and move on.

All the above people believed in settling our western lands and they knew that would mean still more problems. George III had solved that problem by prohibiting settlement beyond the Appalachians. Our founders knew our soon to be Westerners would face new problems needing new solutions that the more settled Easterners would not like. So they designed a Federal government that required other people to follow them to compromise.

That is why we have elections! If you want to blame the Tea Party Republicans, so be it. If not blame the Obama-crats and vote them out. If you don't go to the polls and vote one or the other out, you are to blame!

You think we have problems, try 1862 when the North discovered the South wasn't just going to role over. Lincoln grew old for a very good reason, (like many people he had relatives fighting and dying on both sides) and we are still paying interest on that huge debt which was far greater than our 1862 economy.

That debt was so staggering we even passed the 14th Amendment to assure the future that we the people would someday pay it off. Yet we survived that crisis and we can survive this one. Just start climbing. Heck, we even won WWII. Another debt we are still paying.

So where and how do we climb? Having listening to President Obama and Speaker of the House Boehner dueling with each other over a compromise to raise the debt limit, I have become convinced that both are good guys battling the bad guys with-in their own parties. I am sixty years old, so I don't like hearing about cuts to retirement spending of any kind. If you buy my book I hope to be wealthy, so I don't want my taxes raised either! But compromise, we must.

The Art of the Compromise:

Yet Obama was willing to go to the Democrats and fight for $2.4 trillion in future spending cuts while Boehner was willing to go to the Republicans and fight for $800 billion in future revenue increases (raising taxes on the rich by eliminating their deductions).

Forget the amounts **both were willing to compromise;** the Demo's yelled at Obama so he came back with an additional $400 billion in actual tax increases. Meanwhile the Republicans yelled apparently even louder at Boehner; so he walked out of the talks.

Now, who was wrong? I think neither, both were willing to compromise. That is how we stay together as a nation, we compromise. Thereby Civil Wars are rare.

The alternative is no compromise and we split and go our own way. Pretty soon California goes left while Texas goes right. Then California splits between liberal San Francisco and L.A. the home of Ronald Reagan. Finally, the "Gay" Castro District is too leftist for Sacramento (farm country) to tolerate so Northern California splits.

The same thing happens in Ohio as well as Texas (remember LBJ and his big spending anti poverty bills) because no one will compromise. Sooner or later someone decides to fight, and the New World becomes the Old

World where France and Germany declared war upon the other after 814 (The Treaty of Verdun) and don't quit until 1945, when both are crushed.

Eleven hundred years of war to prove what? Absolutely nothing; this explains why they are at peace today. Because **they finally leaned how to compromise,** do we have to prove we are as stupid as the Germans and French because we can't! Think about it, our history is famous for compromising, The original gang (above) compromised and that is why Washington, D.C. is where it is. The great compromises of 1820 and 1850 which at least postponed our Civil War.

Balance what a wonderful thing, both political parties denounce it as a horrifying thing, I personally could not disagree more. Our founding fathers designed a system so compromise could easily happen. But we must live up to their minimal standards. By being willing to climb up and compromise.

I say look at your Senator or Congressman or woman and if they rejected Obama as a Democrat, vote them out! If your Senator or Congressman or woman rejected Boehner as a Republican, vote them out! I actually am an independent, but I register as if I am a loyal party man.

Many of us live in districts that are very liberal or very conservative. My district is now San Francisco which is so liberal that you should picture demonstrators yelling at President Clinton for trying to prevent another holocaust! Yeah, they did that.

I kid you not, people here were furious that a Democrat would use our military to try preventing another holocaust. So when people make jokes about us, know there probably right. The Republicans have their equivalents; which explains Ron Paul of Texas. Ron Paul is so far to the right he sometimes agrees with the far left. It scares me! But a democracy, we are.

So be brave and look at your Senator or Congressman or woman and be willing to vote them out in the primary. I am a registered Democrat, even though I voted for Bush, Senior twice! Not Bush, Junior, I held my nose, and voted for anyone but Junior. **But vote, that is not only your right but your duty as a citizen.** Otherwise, just welcome Prince Charles as our new king!

But as a registered Democrat I can vote against Nancy Pelosi! If a dedicated opponent runs against her in a primary I might have the power to vote her out! Yes, my vote can matter.

The same goes for very conservative districts. Register as a Republican, it's no more a nasty name than Democrat. You can still vote for whoever you want in the general election just as I voted for Bush Senior twice. I believe in voting for the candidate, like Obama, not the party. The art of the compromise, life ain't perfect, so let's learn how to make a deal and we will see who I will vote for in 2012. Making a deal gets us to the next election, where maybe we can win no matter how you feel. Personally I prefer a balanced approach, so let us:

Quickly review our short History, shall we:

Part one:

First comes George Washington (1789-1797): Politically, I could not disagree more with the rich guy (G.W.) for the rich, but the man; I must go with Colonel Ben Franklin of the French and Indian War (1754-1761): "Now their goes a man (G.W.), that I would gladly follow into battle." . . . "First in war, first in peace and first in the hearts of his countrymen."

Next comes Thomas Jefferson (1801-1809): Who revolutionized our revolution by setting the white man truly free. We decided that who your parents were would not decide your fate. The Federalists and their dreams of the officers of the revolution determining our future alone were now our history like the British Empire. You and you alone now decide your future.

Thirdly comes Andrew Jackson (1829-1837): Who introduced us to the 'Slave' Democratic Party, who warred upon the banks literally forcing them to be our friends.

Then comes Abraham (Abe) Lincoln (1861-1865): Introducing us to the Republican Party. This wise young man, aged by the terrible Civil War, we had all known was probably coming since the 1790's—killed by the last bullet.

Thus the 'Radical' Republicans took over, (1865-1901): Where you can't stop progress, so bow before the ever so concentrated wealth of the future. The right wing or Tea Party Republicans now ruled America. The Democrats, rightly blamed for the Civil War were so unpopular it's a wonder that they survived. Survived they did but they could only win the presidency by out conservativing the Tea Party under Grover Cleveland!

Part Two:

Finally Teddy Roosevelt—Republican (1901-1909) : Introduced us to our modern world, by warring upon the rich Tea Party Republicans. Crushing the giant corporations like U.S. Steel and Standard Oil while passing all kinds of new laws to protect "we the people" like the Income Tax, The Pure Food and Drug Act, and our National Park Service.

Then came the most unpopular war in U.S. history: World War I. Woodrow Wilson (Democrat) gave the world that wonderful thought:

Interruption: for a worldwide revolt, stars here:

The Dream of 1919; Self Determination.

An idea so basic, yet so rejected by the iron clad rulers of this world. Our rulers of this earth had here to fore decreed that you there, you now belong to him, and you over there you now belong to me, because we the rulers of this earth have decided so.

We the people like Thomas Jefferson and the French Revolution rejected our rulers decrees. "We the People," of the world rose up and overthrew the royalty, or the Federalists of old. This was a revolution of the most basic kind, it would take decades to ferment with Gandhi in India of the 1930's, Eleanor Roosevelt pushing the Atlantic Charter onto her husband in 1941, and then into as a founding document of the United Nations in 1945. Only in the 1960's would it explode in the West, as we the people rose up and denounced our rulers actions in the third world.

Woodrow Wilson (1913-1921): Gave WWI to America and we the people rejected it and the Palmer raids to crush the we the people revolt as a result. Thus the Republicans took over as we jointly (both parties) declared war on war itself!

With the rich Tea Party back in charge the rich grew rich beyond belief, and beyond the economy's ability to handle so the Great Depression soon followed. After three years of soaring bread lines we were determined to elect someone who would restore "We the People" back to governance, thus:

Franklin Delano Roosevelt—Democrat (1933-1945): In one hundred days he restored hope to we the people, but little else. Truth be said, he had no more a clue to how to solve the Great Depression than anyone else, so we staggered along in the 1930's with the Jim Crow South quietly ruling America.

Then came WWII and problem solved by massive war spending even while the workers were seduced into buying war bonds on truly massive scales, after all their wasn't much else to buy; but future dreams anyway . . .

Harry Truman (1945-1953): Brought victory and salvation to a broken world while Eleanor brought the Atlantic Charter and Human Rights to the newly created United Nations. While France and Germany tentatively started to talk peace to one another. While America exploded at our communists everywhere according to Senator McCarthy as the Cold War intervened, so taxes continued high into the future . . .

Dwight Eisenhower (1953-1961): Everybody likes Ike! Brought peace and stability to America if that communist agitator Dr. Martin Luther King, Jr. would just go away. The Reverend King would not so . . .

Part Three:

We the People explode:
demanding our dreams be fulfilled, NOW!

John F. Kennedy (1961-1963): Dr Martin Luther King Jr. led a march on Washington that transformed a nation. JFK cut taxes on the rich, man was he popular! Then he probably made the plunge to the left, but assassinated, so we really do not know . . .

Lyndon Baines Johnson—LBJ—(1963-1969) Solves how to get reelected by starting a little war in Vietnam and sponsors the Civil Rights Bill and the Voter Rights Act and the dreamers of 1919 explodes against him as the South soon joins:

Richard Nixon—Republican (1969-1974): Tricky Dickey goes to China, to somehow end the war in Vietnam with honor? Nobody understands what he is doing but only Nixon (the former anti communist house leader of the McCarthy days) could go to China! Meanwhile his Watergate efforts come to light and he is forced to resign.

Gerald Ford—Republican (1974-1977): A nice guy, who never wanted the job.

Jimmy Carter—Democrat (1977-1981): Gave the world a heavy dose of human rights but the Iran hostage crisis did his presidency in.

Ronald Reagan—Republican (1981-1989): Now if it wasn't bad enough with both Democrats and Republicans eliminating the Jackson era Usury Laws for all time. A temporary fix was needed, but permanent? Reagan cut taxes on the rich like JFK, so we the workers of America could benefit from all this "trickling down" effect. I hope you are enjoying all these tax cuts for the rich, now . . . I sure don't! So now you know why Ronnie Reagan is so popular with the Tea Party Republicans!

George Bush, Sr.—Republican (1989-1993): The Cold War suddenly ended when the Dreamers of 1919 at last exploded underneath the communist rulers of Eastern Europe and the Soviet Empire collapsed under Gorbachev who like Churchill was left wondering; what the hell, just happened!

Recognizing a wonderful opportunity offered the Democrats a deal: If you take the heat for cutting domestic spending, I'll take the heat for cutting defense spending and raising taxes on the rich, thus together we will balance the budget.

My kind of Republican!
A real politician like Theodore Roosevelt
would have done far better . . .

Most unfortunately, a politician he never was. GB Sr. had lost in his run for the House, and had moved up by appointment to Nixon and Ford's White House staffs and onto Ronald Reagan's VP. With Reagan's popularity he virtually inherited the White House. Then he raised taxes . . . When the Tea Party Republicans led by Ross Perot exploded at him shouting "Where is the beef?" GB Sr. lost to:

Bill Clinton—Democrat (1993-2001): Who along with the Republican House gladly accepted the credit for balancing the budget! After all Bush Sr. and the Democratic House had agreed to balance the budget over time . . .

George Bush, Jr. Republican (2001-2009): This administration was so bad that quite frankly, I hardly want to start! But this, I must do briefly . . . Bush Junior in my opinion was a nice guy, he was a great spokesperson for the Texas Rangers, apparently, a good spokesperson for the state of Texas, as the Governor, too. Passing a tax cut for the rich, to be popular and surprise, surprise he won re-election . . .

But Dick Rumsfeld led us into the Iraq War and refused to admit he made a mistake . . . Then Katrina . . . and Junior singing on his ranch while thousands of Americans are calling desperately for help and George Junior just sings; "Oh, these are the happiest of days!" . . . ?President?, obviously, a few grades (!) above his level of competence as even the Tea Party Republicans ran as far away from him as they could get, and then . . . the economy melted down . . . 750,000 job losses per month, the not so good ole days . . . Not surprisingly, even a black refrigerator won the Presidency after all!

At last, Barrack Hussein Obama—Democrat (2009—????): Inherited quite a mess but he gave this poor ole world hope and we shall just have to see . . .

So, Where are we . . .

I don't believe in concentrated wealth, not even for me. Yes, like everyone I too want more, but I am not so greedy that I want it all! Unfortunately many people do. That is why the Democrats must be able to impose taxes on those who truly want all the power.

Even a few enlightened Republicans agree with me on that and liberal Republicans like Teddy Roosevelt persuaded congress to pass the Income Tax as a constitutional amendment to get it passed that Tea Party Republicans hate to this day.

Still another liberal Republican George Bush Sr. persuaded a Democratic congress to balance the budget over time. That is what we must do today. But first we have an economy that is still in near Depression mode, and that must come first.

At least if you care for the very poor amongst us, and I do, for unlike some most of us were not born with a hundred million dollars like Mitt Romney's children, already in their nest eggs, or himself the son of the CEO of GM. Do note his dad rose from the bottom, not Mitt. I know it's difficult to believe but many of us have personally known hunger and the fear of how to get dinner on the table, obviously not Mitt. Therefore we do care for we know the very poor could have been us.

So what do we do?

Welcome, to our far, far from perfect world:

Another thing I have been reminded of is Pearl Harbor. Ron Paul reminds me of why America's armed might is needed. In 1939 to 1941 we decided as a people we would not get drawn into another world war. No, not us. NOT US !!! Do u compute?

No, never again would we allow ourselves to get drawn into another world war . . . On December 7th 1941 Japan decided to conquer soft easy, no fight in'em America. Then if that wasn't bad enough Adolph Hitler said let's declare war on them—quoting FDR: "to brave to fight, Americans" on December 8th, 1941.

There are no shortage of idiots in this world. Genghis Khan's, Napoleons, Hitler's and Tojo's the world abounds in. Fortunately the higher up one goes in any country the fewer they become. But the Ahmadinejad 's of Iran, North Korea and Pakistan not to mention Red China and our good ole friend Russia have nukes.

Plus Britain, France, India and Israel have nukes . . . count them including us there are nine country's with or about to have nukes. Please whatever you do, do not disarm, another Pearl Harbor awaits us. But this time with nukes. Please, do think about that.

If the Republicans rule, it will be "trickle down"—Reagan-ism on all us little people. The Tea Party Republicans had their chance to show their strength when in September 2011 they asked the 2012 candidates for president if they would accept a ten part cut in spending in exchange for a one part increase in tax compromise?

They all agreed and raised their hand saying: "No increase in taxes for any reason, we will cut spending and cut it even more, and still more." One of them even called Social Security "fraudulent and unconstitutional!"—and no one, not one objected. The rich could care less about the millions that depend upon it.

For the record, in the worst case scenario (like today) Social Security will be funded to about 55% by today's financing in the future. So, if we are willing *to compromise* in the future we can partially restore its funding. Maybe, if we inaugurate my Investment Plan in Chapter Ten, you might even be better off than old geezers like me!

If the Democrats rule, there is at least some hope . . .

I haven't given up entirely on Obama. Realistically, we the people have little choice, a third party only results in one of the previous parties disappearing, but we do have our Primary System. This is a good system, this is how we the people selected Obama over the established party bosses choice—Hillary.

So, now what do we do?

Realistically a Republican running in the general election will probably be somewhat to the left of the far right above. But not a "we the people" candidate . . .

So to be real and there is no point in not being so, we have to pull Obama to actually represent "we the people" and not Wall Street. We all know he and the Democrats as well as the Republicans bailed out Wall Street. It is now time for us to say:

What about: "We the People!"

So what does "we the people" mean in real terms? I cannot speak for 99% of all Americans; I can only speak for myself. But, I can listen . . . and what have I heard that 99% of Americans would and in my opinion should agree too?

What about big money dominating America . . . Yes, no doubt that it does, in fact just a few years ago our (!!!!) politicians of both parties(!!!!) said to the rich:

Hey, money should be free!

Why should we put restrictions on what big money can buy? I, your politician want your money, why on earth should we outlaw free money! Hey, we can change the law, let us do it! Just like that (our!!!) politicians declared any restrictions on money is a breach of the first amendment!

So, now big money is free to rule.

Well, I think we the people should rise up and defeat the Federalist—It can be done! Fortunately George Washington ain't president. Now to find a Thomas Jefferson . . .

A Teddy Roosevelt would do. Maybe . . . a Barrack Obama can be drafted as a temporary fit. Do you hear me Obama! Maybe, you will do . . . Do you hear me Nancy Pelosi?

You sold out to Wall Street, we know you did. You Democrats are almost as bad as the Republicans so, either join us, or it will be a new Progressive Party, to replace you. Millions of dollars we might come up with, but a hundred million votes; that we do have!

If you want to keep out conservatizing the Republicans the billions of dollars you can have, but not our ninety nine million votes!

It's time to leap to the left!

To make this happen, we must first register. If you don't vote, you have no power, what so ever. So register, now, as in NOW! Remember MLK, he wanted first Eisenhower, then Kennedy and finally LBJ to act, now, it took years of trying but eventually he managed to get a Texan to act, NOW! Bring tears to my eyes, like MLK's by **both registering and then voting!**

If you live in a Democratic District like I do; register as a Democrat. If you live in a Republican District; register as a Republican. That way you have a chance to vote in the primary for at least some one of either party who could be a "we the people" candidate, remember **Teddy** Roosevelt was a Republican and **Eleanor** Roosevelt was a Democrat, so both sides can be on our side! Or perhaps neither, it's their choice!

If neither party is willing to leap to the 99%; we may have to create a new party, we can do that even the Democratic-Republican Party became history like the Federalist Party before it. But for the moment let us try to pull the Obamacrats to

"WE THE PEOPLE's side.

In the mean time get out there and demonstrate, let them know "we mean business," by non violently protesting the continued selling out to Wall Street by both parties, and maybe one party will get the hint and like LBJ say in this too "we shall overcome."

It is time for . . . "WE THE PEOPLE" . . . to rule!

So now you know how to climb, so get off your duff and register, than actually vote and just maybe we will climb by compromising like our founders intended us to.

Those are your orders, but what about me . . .

I hereby this October 7th, 2011 pledge myself to the following:

1—Pledge to give 1/3rd of any and all royalties from this book to the Occupy-Wall Street groups, for now that is hopefully Obama's re election campaign. Another chunk I plan on giving to other groups like San Francisco State University, the University of New Orleans, Delgado Jr. College, and individuals mentioned in this book, like the Kings and four little girls murdered by my race in Birmingham.

2—Allowing for taxes a considerable chunk for me and my brother who has tolerated me all these years. Still, other smaller chunks to others.

So, thinking big, if I collect say $30 million in royalties for sales in 2012 I pledge $10 million to the Occupy-Wall Street groups, do you hear that Obama? I say come join us and "we the people" can be on your side including the ten million above!

3—I pledge to get out there and demonstrate like you!

4—If I collect several million let alone ten million, I plan to help those that I can with a "Walk For America" program. Walk five miles a day for forty dollars. That ain't much, but to many that have been left with nothing, forty dollars a day, would be a small blessing. If so, I say why not!

5—I further pledge to vote in November, So Nancy Pelosi, you have been warned! Stop supporting Wall Street and start supporting:

WE THE PEOPLE!

The End—Thomas Stephen Walters

Occupy Wall Street !!

We the People verses Wall Street is nothing new! Thomas Jefferson fought the Federalist who wanted to make the officers of our Revolution our permanent House of "Lords" in . . . our . . . Senate!

Andrew Jackson warred upon the banks forcing our banks whether local or distant to be our "good neighbors." We the people called these old fashioned laws: "Usury Laws." Only once this was established as the law of the land, then and only then; could we under Abe Lincoln, fight to free all Americans!

**If any are to be free,
then all must be free!**

We the people won that war, but lost the struggle with Lincoln's death. The Bad Guy's, or the One Percenter's took power, this was called "The Gilded Age" where the rich said to we the people: Bow down to concentrated wealth under J P Morgan, Andrew Carnegie and John D. Rockefeller!

We The People soon rose in revolt and elected Theodore Roosevelt our President who warred upon the rich getting the Income Tax passed, and we the people; soon broke up those giant corporations strangling America!

In the 1920's the one per center's retook power and our wealth was quickly re concentrated and they, the One Percenter's gave us the people the Great Depression. In response we the people Re-elected a Roosevelt; FDR, this time, a Democrat . . .

**After Pearl Harbor:
Yes, we can;
Is how we won World War II:**

At a conference in Washington we the people pledged ourselves to victory. The owners agreed: Yes, we can take on a 70% national tax on our income, meaning 80% including state and local taxes. That, is how we won World War II, rebuilt Europe and Japan after the war, rearmed for the Cold War, paid for Social Security, and our economy boomed into the "I like Ike" days of the 1950's! Seventy percent and our economy roared!

Then Kennedy proposed let's cut taxes on the rich. Man was he popular! Then came the 1970's and inflation skyrocketed. So the rich said let us do away with those ancient Usury Laws. Yes, Democrats and Republicans alike said, why not!

Then to top off the celebration Ronald Reagan said let us cut taxes again and we the rich will allow all our wealth to trickle down to the poor. The Tea Party'ers love him to this day. Well, I'm sick and tired of this trickling down! Are You?

I say: WE THE PEOPLE: must retake Washington and New York!!! Theodore a Republican once ruled, Eleanor Roosevelt, a Democrat once ruled and we can force Obama to rule in "We The People's" name. If not, we can impeach him! Remember the words of Martin Luther King; President Obama, in the end; "we too shall overcome!!!"

by Thomas S. Walters

What the rich do not want you to know:

The rich get rich by bowowing money at 5% and earning 20% on that bowowed money. Of course if they can make 30 or 40% they get rich quicker. If you invent a better mousetrap you should be rewarded. Ben Franklin, Robert Fulton, Thomas Edison, Alexander Bell, the Wright brothers and Bill Gates having invented better mousetraps have built fortunes and few of us would or even should object.

What the rich do not want you to know, however is they **stay rich** by getting you, me and every other sucker to lower their taxes. Well, I don't like being a sucker! Do you?

Theodore Roosevelt a Republican, fought tooth and nail to get the Income Tax passed a century ago to tax the rich. But with passage of Social Security for we the people all were soon taxed as our world changed but the taxes on the rich remained higher.

With WWII the highest rates climbed to 70% (seventy percent!) and our economy roared to victory, along with our dads and grand dads actually doing the fighting. Now if one counts state and local taxes this was a marginal rate of 80% (yes, eighty percent!) yet our economy roared out of the post WWII slump of the late 1940's into the 1960's.

Yet, the rich screamed its Socialism, here in America! Others would argue that after the first million it should be 100%. That, is just a matter of opinion. Either way at 70% marginal national tax rates, our economy soared throughout the 1950's! This is because tax rates have almost absolutely no bearing on getting rich.

Yes, tax rates have almost absolutely no bearing on getting rich! In a perfect world it would have zero effect, but this ain't a perfect world. If one invents a better mousetrap at a 100% marginal tax rate, they would never get rich, to begin with. Since I personally, am in favor of better mousetraps we should include exemptions to get rich, but **not to stay rich forever.**

The heirs to the thrones of the Rockefeller's, Carnegie's, Vanderbilt's, Morgan's, and all the other descendents of the rich and powerful want you to believe they create jobs by their earning millions of dollars: **That is a LIE!** They do not create one job. If their millions were taxed away others from overseas would buy into America. Jobs are created by either people bowowing at 5% and earning a profit of say 30% or inventing a better mousetrap (or poem, or book etc.). Now, if we want to work for Americans we should allow the rich to keep some of their money, but never all of it!

So allowing for people to get rich, after the first million than the marginal tax rates should be anywhere from 45% to 80% nationally. But that is strictly my opinion, so I say raise their taxes: If we do that, just maybe, okay let's compromise . . . 40% to 60% and we and . . .

our economy will roar into the future!!!

Thomas S. Walters

My Changing Times:

In the summer of 1963 a preacher man led a March on Washington that had intrigued my interest, but that grown up stuff was of little interest to me a twelve year old. How little I understood how Dr. Martin Luther King Junior's words had changed our world, and more importantly, me:

This is from Ch. 5 of my book: "Why, Must the world be like this!"

In 1962 my parents bought a house in the infant suburban Montclair neighborhood that is now in Fayetteville a few miles from Ft. Bragg, North Carolina where my father worked as a sergeant in the army. About two years later, a friend and I both age thirteen, were walking back into our neighborhood, late one afternoon, when a most telling event occurred.

A middle aged black lady, carrying a purse and a large bag, was walking the opposite way, when my friend suddenly exploded with anger at her. This continued for sometime, I could not understand why this was happening. She had probably been earning some money for her children. I was convinced that this lady had never done my little friend any harm, so why was he yelling and cursing like this, at her?

Finally, I had had enough, I said harshly to my little friend: "Enough is enough, will you just let her be!" My friend then turned his anger on me saying: "What are you a n—lover?"—To a southern white, this was supposed to be, the worst possible insult. I of course, could never be that, so I replied: "No, but enough is still, enough!" My friend just stared at me with tremendous anger . . .

The fact that I was much bigger than him, I think persuaded him to hold his tongue. with-out another word, we continued walking, going our separate ways.

Later that evening, I wondered what had caused my friend to explode like, that? Then I remembered an incident that had occurred about twenty minutes before, the yelling incident. At that time I had thought it was so funny—perhaps it wasn't . . .

We were at Jack's store on Raeford road, a few miles outside Fayetteville (then), buying sodas, I was paying for mine. When my friend (who had already paid for his—we never stole from Jack, 'cause we liked him) turned to me, to say something, as he pushed the glass exit door open, the glass door hit a young black man, in the face coming in. This was a funny accident.

You should have seen the embarrassed looks on both their faces: I could see my little friend's face clearly reflected in the glass door! What followed was not, upon reflection, funny at all:

The two of them would hold a conversation, with their faces only, with not a single word spoken, that would speak volumes to me, about the world, that I lived in:

My friend's initial embarrassment, turned into a smile, as he realized, who (a black) he had hit with the door.

The young black man's embarrassment, now turned to anger, as he realized, that little white boy, was laughing at him!

My friend's smile now turned to fear, as he saw the intense hatred, in the tall young black man's face.

The young black man's face, then turned to a mixture of both anger and fear—as he realized, what would happen to him, if he acted on, what he wanted to do.

My little friend's fear filled face, now turned to worry, as he prayed that no one had seen the fear, on his face—for he knew, that a white was never, never to show fear to a black man.

After a few seconds pause, with both of their recognizably worried faces, frozen upon the glass door, the black man entered, and my little white friend exited, with nary a word spoken. They had both recognized the worry in the other's face, and knew that it was now safe to continue. They both agreed on: The less said about this incident, the better.

The black man knew, that in the world we lived in, no matter what else that might be decided upon, he would be in trouble, for scaring a white boy.

The white boy knew, that in the world we lived in, no matter what else that might be decided upon, he would be in trouble, for having shown fear to a black man.

Upon Reflection

Both the black man and the white boy walked away with bitterness or even hatred in their hearts:

The black man's hatred stemmed from the white boy's intentional slapping him in the face with the glass door and laughing at him.—I'm sure in his mind, he saw it as intentional, because that re-enforced the white boy's smile, which he saw as laughing at him. Ignoring the fact that a little boy, is very unlikely, to pick a fight, with a young man.

The white boy's hatred, stemmed from his own internal hatred, at himself. For he had always been taught to never show fear to a black, because his white world, would always come to his defense; no matter what had transpired. Because, he had shown fear, he had failed to prove he was worthy of manhood (in his own mind), to his white world . . .

This was of course, was why he exploded, with his hatred at the middle aged black lady, carrying a purse in one hand and a large bag in the other who had never done him any harm. He upon spotting her, recognized, that here was his opportunity, to redeem himself internally, with the white adult world that he so wanted to belong to. He knew that this black, would not scare him, certainly not with me walking beside him . . . into our lily white neighborhood, so he launched into his attack . . .

When I said harshly to him: "Enough is enough, will you just let her be!" To him, I was betraying him! Here he was, trying to redeem himself, and I would not let him!

He tried one more time out of desperation, letting me know that my statement, to him was close to treason: "What are you, a n—lover?" When I replied: No, but enough is still, enough! To my little friend, I had indeed betrayed him. I had denied him his opportunity, to redeem himself in his own mind, to his racist world, that he was trying to prove his manhood to. Little wonder that his anger at me had been so intense . . .

That night, as I thought all this through, I decided: Yes, I guess I am a n—lover, for I have been taught: To love all God's children—no matter what, others might call them (or me).

Perhaps a week later I explained to my friend that I would not allow hate filled scenes like that one again. Once again he challenged me by asking: if I was a n—lover. This time I replied: "I lied before, because I was taught to love all God's children, no mater what others might call them." He just looked at me in disbelief. We would gradually drift apart after that though staying friends . . . I wish I could say he changed, but he did not. Our times were a changing, one heart at a time . . . (and not two, at a time).

About thirty years later, I was living in New Orleans when I went shopping at Woolworth's downtown on Canal Street. I remember how happy I was for having purchased so much for so little, as I fought my way through the exit door carrying several large bags onto the street.

As I did so, suddenly I was shoved very hard and went flying off my feet, the packages scattering all about. As I fell, I saw the young black man who had shoved me turn and run away. You can imagine my anger and embarrassment. Two ladies one white and one black helped me gather my bags, but I wanted so much to chase that young man down, but knew I couldn't . . . I could only say thank you to the two ladies for helping me . . .

My anger cooled as I reflected on: Perhaps I was just now the middle aged man with his arms full being paid back by the grandson of that middle aged black lady so long ago . . .

Retelling this long story, some people would ask: Are you really sure he intentionally pushed you? I would answer absolutely yes, because I had "went flying" off my feet. Typing all this out though has forced me to re-think it through, and now I'm not so sure . . .

Was I really shoved, or was I just bumped into at an awkward moment. Further he did not stand there and gloat, instead he ran away . . . Just as the original "funny incident" at Jack's Store had been a true accident, might this too have been one.

In any case no real harm was done except to my pride, and since I have so much, that might even have been a good thing!

Please remember to try to give others the benefit of the doubt and to love all God's children, no matter what others may call them or you.

Thank You, for your time—I hope you enjoyed.

Thomas S. Walters